ROYAL HORTICULTURAL SOCIETY

HOW TO GROW PRACTICALLY EVERYTHING

ZIA ALLAWAY
LIA LEENDERTZ

LONDON, NEW YORK, MUNICH,
MELBOURNE, DELHI

Senior Editor Zia Allaway
Senior Designer Lucy Parissi
Project Editor Caroline Reed
Editors Chauney Dunford, Becky Shackleton
Designer Francesca Gormley
Picture Research Jenny Baskaya, Lucy Claxton
Jacket Design Duncan Turner
Production Editor Joanna Byrne
Production Controller Imogen Boase

Managing Editor Esther Ripley
Managing Art Editor Alison Donovan
Publisher Jonathan Metcalf
Art Director Bryn Walls

RHS Publisher Susannah Charlton
RHS Editor Rae Spencer-Jones

Photography Brian North, Peter Anderson
Additional text Jenny Hendy

First published in Great Britain in 2010 by
Dorling Kindersley Limited,
80 Strand, London WC2R 0RL

A Penguin Company

2 4 6 8 10 9 7 5 3 1

Copyright © 2010
Dorling Kindersley Limited

A CIP catalogue record is available
from the British Library

ISBN: 978 1 4053 2729 9

Printed and bound by Star Standard, Singapore

To find out more about RHS membership, contact:
RHS Membership Department, PO Box 313, London, SW1P 2PE
Telephone: 0845 062 1111; www.rhs.org.uk

IMPORTANT NOTICE
The author and the publishers can accept no liability for any harm,
damage, or illness arising from the use or misuse
of the plants described in this book.

Discover more at
www.dk.com

Foreword

Growing plants is easy when you know how. Most plants will flourish with just a little help, and you don't need any special skills to sow seeds to create beds brimming with flowers and vegetables, or to pot up containers to paint your patio with colour. Follow the step-by-step guides to grow almost anything your heart desires, from spring bulbs and easy-care shrubs in a border, to a tiny orchard or bed filled with tasty root crops. To make life even easier we've included lots of hints and tips to ensure your plants thrive. And if you need inspiration when choosing a plant for a particular place or purpose, take a look at the "Selections" spreads which showcase a range of options.

The book is split into eight chapters: the first is an introduction to plants and soil – a good starting point for beginners before planning or planting. The following chapters offer a feast of ideas for different areas of the garden, fruit and vegetable plot, and your home. There is also a chapter on water and wildlife gardening. Browse through to see what takes your fancy, and use the quick check lists to discover how much time each project will take, and the tools and plants you will need. To conclude, there's advice on garden care and maintenance, as well as tips on keeping pests and diseases at bay, equipping you with everything you need to know to create a beautiful, bountiful garden.

ZIA ALLAWAY

LIA LEENDERTZ

Contents

Gardening Basics

Explore the world of plants and flowers to find out how they grow, and the best ways to care for them. Then, find out more about soil types and aspect to ensure you match your plants to the conditions in your garden. Equipped with this information, the fun can begin: put together a tool kit, decide on your style, design a planting plan, and start choosing plants and seeds. Finally, browse through the "Seasonal Planner" on pages 24–25 to discover what to do when.

Identifying plant types

Does your garden lack colour and structure, or would it benefit from more glitz or a greater sense of permanence? Different types of plant have different roles to play, and understanding what each can bring will help you to make your garden more beautiful, and create year-round interest.

❶ ANNUALS

These plants germinate, grow, flower, set seed and die all in one year. They are bold and colourful, and quickly gone, although hardy ones may self-seed and appear the next year.

❷ BIENNIALS

Much like annuals, biennials are short-lived, but spread their time over two years, growing in the first, flowering in the second. They too are used as colourful bedding plants.

❸ PERENNIALS

Perennials are the mainstays of flower gardens, producing their flowers and foliage year after year. Most die down in winter, and produce a fresh crop of leaves every spring.

❹ GRASSES

Some ornamental grasses are evergreen and keep their leaves all year, while others die back. They create movement and light in the garden, and many have striking winter skeletons.

❺ SHRUBS AND HEDGES

Deciduous or evergreen, these plants form the backbone of the garden. Shrubs have a woody framework and create a permanent structure. Many also produce attractive flowers and autumn berries.

❻ TREES

For privacy, enclosure and a sense of permanence, plant a tree. Evergreens provide colour all year, while deciduous species bring young spring leaves and blossom, autumn colour, and a wintry outline.

❼ CLIMBERS

Scrambling up walls and across trellises, climbers soften the sharp lines of hard landscaping. They can also be grown through trees and shrubs. Many have beautiful flowers, and some are scented.

❽ AQUATICS

If you have a pond, there is a wide range of plants to consider, from marginals with ornamental foliage or flowers that thrive in shallow water, to spectacular deep-water aquatics, such as water lilies.

How plants grow

One of the pleasures of gardening is that it gives you the chance to watch nature at work. As soon as you put a plant in the ground, a cycle of growth and reproduction begins. Learn what plants need to grow strong and healthy, and you can help them to put on their best performance.

Vital supplies

Plants need water, air, nutrients, and light to thrive, and when first planted they are dependent on you to provide them. Neglect them at this stage and they are unlikely to survive.

LIGHT REQUIREMENTS
Plants make energy from sunlight through photosynthesis, and only thrive if they receive the right amount for their needs. Different plants have evolved to survive in different conditions, and while some love shade, others prefer their heads in the sun. Plants also offer clues about the conditions they enjoy — those with small hairy or grey leaves, such as lavender, enjoy sunny sites, and those with large, dark green leaves grow well in shade. When choosing plants, check their light requirements and plant them in an appropriate place. Young plants are particularly vulnerable to poor light conditions and will struggle to establish if the sun is blocked by weeds, so keep the area around them free of competing plants as they mature.

REGULAR WATER SUPPLIES
When young, all plants need regular watering because their small root systems are unable to search for moisture if it doesn't come to them. You can encourage your plants to develop deep, self-sustaining root systems by watering occasionally but deeply, using one large watering can-full per plant. Moisture then seeps deep into the soil, and the roots reach down to find it.

SOIL NEEDS
Plants love to sink their roots into aerated, moist yet well-drained soil. To achieve these ideal conditions, dig in plenty of organic matter, such as well-rotted manure or mushroom compost (*see pp.14–15*) before planting, and spread a thick layer on the soil surface in spring. Earthworms will then drag it down into the soil, where it will gradually improve drainage and water-retention capacity, ensuring your soil contains all the nutrients and moisture necessary for seeds to germinate and roots to explore.

❶ Sunflowers literally love their heads in the sun and their blooms follow its path throughout the day.   **❷** Earthworms produce gums that bind soil particles together, helping to improve soil structure.
❸ Water young plants regularly to help their roots to establish.

∧ Hungry roots
The area close to the root tips is covered in tiny hairs that absorb nutrients dissolved in the soil water. Take care not to damage these.

FOOD FOR THOUGHT

Plants feed via their roots, removing minerals dissolved in water in the soil. They are constantly seeking new areas to exploit and form a large underground network, so that when one area dries out or is killed off, other roots can be relied upon to take over and keep the plant alive. In a natural environment, the plant population will adjust to the nutrients that are available. In a well-stocked garden where plants are growing closely together you will need to top-up the nutrient level regularly by applying fertilizer and organic matter, such as well-rotted manure.

Organic fertilizers are a good choice for borders, as they release nutrients slowly, feeding plants for a season, and do not harm beneficial soil organisms. You can also apply fertilizer directly to the leaves with a foliar feed. If a plant is suffering from a trace element deficiency, such as iron or manganese, a spray of foliar fertilizer can quickly improve its health. Apply fertilizer to the backs of leaves where they can absorb it more easily.

How plants reproduce

Every plant is designed to ensure its survival or that of the next generation, but they go about it in different ways. Some produce copious amounts of seed, while others reproduce vegetatively, extending their root systems through the soil.

MAKING SEED

Plants with colourful, nectar-filled flowers attract pollinating insects that pick up pollen from one flower and transfer it to another. This process activates plants' sexual reproduction, and prompts the flowers to start developing into seeds. The benefit of reproducing sexually is that every seedling has a slightly different genetic make-up, and when adverse conditions hit, only the fittest survive to breed again, strengthening the species.

ROOTING AROUND

Many creepers and climbers throw out long stems above ground that produce roots when they touch the soil. The roots of others clump up and spread gradually, while some send up shoots from long, extended roots. The danger of vegetative reproduction is that it produces a less diverse population, which is more vulnerable to changing conditions. This is why plants that reproduce asexually also flower and set seed, just in case.

❶ Insects, such as bees, transfer pollen from one plant to another, which activates sexual reproduction. ❷ The male pollen grains fertilize female parts of the flower, stimulating the production of seeds. ❸ The arching shoots of brambles start to grow roots when they touch the soil, producing a new plant. ❹ Bamboos throw out long underground roots called "runners", which in turn generate shoots that grow to form new plants.

Understanding soil

Your most important task as a gardener is to gain an understanding of soil. Your soil type determines what will grow well and what will fail, so save yourself heartache and miserable plants by spending a little time getting to know the soil in your garden and how to make the most of it.

TESTING YOUR SOIL

There are two main types of soil particle: sand and clay. Sand particles are relatively large and water drains freely through the spaces between them, while clay particles are tiny and trap moisture in the miniscule gaps. They are also slightly absorbent. This explains why sandy soils are dry and clay soils are moisture-retentive. Most soils are a mixture of both, but tend towards one or the other, but the ideal is "loam", which contains almost equal measures of sand and clay. Loam retains enough water for plant roots to use, but also drains away excess moisture to prevent waterlogging. Test your soil type by digging some up and rolling it between your fingers.

SANDY SOIL

When rolled between the fingers, sandy soil feels gritty, and when you try to mould it into a ball or sausage shape, it falls apart. It is also generally pale in colour. The benefits of sandy soils are that they are light and well-drained, and easy to work. Mediterranean plants are happiest in sandy soil, as they never suffer from soggy roots. However, their poor water-holding capacity makes sandy soils prone to drought and lacking nutrients, because nutrients are dissolved in water.

∨ *Shapeless and gritty*
Samples of sandy soil feel gritty and when you try to roll them into a ball, they simply fall apart, even when wet.

TOP TIP: TESTING ACIDITY

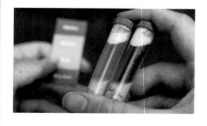

A simple pH test, available from the garden centre, will tell you how acidic (lime free) or alkaline (lime rich) your soil is, and this will determine the range of plants you can grow. Add the supplied solution to a small sample of your soil in the tube provided. Wait until the solution changes colour, then match the colour to the chart.

CLAY SOIL

Roll clay between your fingers and it feels smooth and dense, and retains its shape when moulded into a ball. Soils very rich in clay will not crack even when rolled into a horse-shoe shape. Sticky and impossible to dig when wet; solid, cracked and impenetrable when dry, clay soils are hard work. But in return, when looked after correctly, they have excellent water-retaining properties, and are rich in nutrients. Greedy rose bushes and fruit trees love to sink their roots into them.

∨ *Smooth and sticky*
Like the material used for making pots, clay soils feel smooth and pliable. Roll them into a ball or sausage and they will retain their shape.

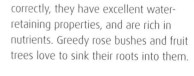

IMPROVING YOUR SOIL

Whether you have a dry sandy soil or a sticky clay, the prescription is the same: lots and lots of organic matter, such as well-rotted farmyard manure, spent mushroom compost and garden compost. These bind together sandy soils and loosen dense clay soils, so ladle them on.

∧ *Fork in manure*
Regular applications of manure and other types of organic matter will help to alleviate every problem related to soil type.

LIGHTENING CLAY

Horticultural grit helps to improve drainage in clay soils. Dig it into the soil over a large area, rather than using it to line the base of planting holes. In heavy downpours grit-lined planting holes act as sumps, and water pools around the roots of plants, which can kill them.

∧ *Add grit*
To improve the structure of heavy clay soil, spread a thick layer of horticultural grit over a large area, and then dig it in.

Sun or shade?

Some plants like a hot spot, and enjoy basking in the sun all day long, while others prefer cool shade. Find out what your garden has to offer before you buy or start planting.

∧ *Using a compass*
Line the red arrow up with north on your compass to discover your garden's aspect.

CHECK YOUR PLOT

Patterns of sun and shade change throughout the day, and a garden that is in full sun at midday may have dark pools of shade by late afternoon, so spend some time watching your garden on a sunny day and make a note of the way shadows move around the plot. You can then plan what to plant where and identify areas for seating. Remember, too, that the patterns change depending on the season. A garden can look very different in low-light winter conditions, and areas that are in full sun for half the day in summer may not get any at this time of the year.

To assess light and shade, take pictures of your garden at different times of the day. This north-west-facing garden has been shot morning, noon, and evening.

1 The patio is partially shaded in the morning. **2** Most of this large garden is sunny at midday because the house is not tall enough to cast shade over it. **3** Sun floods the whole patio in the evening.

ASPECT EXPLAINED

Stand with your back to each of your boundaries and use a compass to work out the direction that they face. Those facing south will be in the sun all day and hot, while those pointing north will be in shade most of the time and cooler. East-facing areas offer morning sun and evening shade, while the opposite applies to those facing west.

Choosing a style

When planning your garden or planting design, start with an idea of the look you want to achieve. Whether it's a formal, ordered scheme or a wild and rambling design you're after, choose a style and then follow it through with appropriate plants and materials.

WHAT DO YOU WANT?

Before deciding on a style, gather together some inspirational images. Take a camera to local open gardens and flower shows, snapping plants or designs that you like. Add pictures from magazines and books and you will soon have a scrapbook of plants and designs. Think, too, about what you want to do in your garden, whether it's to relax and entertain, tend a vegetable plot, or grow a colourful flower border.

< A place in the sun
When planning your garden, locate areas in sun and shade, and plan seating and planting accordingly. Here, the seating area is a sunny terrace, ideal for loungers, surrounded by summer flowers. The ferns in baskets need some shade during the day and plenty of moisture to succeed here, and most of the perennials will die down in winter, leaving bare beds.

MEETING YOUR NEEDS

It is a good idea to focus on a particular style when designing your garden, but you will need to factor in your specific needs too. Write a list of practical requirements and incorporate these into your plans. For example, you may need a space to store bins or bikes, or perhaps room for a greenhouse or shed. Also consider access to utility buildings. When planning a dining area, consider how many people you will need to seat around a table, and calculate the size of a proposed patio to accommodate them.

∧ Bicycle sculpture
The problem of storing bikes in a small front garden is solved here with these cleverly designed racks that not only keep them secure, but transform them into a sculptural feature.

∧ Beautiful bins
Most households have recycling bins that take up space and look unsightly. Here, a small cupboard with a roof planted up with mind-your-own-business (Soleirolia soleirolii) hides them neatly away, and blends discreetly into the garden.

∧ Raised vegetables
Growing fruit and vegetables in raised beds makes them easier to tend. The beds can also double as seats where space is limited.

Planting styles

The type of plants you choose, and the way in which you group them, will affect your designs. For instance, packing lots of different plants together lends an informal note, while using just a few species creates a modern, urban look.

THEME YOUR PLANTING

Use your favourite plants to evolve a garden style to suit you. If you love large, leafy plants, consider a tropical theme. Summer annuals lend themselves to traditional cottage gardens, while spiky succulents and drought-tolerant plants suit gravel gardens.

❶ Spiky yuccas and hardy bananas create a lush tropical flavour. ❷ Relaxed planting best suits the cottage-garden style. ❸ The tepee and butterfly-friendly plants make this garden a haven for children. ❹ Strong lines and few plants reflect a stark Modernist style. ❺ A circular lawn and grassy borders update a traditional theme. ❻ Sun-loving succulents sit happily in this desert-style bed.

Planning your planting

The plants you choose for your garden will depend on your taste and the style you want to achieve, but there are some basic rules about placing and grouping them that are relevant to all designs. If you have just inherited a garden, wait a couple of seasons to see if any plants appear that are worth keeping.

ASSESS YOUR PLANTS

As well as making a list of the plants you want to include in your garden, also note those you have already. Think carefully before removing trees and large shrubs, since these will take the longest time to replace if you subsequently regret your decision. You may find that a hedge or shrub bed is sheltering the garden from prevailing winds, or a tree could be masking an ugly view or neighbour's window. Remember, too, that clumps of perennials and bulbs are easy to move, or split into smaller groups.

Shrubby shelter belt >
The shrubs surrounding this patio shelter it from wind, and provide shade and privacy. When deciding whether to keep or remove large plants, try to visualize the garden without them, or cut them back first to see the effect.

^ *Stairway to heaven*
To create this beautiful landscape, plant the shrubs first, and fill in between them with perennials and grasses. Plants that require good drainage are squeezed between large boulders.

^ *Planting plan*
When planning a tree in a border, take note of its spread, which will affect the light and water available to plants beneath it. The light leaf cover of this Acer *allows dense planting below.*

PLAN THE STRUCTURE FIRST

First, mark out the area for a bed or border with non-toxic spray paint, sand from a bottle, or a hosepipe (*see p.28*), and make a rough paper plan by scaling down the length and breadth to, say, 1cm (½in) on paper to 10cm (4in) on the ground, or 1cm (½in) to 20cm (8in). Then start plotting areas for the main structural plants, such as shrubs and trees. Check their heights and spreads to ensure they will have space to grow where you want them. Then draw circles with diameters that represent the spread of each plant on your paper plan. Alternatively, draw circles with sand from a bottle or non-toxic spray paint marking the positions of the plants on the actual bed.

The next step is to plan the planting around these large specimens. Make sure that perennials will be a good distance from the central stems of trees and shrubs; spring bulbs that flower before the canopies are in leaf can be planted closer.

GROUPING PLANTS

Specimen trees and shrubs look great as individual statements, but bulbs and perennials have greater impact when planted *en masse*. Bulbs are best planted in large groups of 10 or more if you have space — weave them between later-flowering plants. Perennials work well in swathes of five or more. You can achieve a naturalistic design by interlocking sausage-shaped groups together, or for a modern look, plant in more regimental square or rectangular shapes. You can also add rhythm and continuity to your design by repeating the same plants throughout the garden, and try combining contrasting leaf shapes as well as flower colours for a rich, textured look.

Creative contrasts >
Although the predominant colour in this border is green, the bold groups of perennials with contrasting leaf shapes and forms more than compensate for the limited colour palette.

CHOOSING A COLOUR THEME

Skilful garden designers are adept at matching colours to create harmonious planting displays, and by applying their methods you can create similar effects. For a bright bold display, choose hot colours, such as canary yellow, fuchsia pink, red, and orange. Or use cool blues, mauves, purples, and white to create a calming, mellow mood. Alternatively, mix the two schemes, placing blue next to yellow, or purple with red, to achieve a more balanced effect, but avoid too many different hues or your scheme will look disjointed and messy. Another option is to limit the palette to just one or two colours for an elegant mono- or duo-tone scheme.

< ∧ Lively or low key
Red tulips and yellow wallflowers toned down with blue forget-me-nots create a bright, exciting design to herald spring (left). At the opposite end of the spectrum, this blue and white scheme of grasses, daisies, Bergenia and Euphorbia has a tranquil effect (above).

Get ready to plant

Having assessed your site and soil conditions, you are now equipped with the information you need to buy the best plants for your garden. Browse through the rest of the book for ideas and plans, and make a list of your favourites.

Make your choices

When buying plants at a garden centre or nursery, take the list of those you want with you, and try to stick to it. Remember, perennials look best planted in groups of three or more, while shrubs will need space to grow.

CHOOSE CAREFULLY
If some of the plants you have chosen are not available at your local garden centre, it is tempting to select a similar plant, but take care to check the labels for heights, spreads and growing conditions first (*left*). Different species of the same type of plant may grow to very different proportions from the one on your list.

∧ *Small selections*
Garden centres often stock a large range of plants, but only a small selection of each species. For a greater choice, use specialist nurseries; many offer a mail-order service.

BUYER BEWARE
Before buying a plant, give it a quick check to ensure you take home the healthiest specimen. First look at the leaves and stems for signs of pests and diseases, and reject any plant with wilted foliage. Large weeds growing in the pot are also a sign of neglect. Then, turn over the pot. If there is a mass of roots growing through the drainage holes, the plant has been in its pot too long — a condition known as "root bound". Finally, look for plants with lots of leafy stems and fat flower buds.

∧ *Cause for concern*
Of the two climbers shown here, the one on the left is the best choice, with lots of leafy stems.

< *Root check*
Just a few roots showing through the drainage holes suggest that the plant has a well-established root system but has not been in its pot for too long.

Storing plants

It is best to plant your purchases within a day or two of bringing them home, but if this is not possible, store them carefully and they should continue to flourish until you have time to plant them, or the weather improves.

∧ *Cool conditions*
Store new plants in a cool, shady spot, and water daily before planting.

∧ *Bare-root storage*
If you are unable to plant bare-root plants immediately, simply bury their roots in the ground to keep them protected and moist.

TEMPORARY HOMES

Do not plant if the soil is waterlogged or frozen; the roots of young plants will not survive in either of these conditions. Planting in a drought is also not advisable because you will bring cooler, damp soil from beneath the ground up to the surface and lose precious moisture. In either case, store your new plants in a sheltered area in the shade, and water daily until the conditions improve.

Prepare the ground

Taking a few hours to prepare the soil before you plant always pays dividends, and often ends up saving time in the long run. Removing weeds and enriching the soil are essential jobs that are best done in the autumn or early spring.

REMOVE ALL WEEDS

First, dig out all of the weeds from the site by hand, or apply a weedkiller to pernicious types, such as bindweed or ground elder (*see pp.402–403*). If the weeds are really problematic, consider covering the soil with old carpet for a few seasons. This excludes light and moisture, as well as forming a physical barrier against weed seeds, and should kill off even the most troublesome types.

DIG IN DEEP

If you have taken on a neglected plot, or want to improve all the soil in your garden, try "single digging". This involves digging a trench across your plot, one spade wide and deep. Move the excavated soil to the far end of the plot and add manure to the base of the trench. Dig a second trench next to the first, filling the first with the excavated soil. Then add manure to the second trench. Repeat across the plot. This is hard work, but well worth the effort.

∧ *Time saver*
When weeding try to completely remove the root systems to prevent the plants from regrowing.

< *Fertile ideas*
By digging in well-rotted manure or garden compost over the whole plot you will not have to worry about adding it to individual areas each time you plant.

Essential tools

You don't need to spend a fortune when you start gardening, but a few basic tools are essential if you want to perform more than the smallest tasks. When you have more than three or four tools, consider investing in a small shed or box to keep your collection clean, dry, and free from rust.

YOUR TOOL KIT
A beginner's kit should include a watering can, fork, spade, rake, trowel, and a hand fork. Add to these as your interest increases, and the list of jobs you carry out diversifies. If you find yourself doing a particular task frequently, such as digging the vegetable patch, invest in one tool of particularly good quality to make the job easier and more pleasurable.

DIGGING, PLANTING AND HARVESTING
Spades and forks are both used to cultivate the soil but they have distinct roles. Use a fork to dig heavy soil, lift root crops, handle bulky material, such as garden compost, or to incorporate organic matter, such as manure, into the soil. Spades are best for digging holes and trenches, and shifting large quantities of soil; they cope better with light soils that fall through the prongs of a fork. However, if you find a spade too heavy, buy a border spade, which has a smaller head.

❶ A sturdy garden fork is an essential tool, ideal for digging heavy soil and aerating lawns. ❷ Buy a lightweight trug for weeding and moving plants around the garden. ❸ If you are tall, invest in a long-handled spade and fork, which will help to prevent back injuries. ❹ Trowels are ideal for planting seedlings and filling pots with compost. ❺ Use a hand fork for small planting jobs and removing weeds. ❻ A standard rake is used to level seedbeds and tamp down soil; buy a spring-tined fork for removing moss from lawns.

PRUNING AND CUTTING
The cutting tool you require depends on the thickness of the material you need to remove. There are lightweight clippers for cutting flowers and shaping fine topiary; secateurs for pruning stems of around pencil thickness; and loppers and pruning saws for larger branches. Choose the right pruning tool for the job, as secateurs may be damaged by material that is too thick, and a pruning saw will be too rough and unwieldy for small branches. Using the right pruner also makes the job much easier.

∧ *Pruning with secateurs*
Invest in a good-quality pair of secateurs if you have shrubs and trees to prune. Look for those with long-term guarantees.

∧ *Coping with larger branches*
Small branches should be cut with a pruning saw, which has a curved blade to make sawing easier, and fits into awkward spaces.

WATERING

In summer, watering becomes the main task in the garden, and a basic watering can serves most needs. Fit a rose on the spout to sprinkle water on delicate seedlings or new plants after planting. An additional benefit is that watering cans fit easily under a rainwater butt tap.

In larger gardens, or if you have lots of pots, you may find it necessary to use a hose. Look for one with adjustable settings so that you can gently sprinkle water on to containers or spray established plants. You can also buy long-handled hoses for watering hanging baskets.

∧ *Shower young plants*
Use a garden hose with a spray fitting to water newly planted areas with a gentle shower.

∧ *Watering cans for all jobs*
Use a full watering can to soak the roots of new plantings, and for large potted trees and shrubs.

∧ *Good slicing action*
Keep your hoe sharpened and it will sever the roots of annual weeds more efficiently.

∧ *Dealing with deep roots*
A weed grubber can lever tap roots out of the soil, preventing regrowth.

WEEDING

The most useful tool for weeding is a hoe, which you push along the surface of the soil to slice through the necks of weeds, where the stems meet the soil. Although hoeing kills annual weeds instantly, perennials chopped off in this way will survive and regrow. Weeds with tap roots, such as dandelions, are better dealt with using a weed grubber — a long pointy tool that penetrates deep into the soil. Use a spade or trowel to tackle perennials without tap roots, such as dock.

CLEANING AND CARE

Clean your tools regularly to keep them in good condition. Oil secateurs every few months to prevent them from rusting and check that the blades are tight so they cut efficiently. Brush soil from spades and forks regularly, and apply oil to the blades and prongs once or twice a year to deter rust. Before trimming or pruning a plant, help to prevent the build-up of plant diseases, such as box blight (see p.99), by cleaning your cutting tools, including saws and secateurs, with household disinfectant.

❶ Clean all pruning tools before each use to avoid spreading diseases from one plant to another. ❷ At the end of the season, clean and oil spades to prevent rust. ❸ Wipe pruning saws with a soft cloth and oil them.

Seasonal planner

Every season brings its own tasks in the garden, whether it's making long-term changes, preparing for the months ahead, or maintaining it in the here and now. Do these jobs at the right time and in the correct order, and caring for your garden will be easier, quicker, and more satisfying. Your plants will benefit, too.

❶ Sow annual flowers and vegetables inside in spring for earlier displays and crops.
❷ Deadhead flowering plants throughout spring and summer, to encourage more blooms. Store dahlia tubers in a frost-free place for the winter.   ❸ Check all vegetable and fruit crops regularly, and harvest them when they're at their best.   ❹ Rake up fallen leaves from the lawn in late autumn to keep the grass green. Use them to make leafmould.

Spring

EARLY SPRING
- Cut back ornamental grasses (*pp.52–53*), prairie-style borders, (*pp.70–71*) and autumn-flowering perennials (*pp.94–95*).
- Prepare beds and borders for planting; weed and dig over the soil; add organic matter where appropriate (*p.249*).
- Prune late-flowering shrubs, early summer-flowering clematis and roses (*pp.412–415*).
- Pollard willows and coppice dogwoods (*pp.230–231*).
- Cut lavender hedges back (*p.199*).
- Apply a granular fertilizer around shrubs, trees, and perennials (*p.404*).
- Sow half-hardy annuals indoors (*pp.108–109*).
- Pot up plug plants indoors (*pp.120–121*).
- Lift and divide established clumps of perennials (*p.416*).
- Plant hardy grasses (*pp.52–53*).
- Plant snowdrops "in the green" (*p.41*).
- Regularly deadhead spring-flowering bulbs and bedding plants.
- Repot Christmas trees (*pp.158–159*).

MID–LATE SPRING
- Plant perennials (*pp.28–31*); summer-flowering bulbs (*pp.124–125*); and pond plants (*pp.326–327*).
- Inside, plant Thai herbs (*pp.302–303*)
- Plant indoor hanging baskets (*pp.370–371*).
- Sow hardy annuals directly outdoors; sow tender annuals indoors (*pp.208–209*).
- Sow vegetables (*pp.248–289*), and plant potatoes (*p.252*).
- Sow a wildflower meadow (*pp.348–349*).
- Mulch the soil (*p.495*).
- Start weeding (*p.23 and pp.402–403*).
- Prune early-flowering shrubs and early clematis after flowering (*p.412; p.416*).
- Stake herbaceous perennials(*p.67*)
- Start mowing the lawn (*pp.422–423*).

Summer

EARLY SUMMER
- Harden off tender seedlings sown indoors (*pp.108–109*).
- Plant out summer bedding and vegetable plants.
- Plant up containers (*pp.110–111*) and hanging baskets (*pp.130–131*).
- Protect young plant growth from pests, especially slugs (*pp.424–429*).
- Put houseplants, including citrus (*pp.304–305*), outside for summer.
- Feed flowering shrubs and roses with a rose fertilizer to promote flowering (*pp.404–405*).
- Prune evergreen shrubs (*p.411*), and hornbeam, cherry and pear trees (*p.413*) after flowering.
- Earth-up potatoes and harvest after flowering (*pp.252–253*).
- Sow beetroot (*p.254*), radish (*p.260*), spinach (*p.263*), and lettuce (*p.286*) every two weeks.
- Take softwood cuttings (*p.420*).

LATE SUMMER
- Sow spring cabbages (*p.262*).
- Trim lavender hedges after flowering (*p.199*).
- Prune wisteria to restrict growth (*p.226*).
- Take semi-ripe wood cuttings (*p.421*).
- Make an insect hotel in time for winter hibernation (*pp.354–355*).

ALL SUMMER
- Water containers and new plantings frequently, particularly in hot weather (*pp.406–407*).
- Weed beds and borders.
- Mow the lawn as required.
- Deadhead flowering plants to extend blooming.
- Prune hedges and topiary as required.
- Tie climbers in to their supports.

Autumn

EARLY AUTUMN
- Prepare beds for spring planting (*p.249*).
- Plant spring bulbs, except tulips, in beds (*pp.40–41*) and lawns, (*pp.210–11*).
- Plant containers and baskets for winter colour (*pp.156–157*).
- Take hardwood cuttings (*p.419*).
- Sow sweet peas for an early display the following year (*pp.228–229*).
- Plant wallflowers for spring colour (*p.114*).
- Bring houseplants back indoors, checking for pests and diseases first.
- Protect slightly tender exotics from frost by wrapping in fleece (*p.181*).
- Cover slightly tender perennials with a thick mulch of straw or bark chippings.
- Move tender dahlia tubers and cannas inside (*pp.86–87*).
- Turf or sow lawns (*pp.206–208*).
- Apply an autumn lawn fertilizer to established lawns (*pp.422–423*).
- Lay chamomile lawns (*p.209*).
- Make a woodpile shelter for wildlife (*pp.354–355*).
- Prune hedges for the last time.

LATE AUTUMN
- Plant shrubs (*pp.20–21*); roses (*pp.92–93*); trees (*pp.178–179*); hedges (*pp.192–197*); climbers (*pp.212–213*); and fruit bushes (*pp.292–293*).
- Plant tulips (*pp.40–41*).
- Sow broad beans (*see p.283*).
- Plant onions and garlic (*pp.270–271*).
- Grow trees from seed (*pp.188–189*).
- Indoors, plant amaryllis bulbs (*pp.366–367*), and prepared hyacinths and narcissi (*pp.378–379*).
- Trim late-flowering shrubs to reduce winter wind-rock (*p.412*).
- Rake up fallen leaves and make leafmould (*pp.360–361*).

Winter

- Plant bare-root trees and hedges (*pp.192-193*).
- Take root cuttings from perennials (*p.418*).
- Prune wisteria (*pp.226–227*), and most trees, including apples and pears (*pp.410–411*).
- Prune late-flowering clematis (*p.414*).
- Prune trees to create multi-stemmed specimens (*p.182*).
- Harvest winter crops (*pp.264–265*).
- Chit potatoes in late winter to plant in spring (*pp.252–253*).
- Plan your vegetable and flower beds.
- Order flower and vegetable seeds.
- Group containers for stability in high winds and for insulation.
- Wrap terracotta pots in bubble plastic or hessian for frost protection (*p.409*).
- Build a raised bed (*pp.254–255*).
- Put up new bird boxes (*p.363*).

ANY TIME OF YEAR
- Make a compost bin; fill, turn and empty when necessary (*pp.358–359*).
- Make a wooden obelisk (*pp.216–218*).
- Create a bog garden (*pp.330–331*).
- Dig out a pond (*pp.324–325*).
- Make a border and lawn edge (*pp.32–33*).
- Make a rose arch (*pp.222–223*).
- Check tree ties, and loosen if necessary (*p.179*).
- Look out for pests and diseases, and take appropriate action (*pp.424–433*).
- Cut out dead or diseased wood (*pp.410*).
- Clean all cutting tools after use to prevent spreading plant diseases (*p.23*).

Beautiful Beds

In this chapter you will find everything you need to know to make stunning beds and borders, from digging out a new site, to creating a group of grasses or a sparkling winter display. Learn how to plant bulbs, perennials, and shrubs, and then create a range of beautiful planting designs – either copy the ideas here or use them as inspiration for plans of your own. From old-fashioned cottage perennials to modern architectural foliage plants, there's something for everyone.

Create a new border

Before you start digging a new border, think about the best place for it. Try taking a photograph of your garden from an upstairs window, or from a seating area, to see where you need colour and interest. Also consider where the sun falls at different times of the day, and the types of plant you would like to use. Many summer-flowering plants need sun to bloom well, while large leafy types often prefer shade; others are happy with both, so check what your chosen plants need before buying them.

» **WHEN TO START**
Early autumn

AT ITS BEST
Summer

TIME TO COMPLETE
🕐 2 days

YOU WILL NEED
🛈 Tape measure
Hosepipe
Half-moon turf cutter
Spade
Fork
Rake
Well-rotted organic matter, such
  as farmyard manure
Horticultural grit (for clay soil)
Granular fertilizer
Watering can

Plants used in this border:
Achillea
Crocosmia masoniorum
Verbena bonariensis

1 MARK OUT THE BORDER

With a tape measure, mark out the length and breadth of your border, making sure that it is not too narrow – a minimum width of 1m (3ft) is best. Use broad sweeping curves or a geometric design; avoid wiggly shapes, which look messy. Use a garden hose to mark out curved borders or pegs and string for straight edges. Carefully following the outlines, cut through the grass using a half-moon turf cutter or a spade.

2 LIFT THE TURF

Cut the turf into squares within your marked out area. Turf is quite heavy so to make the squares easier to remove, make them a little smaller than the width of a spade blade. Use the spade to slice through the grass roots under each square before lifting the turf.

3 PREPARE THE SITE

Remove the turves and store them upside–down and out of the way (*see Top Tip, right*). Clear the site of large stones, debris, and weeds, removing the roots of perennial species, such as dandelion, dock and bindweed. Break up large clods of soil with a garden fork to give an even texture. Then, check your soil to see if it is sandy or rich in clay (*see pp.14–15*).

4 ENRICH THE SOIL

Whatever your soil type, it will benefit from an application of well-rotted organic matter, such as farmyard manure or garden compost. Either use the "single-digging" method (*see p.21*), or dig in organic matter by spreading an 8cm (3in) layer over the border and mixing it into the top 15cm (6in) of soil. If you have heavy clay, also dig in some horticultural grit to improve drainage. Rake the surface smooth.

continued...

TOP TIP: RECYCLING TURF

You can use turf removed from the border to patch up holes in lawns elsewhere in the garden, or pile it up and leave for about a year to rot down. Grass turves make excellent compost, which you can apply as a mulch to your border in early spring, before the perennials start to shoot.

5 SET OUT YOUR PLANTS

Now that the border is prepared, it is time to start planting. Make sure you buy plants that will suit your site and soil conditions, and the style you wish to create (*see pp.14–17*). This free-draining, sunny site suits a prairie-style scheme. Set out your plants in their pots, and step back to see how the arrangement looks.

6 WATER PLANTS WELL

Check that tall plants will not shade the smaller ones, and position the perennials in groups of three or more. Water them well before planting, either with a watering can, or by plunging the pots in a bucket of water, waiting for the bubbles to disperse, and then removing the plants to drain.

7 CHECK PLANTING DEPTHS

For each perennial plant (*see p.36 for planting shrubs*) dig a hole twice as wide as the pot, and a little deeper. Place the pot into the hole to check that the plant will be at the same depth as it is in its pot after planting. Lay a garden cane across the hole to help judge the right depth.

8 REMOVE PLANTS FROM POTS

Fork the bottom of the hole to break up any compacted soil. Then squeeze the sides of the pot and turn it upside down. With your fingers threaded through the stems and holding the compost, give the bottom of the pot a tap. The plant should slide out easily, but if not, tap the pot until it does.

10 FINISHING TOUCHES

When you have planted the whole border, use a hose to water the plants thoroughly. A good soaking will settle the soil around the plants, helping them to establish. If any roots are exposed by the water, cover them with soil.

9 FIRM IN

If the roots have circled round the root ball, gently tease them out (*see Top Tip, opposite*). Place the plant in the hole. Add some granular fertilizer to the excavated soil, and use this to fill in around the plant. Firm it in with your hands.

11 **CARING FOR YOUR PLANTS**
Apply a mulch (*see p.405*) to the whole border. Perennials take about a year to establish fully, and if planted in spring, they should have a healthy root system by the autumn. Until then, the plants will need to be watered regularly, even daily during periods of drought. After planting, feed them every year in spring with an all-purpose fertilizer and reapply a mulch.

TOP TIP: TEASING OUT ROOTS

When planting, you may see the roots growing round in a tight circle, where they have been restricted by the pot. This is known as "root-bound", and will limit the plant's development. Remedy the problem by gently teasing out the roots so that they will grow away from the ball into the surrounding soil.

Planting depths

The depth at which you plant can have a great impact on growth. Most plants, including shrubs (*see pp.36–37*) and perennials should be planted at the same depth as they were in their pots. However, there are exceptions, including those mentioned below. Most trees also have specific planting needs (*see pp.178–179*).

PLANTING PROUD
Some plants perform best when planted slightly above the surrounding soil level. These include irises, whose rhizomes (*bulb-like structures – see right*) will rot if buried, and other plants sensitive to wet soils, including *Verbascum, Sisyrinchium, Sedum,* and other hardy succulents. Plant these 2–3cm (1in) proud of the surface, leaving iris rhizomes exposed; for other plants, raise the soil in a mound around the rootball, so that water drains off.

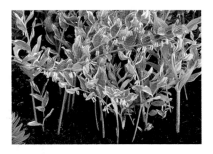

DEEP PLANTING
Moisture-loving plants often prefer to be planted more deeply in the soil, so that their roots are not exposed to the drier conditions near the surface. Plant hostas with their roots 2cm (1in) below the surface, and bury Solomon's seal, *Polygonatum*, at a depth of 10cm (4in).

Build a decorative edge

Edging is both practical and aesthetic. At its most useful it marks out the boundary of a lawn, while also allowing you to simply run the mower over it. With a wide variety of materials to choose from, edging can be a decorative feature in its own right, chosen to complement the plants it contains.

 WHEN TO START
Any time
AT ITS BEST
All year round

TIME TO COMPLETE

5 hours

YOU WILL NEED

 Bricks
String and pegs
Sharp spade
Wet mortar mix
Dry mortar mix
Rubber mallet
Spirit level
Trowel
Brush

1   USE STRING AS A GUIDE
Use one brick to measure the correct distance from your raised bed (or border) and set up a line of string between two pegs from which to work. Cut through the turf along the line using the sharp edge of a spade.

2   REMOVE A STRIP OF TURF
Dig out a strip of turf deep enough to accommodate the bricks plus a 2.5cm (1in) layer of mortar. First slice the turf up into manageable sections, then slide the spade underneath and lift them out onto a piece of tarpaulin.

3 LEVEL THE GROUND

Use the spade to roughly level out the ground. Mix wet mortar and add a 2.5cm (1in) layer to the bottom of the trench to bed in the bricks.

4 LAY BRICKS ON MORTAR

Place the bricks on the mortar and set slightly below the level of the turf. Leave a small gap between each. Use a spirit level to check they are horizontal, and firm them using a rubber mallet.

5 APPLY A DRY MIX

Finally use a dry mortar mix to fill the joints between the bricks, working the mixture in with a trowel. Clean off the excess with a brush.

Edging options

Different edging materials will bring different looks to your garden, from delicate and ephemeral to solid and hard working. Copper piping, bent into a graceful curve (*above*), provides a pretty edge that echoes the colours of the planting.

❶ In an informal area, allow your plants to spill over onto solid brick paving.
❷ Geometric Victorian-style brick edging suits both formal and cottage-style gardens.   ❸ The attractive soft grey of slate chippings provides a perfect foil for edging plants.   ❹ Log edging is the ideal choice for seaside-themed gardens, especially when used with a shingle mulch, mixed with larger pebbles.

First flush of spring

Awkward areas of bare ground beneath trees or shrubs are perfect for spring-flowering perennials and bulbs that bloom before the trees' leaves are out and casting shade. Choose woodland dwellers, such as snowdrops and hellebores, for dense areas of shade, and sun-loving crocuses for the edge of the border.

›› WHEN TO PLANT
Spring for snowdrops
Autumn for bulbs and plants

AT THEIR BEST
Early spring

TIME TO COMPLETE
🕐 2 hours

YOU WILL NEED
Slim trowel or bulb planter
Spade
Well-rotted leafmould

1. Snowdrop, *Galanthus nivalis*
2. Winter aconite, *Eranthis hyemalis*
3. *Crocus tommasinianus*
4. *Helleborus* x *hybridus* (purple)
5. *Helleborus* x *hybridus* (pink)

1 PREPARE THE GROUND
Woodland bulbs enjoy a moist, open-textured soil, rich in organic matter, so add plenty of well-rotted leafmould before planting (*see p.360*).

2 PLANT THE BULBS
Most spring bulbs are planted in autumn, but snowdrops do best when transplanted "in the green" – after flowering but while their leaves are intact. For a natural effect, plant bulbs in drifts.

3 AFTER FLOWERING
In rougher corners of the garden, dying bulb leaves can just be left, but if you feel the need to tidy, make sure the leaves have died down completely before you remove them. Give all plants an annual mulch of leafmould.

Plant a shady border

A border set in deep shade can be a real bonus in the garden if you choose your plants carefully, as some of the most beautiful shrubs will only grow well in low light conditions. These areas may lack the drama of a sunny spot, but they have a cool and understated sophistication of their own.

 WHEN TO START
Autumn

AT ITS BEST
Spring

TIME TO COMPLETE
 2 hours for preparation
3 hours for planting

YOU WILL NEED
 Spade
Organic matter, such as
well-rotted leafmould

Shrubs such as:
Camellia and flowering currant,
Ribes sanguineum.
Underplanting, for example
Bergenia, *Dicentra spectabilis*,
ferns and hellebores.

1 BEFORE YOU PLANT
Many plants that enjoy living in shady conditions grow naturally in woodlands, and need a cool, moist soil, which has been enriched with leafmould. In autumn, clear the area of all weeds, then mix plenty of leafmould into the soil (*to make leafmould,* see *pp.360–361*).

2 DIG PLANTING HOLES
Buy your shrubs in autumn or spring, and plan carefully where you are going to plant them, taking into account their final size. The shrubs go towards the back of the border, with the underplanting below them, and in front. The planting holes should be twice as wide and slightly deeper than the pots.

3 CHECK PLANTING DEPTHS
Put some leafmould in the bottom of each hole and then place a plant on top of it. Use a cane across the hole to check the plant will be at the same depth as it was in its original pot when planted.

4 WATER IN WELL
Fill in around the plant with soil and leafmould, and water in well. Water regularly until the plant is established. Mulch with organic matter, like leafmould, leaving the area around the stems clear.

TOP TIP: FEEDING SHRUBS

Shrubs need regular feeding to thrive. Early spring is the best time to sprinkle a fertilizer, such as blood, fish and bone meal, around the base of the plants. Repeat each year to keep growth vigorous and healthy.

Planting options

Shade-tolerant shrubs that are grown for their flowers, such as camellias, need a little light. The selection below is best planted where some sun can filter through, such as near deciduous trees or a trellis.

❶ *Daphne laureola* subsp. *philippi*; ↕45cm (18in) ↔60cm (24in) ❷ *Rosa rugosa* 'Rubra'; ↕↔2m (6ft) ❸ *Paeonia delavayi* var. *lutea*; ↕2m (6ft) ↔1.2m (4ft) ❹ *Hydrangea aspera* Villosa Group; ↕↔3m (10ft)

< *Kept in the dark*
This beautiful white form of flowering currant, Ribes sanguineum, *and pink camellia are underplanted with a golden-leaved bleeding heart,* Dicentra spectabilis *'Gold Heart', and other shade-lovers.*

Spring bulbs

Spring bulbs brighten the garden from the depths of winter to the beginning of summer. The first out is always the snowdrop, often pushing its pale little flowers through a layer of snow. At the end of the season, alliums come into their own, heralding the start of summer with their globe-like purple flowerheads, floating above early perennials. Plant your bulbs in autumn and your efforts will be rewarded come the spring.

SELECTIONS》

❋❋❋ fully hardy   ❋❋ hardy in mild regions/sheltered sites   ❋ protect from frost over winter
☼ full sun   ☀ partial sun   ☀ full shade   ◊ well-drained soil   ◐ moist soil   ● wet soil

❶ *Allium hollandicum* 'Purple Sensation'; ↕1m (3ft) ↔10cm (4in) ☼ ◊ ❋❋❋   **❷** Grape hyacinth, *Muscari armeniacum*; ↕20cm (8in) ↔5cm (2in) ☼ ◊ ◐ ❋❋❋   **❸** *Tulipa* 'Prinses Irene'; ↕35cm (14in) ↔10cm (4in) ☼ ◊ ❋❋❋   **❹** *Scilla siberica*; ↕20cm (8in) ↔5cm (2in) ☼ ☀ ◊ ◐ ❋❋❋   **❺** *Crocus corsicus*; ↕10cm (4in) ↔5cm (2in) ☼ ◊ ❋❋❋   **❻** *Narcissus* 'Canaliculatus'; ↕15cm (6in) ↔5cm (2in) ☼ ☀ ◊ ◐ ❋❋❋   **❼** *Narcissus* 'Tête-à-Tête'; ↕15cm (6in) ↔5cm (2in) ☼ ☀ ◊ ◐ ❋❋❋   **❽** *Hyacinthus orientalis* 'Blue Jacket'; ↕20cm (8in) ↔8cm (3in) ☼ ☀ ◊ ❋❋❋   **❾** Fritillary, *Fritillaria raddeana*; ↕60cm (24in) ↔10cm (4in) ☼ ◊ ❋❋❋   **❿** *Tulipa sprengeri*; ↕50cm (20in) ↔10cm (4in) ☼ ◊ ❋❋❋   **⓫** Snowdrop, *Galanthus nivalis*; ↕10cm (4in) ↔10cm (4in) ☀ ◐ ❋❋❋

Plant a bed of spring bulbs

Harbingers of spring, bulbs transform sleeping gardens into oceans of colour as the seasons turn. Starting with the first brave snowdrops that peek through the soil in winter, and closing with a spectacular display of tulips and alliums at the end of spring, bulbs provide a long period of interest. Plant them in autumn – leave tulips until late in the season – and they will flower the following year.

WHEN TO START
Mid-autumn

AT ITS BEST
Early to late spring

TIME TO COMPLETE
30 minutes for planting

YOU WILL NEED
Fork
Spade
Horticultural grit
Bulb planter or trowel
Chicken wire
Selection of spring bulbs

1 PREPARE TO PLANT

All bulbs need well-drained soil, so if you have heavy clay, either dig in plenty of grit before you start, or grow them in pots (*see pp.106–107*). You can either plant bulbs individually, using a bulb planter or trowel, or dig a wide hole and plant them *en masse*, which is an easier method, and more naturalistic.

2 DIG A HOLE

Dig to a depth of about two to four times the height of your bulbs (*see right*). Place the bulbs in the planting hole with the pointed growing tip facing upwards. Discard any bulbs that are mouldy or soft.

3 COVER BULBS

Fill in the hole with soil, taking care not to damage the growing tips, and firm it down with your fingers. Cover with chicken wire to prevent animals digging up the bulbs; remove it when the first shoots appear.

TOP TIP: PLANTING SNOWDROPS

Snowdrops have tiny bulbs that dehydrate quickly, and often fail to flower if planted in autumn. Instead, buy pot-grown bulbs in leaf in the spring and plant them so that the pale bases of the stems are just below the soil surface. If you already have large clumps of snowdrops, lift and divide them in spring, after flowering (*see pp.416–417 for tips on dividing plants*).

How deep?

For bulbs to succeed, you need to plant them at the right depth, usually two to four times the height of the bulb. Plant too shallowly, and they may not flower; too deep and they might not grow at all.

❶ Tulips prefer to be planted deeply, four times their own depth; 5cm (2in) bulbs are planted 20cm (8in) deep. ❷ Daffodils are planted three times their own depth; 5cm (2in) bulbs are planted 15cm (6in) deep. ❸ Plant grape hyacinths (*Muscari*) at three times their depth; 2cm (¾in) bulbs are planted at a depth of 6cm (2½in). ❹ Alliums are also planted at three times their depth; 3cm (1¼in) bulbs should be planted 9cm (3½in) deep.

Seasonal pastels

Many of the bulbs and flowers of early summer come in pastel shades that can be easily combined to create a harmonious scheme. Striking alliums dotted through the border provide a touch of drama.

≫ **WHEN TO PLANT**
Autumn and early spring
AT THEIR BEST
Early summer

TIME TO COMPLETE
🕐 5 hours

YOU WILL NEED
ℹ Horticultural grit
Spade
Bulb planter or slim trowel

1. Foxglove, *Digitalis purpurea* f. *albiflora*
2. *Allium hollandicum* 'Purple Sensation'
3. *Aquilegia vulgaris* 'Nora Barlow'
4. Perennial wallflower, *Erysimum* 'Bowles's Mauve'

1 PREPARE THE SOIL
Many bulbs and most of these plants prefer a well-drained soil, and suffer if left to sit in damp conditions over winter. If your soil is heavy, dig in horticultural grit to improve drainage.

2 PLANT UP
Plant the alliums in autumn and mark their positions with labels. In spring, plant the perennial wallflowers and the aquilegias around the alliums in drifts. Plant the tall foxgloves at the back.

3 AFTERCARE
Alliums have beautiful seedheads, so leave for as long as they look good. Aquilegias can be cut back after flowering to promote fresh growth. Alliums and aquilegias come up each year, foxgloves self-seed, but the wallflowers may need replacing after a few years.

Grow acid-lovers

If you have tested your soil (*see p.14*) and found that it is acidic, some of the most beautiful flowering and foliage shrubs, including Japanese maples, camellias and rhododendrons, will thrive in your garden.

WHEN TO PLANT
Autumn or early spring
AT THEIR BEST
Spring

TIME TO COMPLETE
 2 hours

YOU WILL NEED
Well-rotted organic matter, such as farmyard manure
Spade
All-purpose fertilizer for acid-loving plants

Selection of acid-loving shrubs:
Japanese maple, *Acer palmatum*
Flowering dogwood, *Cornus florida*
Korean rhododendron, *Rhododendron mucronulatum*

1 SPACING THE PLANTS
You can use any *Acer palmatum* or rhododendron for this scheme but they may have different growth habits to these, so check labels for sizes and allow space between plants for a few years' growth.

2 ADD ORGANIC MATTER
Choose a partly-shaded site, sheltered from cold, drying winds. Before planting, dig into each square metre of soil a bucketful of well-rotted organic matter. Water the plants well, and then plant according to the instructions for shrubs on page 36.

3 CARING FOR ACID-LOVERS
Each spring, apply an all-purpose fertilizer for acid-loving shrubs, and mulch annually (*see p.405*) to aid soil moisture retention. In spring, after flowering, trim back lightly any wayward growth.

Planting in containers

If you have an alkaline soil but would like to grow acid-loving plants, try planting them in containers filled with ericaceous compost, which is specially designed for them.

CREATING THE RIGHT CONDITIONS
Choose a large container or make a raised bed (*see pp.254-255*) for shrubs, such as camellias, azaleas and rhododendrons. Fill your planters with ericaceous soil-based compost, such as John Innes types, and each spring, replace the top layer in the bed or pot with fresh compost mixed with fertilizer for acid-loving plants.

∧ *Acid colours*
Azaleas come in a range of fiery shades that set off simple white containers beautifully. If leaves start to yellow, which is a sign of iron deficiency, give them a dose of fertilizer for acid-lovers.

Planting options

Combine the spring shrubs in this scheme and below with summer-flowering blue hydrangeas, *Kalmia latifolia* and fragrant summersweet, *Clethra,* to extend the season. Alternatively, create a conifer and heather garden which will thrive in acid conditions.

1 *Enkianthus deflexus*; ↕↔3m (10ft)
2 *Grevillea rosmarinifolia*; ↕1.8m (6ft)
↔2.5m (8ft) **3** *Cercis canadensis* 'Forest Pansy'; ↕↔10m (30ft) **4** Winter heath, *Erica carnea*; ↕15cm (6in) ↔45cm (18in)

< *Candy colour mix*
This sumptuous mix of blowsy pink rhododendron flowers (Rhododendron mucronulatum), dark purple maple leaves (Acer palmatum var. dissectum 'Garnet') and elegant red dogwood stems makes a stunning spring display.

Fiery border

Hot-hued plants in shades of orange, red, and yellow are guaranteed to brighten up your garden. Plant them in a sunny spot, and position them against a dark background for maximum impact.

>> **WHEN TO START**
Late autumn to early spring
AT ITS BEST
Mid- to late summer

TIME TO COMPLETE
1 hour preparation; 3 hours to plant

YOU WILL NEED
Organic matter
All-purpose fertilizer
Stakes and twine

1. *Clematis x diversifolia*
2. *Kniphofia* 'Bees' Sunset'
3. *Dahlia* 'David Howard'
4. Feather grass, *Stipa tenuissima*
5. *Achillea* Summer Pastels Group
6. *Helenium* 'Moerheim Beauty'
7. *Crocosmia* 'Lucifer'
8. *Dahlia* 'Bishop of Llandaff'

1 PREPARE THE SITE
Between late autumn and early spring, remove all weeds from the site and dig in well-rotted organic matter (*see also p.29*). Buy plants in spring.

2 SET OUT THE PLANTING PATTERN
First plant the clematis against the screen (*see p.219*). Set out the other plants in pots and arrange them in groups of three or more, with the dahlias, *Kniphofia* and *Crocosmia* at the back.

3 PLANT AND STAKE
Plant as for perennials (*see pp.30–31*) and include some all-purpose fertilizer in the planting holes. Insert a stake next to the dahlias, and tie in the stems as they grow. Water well after planting and during dry spells for the first year. Overwinter dahlia tubers in a frost-free place (*see p.86*).

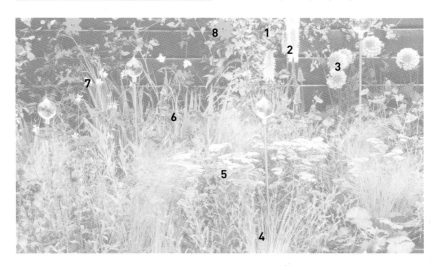

Delicious scents

Even the most beautifully designed and colourful garden is lacking an essential ingredient if it contains no fragrant plants; some emit strong scents that fill the garden, others are best appreciated at close quarters. Use perfumed plants next to seating areas or alongside walkways to experience them in full. Most flower from spring to summer, but include mahonia or Christmas box for delicious scents in the depths of winter.

SELECTIONS 《》

✾✾✾ fully hardy   ✾✾ hardy in mild regions/sheltered sites   ✾ protect from frost over winter
☼ full sun   ☀ partial sun   ☀ full shade   ◊ well-drained soil   ◉ moist soil   ◆ wet soil

❶ Mock orange, *Philadelphus* 'Burfordensis'; ↕3m (10ft) ↔2m (6ft) ☼ ☀ ◊ ✾✾✾   ❷ *Daphne* x
burkwoodii 'Somerset'; ↕1.5m (5ft) ↔1.5m (5ft) ☼ ☀ ◊ ◉ ✾✾✾   ❸ Wallflower, *Erysimum cheiri*
'Fire King'; ↕25cm (10in) ↔20cm (8in) ☼ ◊ ✾✾✾   ❹ Chocolate plant, *Cosmos atrosanguineus*; ↕75cm
(30in) ↔45cm (18in) ☼ ◊ ◉ ✾✾   ❺ *Mahonia* x *media* cultivar; ↕5m (15ft) ↔ 4m (12ft) ☼ ☀ ◊ ◉ ✾✾✾
❻ *Rosa* Escapade; ↕75cm (30in) ↔60cm (24in) ☼ ◉ ✾✾✾   ❼ *Lavandula angustifolia* 'Munstead';
↕45cm (18in) ↔60cm (24in) ☼ ◊ ✾✾✾   ❽ Pink, *Dianthus* 'Bovey Belle'; ↕30cm (12in) ↔30cm (12in)
☼ ◊ ✾✾✾   ❾ *Rhododendron luteum*; ↕4m (12ft) ↔ 4m (12ft) ☀ ◉ ✾✾✾   ❿ Christmas box,
Sarcococca confusa; ↕2m (6ft) ↔1m (3ft) ☀ ☀ ◉ ✾✾✾   ⓫ *Viburnum carlesii* 'Aurora'; ↕2m (6ft)
↔2m (6ft) ☼ ☀ ◊ ◉ ✾✾✾

Fragrant combination

Scent is one of the most evocative senses, and this profusion of perfumed plants is sure to tempt you closer to enjoy the fragrant flowers of old-fashioned roses, lilies, lavender, and pinks.

WHEN TO PLANT
Early spring

AT ITS BEST
Summer

TIME TO COMPLETE
3 hours

YOU WILL NEED
Well-rotted organic matter, such as farmyard manure
Grit
Spade
All-purpose granular fertilizer

1. Bronze-leaved fennel
2. Easter lily, *Lilium longiflorum*
3. Pink, *Dianthus* 'Super Trooper'
4. Silver-leaved thyme
5. French lavender, *Lavandula stoechas*
6. *Rosa* 'Gertrude Jekyll'

1 PLANT THE ROSES
Most of the plants here prefer free-draining soil, so dig plenty of grit into clay soils to improve drainage. The roses require more moisture: plant these as recommended on page 93.

2 COMPLETE THE PLANTING
Plant a line of lavender and lilies in front of the roses, and position the thyme and pinks along the front edge. Mulching with gravel will keep plant stems dry, and help stop them rotting off.

3 AFTERCARE
Keep the bed well watered for the first year, and during any prolonged dry spells thereafter. To ensure a good display, feed the plants each spring with a granular fertilizer, and regularly remove any faded rose and *Dianthus* flowers as they appear to extend their performance.

Grassy border

Decorative grasses produce fabulous textural effects and look stunning when grouped together. Most are easy to maintain, and have a long season of interest, with plumes of flowers in summer followed by seedheads and stems that offer colour and structure in winter.

WHEN TO PLANT
Autumn or early spring
AT ITS BEST
Summer to early autumn

TIME TO COMPLETE
2½ hours

YOU WILL NEED
Well-rotted organic matter
Spade
All-purpose fertilizer

1. Pampas grass, *Cortaderia selloana* 'Aureolineata'
2. *Cortaderia selloana* 'Pumila'
3. Feather grass, *Stipa calamagrostis*
4. *Stipa splendens*
5. *Miscanthus sinensis* 'Malepartus'

1 PREPARE A BORDER
Choose an open, sunny site for your border. Grasses generally tolerate a wide range of soil conditions, but it is always wise to dig in well-rotted organic matter before planting your border. If you have heavy clay, incorporate some horticultural grit to increase drainage.

2 SET OUT THE PLANTS
The *Miscanthus* and pampas (*Cortaderia*) are the tallest grasses, so set them towards the back of the border, leaving space at the front for the feather grasses (*Stipa*). Allow about 1.2m (4ft) between the larger grasses for them to spread, and 75cm (30in) between the smaller ones.

3 PLANTING AND AFTERCARE
Plant grasses at the same depth as they were in their original containers and mulch with gravel to help suppress weeds. Keep the plants well watered for the first year until they are established. Leave the dried stems on the plants to overwinter, and in early spring, cut them down almost to ground level to allow new growth to emerge.

Rustle and sway >
This bold group of grasses creates a dynamic effect as their plumes and foliage dance in the breeze. The tall grasses grow to about 1.8m (6ft), while the shorter feather grasses (Stipa) at the front reach 1m (3ft) in height.

Planting options

There are many grasses to choose from and most require free-draining soil and a sunny site. For a smaller area, select the more compact cultivars – you will find a large selection available via mail order from specialist nurseries.

1 *Helictotrichon sempervirens*; ↕1m (3ft) ↔1m (3ft) **2** *Miscanthus sinensis* 'Morning Light'; ↕1.5m (5ft) ↔1m (3ft) **3** *Miscanthus sinensis* 'Zebrinus'; ↕2.5m (8ft) ↔1.2m (4ft) **4** *Pennisetum alopecuroides*; ↕75cm (30in) ↔1m (3ft)

Make a family garden

Creating a plot that children and parents will both enjoy is not easy. The key is to provide kids with space to play without filling it with garish toys, while setting aside a relaxing area for grown-ups to chill.

∧ *Green fingers*
Children enjoy the responsibility of looking after their own projects, so why not encourage them to grow some fruit and vegetables, and learn how plants develop?

COMBINING PLAY WITH PLANTING

Research shows that children and adults benefit mentally and physically from being in a natural environment. So although it is tempting to buy a plastic play gym and set it in the centre of the lawn, it may not be very beneficial for your children in the long run. Instead, surround play areas with plants that children will enjoy, such as cheerful sunflowers (*see pp.64–65*) and those that attract butterflies (*see pp.352–353*).

Children's interests change rapidly, and what they like one year will be passed over the next. Prevent boredom setting in by providing toys that are not permanent fixtures, and will seem new and exciting time after time. Tents are a great choice, appealing to all ages, and offering limitless opportunities for imaginative play. All you need is an area of lawn to pitch one on.

Growing fruit and vegetables allows children to take a real interest in gardening; sowing seeds and watching their plants grow gives young ones a real sense of achievement. Plastic sandpits often languish unloved once the novelty has worn off, but one made from a raised bed can be easily converted into a small vegetable plot, the perfect size for little hands to tend their first crops.

TOP TIP: SIMPLE SWINGS

You can make a simple swing from a thick rope attached securely to a sturdy tree branch. Tie an old tyre to it to make a traditional swing, checking that it will hold your child by swinging on it yourself first. Alternatively, knot the rope at intervals for children to climb up. Adult supervision is always advisable when small children are using any type of play equipment.

∧ *Raise your play*
This sandpit is made from a timber raised bed, which you can buy as a kit, or make yourself (see pp.254–255). When children tire of the sand, fill the bed with colourful sunflowers, edible flowers, such as nasturtiums, and quick-growing vegetables.

∧ *Swing seat*
Play equipment need not be expensive or shop-bought. A rope and old tyre are all you need to keep children happy. Just make sure your child is strong enough to hold on to the rope when swinging.

Water and wildlife

If your children can swim and are old enough to understand the dangers of water, ponds offers more play opportunities than almost any other garden feature. They are easy to build (*see pp.324–327*) and will soon attract a wealth of wildlife to your garden.

BE SAFE

Small children can drown in just a few centimetres of water, so wait until yours are old enough to appreciate the dangers before installing a water feature. If you have older children with younger siblings, fit a custom-made metal grille over the water surface and ensure it will take the weight of a child, should he or she fall.

WILDLIFE HAVEN

As soon as your pond is installed, birds and small animals will visit to drink and bathe, and many other creatures will become permanent residents. Make sure the sides are sloped so they can get out if they fall in, and plant around the sides to provide them with cover and habitats. Frogs and toads will be drawn to any pond, large or small, and in spring will fill the water with spawn. Other creatures to look out for include water beetles, pond skaters, water snails, newts, damselflies and dragonflies.

∧ *Aquatic homes*
Wrap planting around your pond to create shelter for wildlife, such as birds, small mammals, frogs, and toads.

< *Beauty and the beast*
Look out for dragonfly nymphs as they climb from the water and shed their skins, before emerging as adults.

Plots for pets

Sharing your garden with pets can be a fun and fulfilling experience, and by catering for their needs, as well as your own, you can all live happily together in the same plot.

PET SPACES

Small pets, such as guinea pigs and rabbits, are happiest in a secure run on a lawn. If you move the run every few days, you may even eliminate the need to mow the grass altogether.

Dogs who have free reign of the garden can present problems if they are not trained. Set aside a quiet area, such as behind a shed, for your dog to use as a toilet. After a few weeks, and treats for good behaviour, he or she will only go there. Raised beds and borders edged with low hedging will also help deter your dog from rampaging through your favourite flowers.

Cats are not as easily trained as dogs, especially in their toilet habits. Encourage them to use a litter tray, and deter them from using the borders by inserting short pieces of cane in the areas where they are likely to dig. Cats like bare soil, so these are the areas to concentrate on.

< *Dog territory*
Boisterous dogs can devastate gardens by trampling plants, so grow your favourites in raised beds to help reduce the risk. Also, weigh down containers to stop them from being knocked over.

Kitty treat >
Cats adore the scent of catmint (Nepeta) and love to roll around in it. Give your pet a treat and set aside a bed for this pretty plant.

Make a shady rockery

Transform a dull, shady corner into a rockery for spring interest. Many shade-loving plants, such as ferns, ivies, and violas, love the cool, moist but well-drained conditions and will thrive here.

 WHEN TO START
Autumn
AT ITS BEST
Spring

TIME TO COMPLETE
6 hours: preparation and planting

YOU WILL NEED
Topsoil (if not working on a sloping site)
Attractive large stones
Bugle, *Ajuga reptans*
Creeping phlox, *Phlox stolonifera*
Dog's-tooth violet, *Erythronium*
Hardy ferns
Hostas
Ivies, *Hedera*
Violas

1 PREPARE THE SOIL
If you have a flat site, create a slope with weed-free topsoil in autumn, so it has time to settle. If you have a slope already, weed it thoroughly. Dig in some grit if the drainage is poor.

2 SELECT AND PLACE STONES
Set rocks into the soil, with larger ones at the base of the slope and smaller ones at the top. Bury one third of each stone, and angle them so that rain will run off into the soil.

3 CHECK PLANTING POSITIONS
In spring, buy your shade-loving plants. Arrange them around the rockery, while they are still in their pots, to see where they will look best, before deciding on their final planting positions.

4 PLANT AND MULCH
Plant in the pockets between the stones, then water well. Mulch with composted bark, or similar, to help keep moisture sealed in and to suppress weeds. Water regularly for the first year.

Versatile ferns

Ferns are a wonderful choice for shady areas. They will grow in the tiniest of dank crevices, as long as they have enough moisture and a glimmer of light. Sunken pits echo the way ferns sometimes lodge themselves in subterranean drains, and peer up from the gloom. You can also try growing them under a bench, where little else will thrive. For dry sites under trees or close to walls, try the male fern, *Dryopteris filix-mas*, or the evergreen hart's tongue fern, *Asplenium scolopendrium*. The royal fern, *Osmunda regalis*, is perfect for damp areas and looks very effective planted near water.

∧ *Cool perspective*
Ferns don't mind shade, so grow them where little else will thrive, such as under garden furniture.

< *Star performers*
Ferns are ideal for these mesh-covered troughs, which were designed as a green car-parking bay.

Dry shade solutions

Shady, dry areas, such as those beneath trees and large shrubs, are some of the trickiest for plants to cope with. Choose sun-lovers for these sites and you will have mean, dried-out plants stretching for light. However, there are a few stalwarts that will not only cope, but thrive in such a spot. To give them a head start, dig large planting holes and mix plenty of well-rotted manure with the soil, then apply lots of water while they settle in.

❋❋❋ fully hardy **❋❋** hardy in mild regions/sheltered sites **❋** protect from frost over winter
☼ full sun ☼ partial sun ☼ full shade ◊ well-drained soil ◊ moist soil ● wet soil

❶ *Kerria japonica* 'Golden Guinea'; ‡2m (6ft) ↔2.4m (8ft) ☼ ☼ ◊ ❋❋❋ ❷ Deadnettle, *Lamium maculatum* 'White Nancy'; ‡15cm (6in) ↔1m (3ft) ☼ ☼ ◊ ◊ ❋❋❋ ❸ Lungwort, *Pulmonaria* 'Lewis Palmer'; ‡35cm (14in) ↔ 45cm (18in) ☼ ☼ ◊ ❋❋❋ ❹ *Saxifraga stolonifera* 'Tricolor'; ‡30cm (12in) ↔30cm (12in) ☼ ☼ ◊ ◊ ❋❋ ❺ *Brunnera macrophylla* 'Dawson's White'; ‡45cm (18in) ↔ 60cm (24in) ☼ ☼ ◊ ◊ ❋❋❋ ❻ *Viburnum davidii*; ‡1.5m (5ft) ↔1.5m (5ft) ☼ ☼ ◊ ◊ ❋❋❋ ❼ *Cyclamen coum* Pewter Group; ‡8cm (3in) ↔10cm (4in) ☼ ☼ ◊ ❋❋❋ ❽ Jacob's ladder, *Polemonium caeruleum*; ‡60cm (24in) ↔30cm (12in) ☼ ☼ ◊ ◊ ❋❋❋ ❾ *Euonymus fortunei* 'Emerald 'n' Gold'; ‡60cm (24in) ↔90cm (36in) ☼ ◊ ◊ ❋❋❋ ❿ *Aquilegia vulgaris* 'Nivea'; ‡90cm (36in) ↔ 45cm (18in) ☼ ☼ ◊ ◊ ❋❋❋ ⓫ Fringe cups, *Tellima grandiflora*; ‡80cm (32in) ↔30cm (12in) ☼ ☼ ◊ ◊ ❋❋❋

Tropical retreat

You don't need to live in the tropics to create a lush, leafy, jungle-like corner in which to hide away from the stresses of the world. Choose sculptural plants with dramatic leaves in shades of green.

》 WHEN TO START
Spring

AT ITS BEST
Summer

TIME TO COMPLETE
🕐 4 hours

YOU WILL NEED
🛈 Spade
Well-rotted organic matter
Mulch

1. Loquat, *Eriobotrya japonica*
2. *Phormium cookianum* subsp. *hookeri* 'Tricolor'
3. *Polystichum setiferum*
4. Arum lily, *Zantedeschia aethiopica*
5. *Musa basjoo*

1 CHOOSE THE SITE
All these plants prefer a sunny site, but will tolerate light shade. They also need to be sheltered from strong winds, which could damage their foliage.

2 PREPARE TO PLANT
Clear the border of weeds and dig in organic matter over the site. Arrange the plants in a tiered jungle effect, then plant and water well (*see pp.30–31 for planting method*). Mulch with bark to give the feel of a forest floor.

3 AFTERCARE
All of these plants are quite hardy, except *Musa basjoo*. In winter, surround it with chicken wire attached to stakes and fill with hay (*see also p.408*). In mild areas, wrap it with garden fleece.

Plant bare-root bamboo

Bare-root bamboo plants are significantly cheaper than those grown in pots, and are a good option if you need several to create a screen, as shown here. You may also get a bare-root plant if a friend has sections to spare. Plant them as soon as you get them home to prevent the roots drying out.

WHEN TO PLANT
Autumn

AT THEIR BEST
Summer

TIME TO COMPLETE
1–2 hours

YOU WILL NEED

Bare-root bamboo
Plastic bag
Spade
Compost
Watering can
Root barrier
Garden moss

< *Elegant screen*
Bamboo makes a perfect screen to hide ugly objects in the garden or to ensure privacy. Evergreen, clothed in foliage all the way up the stem, and with an upright habit, it takes up less space, if controlled, than the average hedge.

1 KEEP ROOTS MOIST
As the roots are not in soil and will dry out and die very rapidly, you must keep them moist before planting. Place a plastic bag filled with garden moss around the roots, and keep the moss damp until the last minute, when you are ready to plant.

2 ADD ORGANIC MATTER
Dig a hole larger than the rootball and break up the base using a fork. In the bottom, add a layer of well-rotted organic matter, such as garden compost or farmyard manure, and mix it in lightly. Add more organic matter to the excavated soil from the hole and mix this together.

3 PLACE BAMBOO INTO HOLE
Unwrap the bamboo, gently tease out the roots and carefully lower it into the planting hole. Keeping the plant upright, add the organic matter and soil mix, firming down as you go to make sure there are no air pockets between the roots.

4 PLANT AND FIRM IN BAMBOO
Fill in the hole around the stems, making sure the plant is at the same level as originally planted. To do this, look for an earthy tidemark on the stems, showing where the soil had previously come up to. Firm well and water.

5 AFTERCARE
Keep the immediate area weed-free while the plant is establishing. Water regularly during dry spells to ensure the plant roots do not dry out. Thin out and tidy established clumps every two years in early spring, before they begin shooting. Cut any dead or weak stems down to ground level.

TOP TIP: CONTROLLING BAMBOOS

Some bamboos are "runners" and once established will send out roots all over the garden. These plants need containing with a root barrier made from a non-perishable material, such as rigid plastic or slate. Dig a narrow trench round the clump and insert your barrier. Cut and remove all peripheral roots, then fill in with soil.

Sow an annual border

Annual bedding plants are great in pots and window boxes, but they can also be planted straight into the summer border, where they offer a quick and colourful way to fill bare patches in new gardens.

Sunflowers

From towering giants to knee-high midgets, sunflowers are real crowd pleasers, and always a hit with children.

>> **WHEN TO SOW**
Spring
AT THEIR BEST
Mid- to late summer

TIME TO COMPLETE
🕐 20 mins to sow; 20 mins to plant

YOU WILL NEED
ⓘ Sunflower seeds
7cm (3½in) pots
Seed compost
Garden canes
String

1 PLANT SEEDS
In spring, sow sunflower seeds indoors in a light, warm spot. Sow a single seed into each pot, as they make large seedlings. Coir pots (*above*) can be planted whole, straight into the soil.

3 SUPPORT YOUNG PLANTS
Prepare a suitable area of soil outside, and once the risk of frost has passed, plant the sunflowers out into the garden. As their young stems bend easily, tie them to short canes. For extra big sunflowers, choose a large cultivar. Feed and water the plants all summer.

2 WATER FREQUENTLY
Water seedlings regularly, and keep them indoors or in a warm greenhouse until mid-spring. Then put them outside during the day, bringing them indoors at night, to harden off.

Planting options

Flowering annuals come in a wealth of shapes and sizes, and even scents; many are tender, so plant outside after the frosts.

Cosmos has delicate, ferny foliage, with flowers that float on tall, delicate stems. In contrast, *Iberis* scrambles across the soil and offers useful groundcover. *Senecio*'s silvery foliage provides a wonderful foil for flowers, and low-growing *Gazania* is a dazzler, adding vivid colour to a sunny spot.

❶ *Cosmos bipinnatus*; ↕1m (3ft) ↔45cm (18in)
❷ *Senecio cineraria*; ↕↔60cm (24in)
❸ *Gazania*; ↕20cm (8in) ↔25cm (10in)
❹ Candytuft, *Iberis umbellata*; ↕30cm (12in) ↔23cm (9in)

< Pot of gold
Not all sunflowers are giants. The shorter varieties, 'Teddy Bear' and 'Dwarf Yellow Spray', are planted alongside bedding geraniums (Pelargonium), Salvia farinacea 'Strata', nasturtiums, and black-eyed Susan (Thunbergia alata), in this colourful bed.

Cottage dream

The gentle hues and varying textures of cottage garden perennials can be used to create beautiful combinations in an informal planting scheme. This is the classic sun-loving border of many gardeners' imaginations, with spires of lofty delphiniums piercing through lower mounds of colourful flowers.

WHEN TO START
Autumn

AT THEIR BEST
Midsummer

TIME TO COMPLETE
2 hours preparation; 3 hours to plant

YOU WILL NEED
Spade
Well-rotted organic matter
Grit

1. *Delphinium* Black Knight Group
2. *Anchusa azurea*
3. *Alstroemeria ligtu* hybrids
4. *Achillea filipendulina* 'Gold Plate'
5. *Salvia sclarea var. turkestanica*
6. *Verbascum olympicum*

1 PREPARE THE SOIL

In autumn, clear the border of all weeds. Dig in organic matter, such as garden compost or well-rotted farmyard manure. Ideally you should dig down one spade depth (*see p.21*), incorporating organic matter into the top 15cm (6in) of soil. On heavy soils, spread a layer of grit over the whole area, and dig it in to improve drainage.

2 SET OUT THE PLANTING PLAN

Buy plants in spring and set them out across the border, taking time to arrange them and to visualize how they will grow in relation to each other. The classic arrangement is taller plants at the back and shorter plants at the front, but consider using tall, airy types, such as *Achillea* or *Verbena bonariensis*, further forward.

3 AFTERCARE

Some of the plants will need staking as they grow (*see right*), and in their first year they will require regular watering to help them to establish. Although these herbaceous perennials die back in winter, where possible, leave their stems to stand until spring. Then cut everything back to the ground to tidy the border and allow space for new growth. This is also a good time to apply a general-purpose granular fertilizer and a mulch of well-rotted organic matter.

TOP TIP: STAKING

Many perennials, such as delphiniums and *Achillea*, become top-heavy and require support. If you provide supports early in the season, plants will grow through and disguise them, and they will still look natural and attractive. Plants staked at a later date, once they have already flopped, always tend to look trussed up.

∧ *Stop the flop*
Use short canes to support tall flowers, such as delphiniums (top left). Plants with mound-like growth will grow through and be supported by twiggy sticks put in place in spring (top right). Linked metal stakes serve a similar purpose (above).

Cottage garden plants

There are so many different plants that suit a cottage garden, but as a rule, the simpler ones that have not been highly bred look most at home in such a scheme. Plants such as anemones, *Cirsium* and *Anthemis* create easy-going, loose arrangements, while the tall flower spires of lupins and hollyhocks provide structure. Cottage garden plants are generally loved by bees and other nectar-seeking insects.

❀❀❀ fully hardy   ❀❀ hardy in mild regions/sheltered sites   ❀ protect from frost over winter

☼ full sun   ☼ partial sun   ☀ full shade   ◊ well-drained soil   ◐ moist soil   ● wet soil

❶ Monkshood, *Aconitum carmichaelii* Arendsii Group; ↕1.2m (4ft) ↔30cm (12in) ☼ ☼ ◊ ◐ ❀❀❀
❷ Golden marguerite, *Anthemis tinctoria* 'E.C. Buxton'; ↕60cm (24in) ↔90cm (36in) ☼ ◊ ❀❀❀
❸ *Aquilegia formosa*; ↕60cm (24in) ↔45cm (18in) ☼ ☼ ◐ ❀❀❀   ❹ *Coreopsis verticillata*
'Moonbeam'; ↕50cm (20in) ↔60cm (24in)☼ ☼ ◊ ❀❀❀   ❺ *Cirsium rivulare* 'Atropurpureum';
↕1.2m (4ft) ↔60cm (24in) ☼ ◊ ◐ ❀❀❀   ❻ Bleeding heart, *Dicentra spectabilis* 'Alba'; ↕1.2m (4ft)
↔45cm (18in) ☼ ◐ ❀❀❀   ❼ *Anemone hupehensis* 'Hadspen Abundance'; ↕60cm (24in) ↔40cm
(16in) ☼ ☼ ◐ ❀❀❀   ❽ Meadow cranesbill, *Geranium pratense* 'Mrs Kendall Clark'; ↕60cm (24in)
↔60cm (24in) ☼ ☼ ◊ ◐ ❀❀❀   ❾ Lupin, *Lupinus* 'Inverewe Red'; ↕90cm (36in) ↔60cm (24in)
☼ ☼ ◊ ❀❀❀   ❿ Hollyhock, *Alcea rosea* Chater's Double Group; ↕2.4m (8ft) ↔60cm (24in)☼ ◊ ❀❀❀
⓫ *Astrantia major*; ↕60cm (24in) ↔45cm (18in) ☼ ☼ ◐ ❀❀❀

∧ Autumnal tones
This scheme looks beautiful in autumn, when the seedheads of late-flowering perennials offer shades of copper and bronze.

∧ Winter structure
The plants have a strong structure, so their stems and seedheads remain intact all winter, to the benefit of birds and wildlife.

Prairie partners

Popularized by Dutch garden designer Piet Oudolf, prairie planting schemes use dramatic swathes of grasses, alongside perennials that have a strong winter structure. Particularly suitable for larger gardens, these borders are often at their most beautiful in autumn and winter, a time when many perennial beds are lacklustre and dull.

》 **WHEN TO START**
Spring or autumn

AT ITS BEST
Late summer to early winter

TIME TO COMPLETE
🕐 4 hours

YOU WILL NEED
🛈 Well-rotted organic matter, such as farmyard manure
Horticultural grit for clay soils

1. *Deschampsia cespitosa*
2. *Sedum spectabile*
3. *Echinacea purpurea* 'Rubinstern'
4. *Lythrum virgatum*
5. *Eupatorium*

1 PREPARATION
It is important to dig over the soil thoroughly and incorporate plenty of organic matter, such as well-rotted manure, before you start planting. This style of gardening uses groups of plants that enjoy similar well-drained but moist soil, so you will also have to incorporate grit into heavy clay soil (*see pp.14–15*).

2 PLANTING LAYOUT
The prairie planting style uses interlocking swathes of plants, with each swathe comprising just one species or type of plant. To create this effect, you will need lots of plants, so buy young ones to minimize costs. If you have a small garden, follow the same rules for larger plots but reduce the number of different species used. Set your plants out in teardrop-shaped swathes, with the narrow sections neatly slotting together.

3 CUT BACK IN SPRING
This border is designed to look good all winter long, so you must resist the temptation to cut it all back or tidy it too much in autumn. Most cutting back can be left until early spring, when new shoots appear at the base of the plants. If some areas start to look really messy, tidy stray stems earlier.

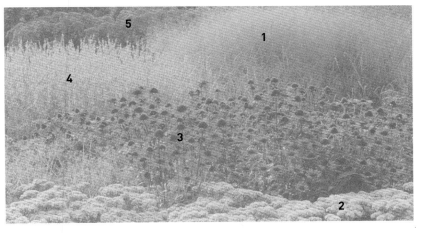

Flowers for cutting and drying

One of the greatest pleasures of owning a garden is growing an abundance of flowers, many of which can be picked and brought indoors to decorate the house as well. Some are particularly well suited to cutting, while others can be harvested and dried to last into winter and beyond.

Cutting

Many plants can be cut frequently with little impact on the garden display; they just keep on producing more flowers. Plant a cut-flower border full of such varieties.

FLOWERS FOR CUTTING

Allium	Dahlia
Alstroemeria	Foxglove, *Digitalis*
Antirrhinum	Peony (*above*)
Chrysanthemum	*Rudbeckia*
Cleome	Sunflower
Cornflower,	Sweet pea
Centaurea	Sweet William
Cosmos	Tulip
Daffodil	*Zinnia*

>> **WHEN TO START**
Autumn or spring

AT THEIR BEST
Spring to late summer

TIME TO COMPLETE
🕐 5 hours for sowing and pricking out
2 hours for planting

YOU WILL NEED
💧 Seeds of annuals
Bulbs
Perennials
Spade
Well-rotted organic matter, such
 as farmyard manure
Watering can

1 PLANT IN SWATHES
Clear the area of weeds, and dig in organic matter. In autumn, plant bulbs and mark their positions (*see pp.40–41*). Then, in spring, plant large swathes of perennials and annuals (*see pp.30–31 and pp.108–110*), so that you can cut the flowers regularly without leaving large gaps in your border.

2 PICK AND MIX
When you are planning to pick your flowers, water the area well the night before. This helps the stems to plump up, and the cut flowers will keep for longer. It is best to cut first thing in the morning, plunging the stems immediately into a deep bucket of water. Always cut to just above a leaf.

Drying

Some flowers retain their colours and scents when they are cut and dried, and can be used in flower arrangements throughout the year. Seedheads look striking in indoor arrangements too, but leave some on the plants if you want a dramatic winter border.

》 **WHEN TO START**
Summer to autumn

AT THEIR BEST
All year

TIME TO COMPLETE
About 2 weeks for drying

YOU WILL NEED
Flowers for drying
Rubber bands
Tacks or pins
Hooks or paperclips
String

1 PLANT AND SOW
Several perennials are useful as dried flowers, but you may want to sow some annuals too. Sow half-hardy annuals into modules or pots indoors in spring, planting out when all risk of frost has passed (*see pp.108–110*). Hardy annuals can be sown direct in autumn or spring. Water, feed, and deadhead as you would any other plant.

2 CUT IN DRY WEATHER
Pick flowers for drying in fine weather to avoid excess moisture on the foliage and petals. Most flowers will dry better if they are cut before they are fully open. Pick roses just as the buds begin to open, and lavender stems as the top petals start to emerge.

3 AIR DRY THE BLOOMS
Tie a few stems together with a rubber band or string. Use a kitchen hook or a paper clip to attach the bands to a line of string, or tie them to a bamboo cane (*below*). Then fix the string or cane to the ceiling in a cool, airy place. As strong light will bleach out the colours, it is best to hang them in the dark, or in low light.

FLOWERS FOR DRYING

Achillea (above)	Quaking grass,
Cornflower,	*Briza*
Centaurea	Sea holly,
Globe thistle,	*Eryngium*
Echinops	Statice,
Hare's tail,	*Limonium*
Lagurus	(above)
Lavender	Strawflower,
Love-in-a-mist,	*Xerochrysum*
Nigella	(below)

Textured edge

A striking scheme such as this should be treated as a modern take on bedding. The perennials will last far longer than annual plants, but the formal effect will eventually lose its crispness as they grow.

WHEN TO PLANT
Autumn or spring

AT ITS BEST
Early summer

TIME TO COMPLETE
2 hours

YOU WILL NEED
Sand or string
Well-rotted organic matter, such as farmyard manure

1. *Iris chrysographes* 'Black Knight'
2. *Salvia x sylvestris* 'Mainacht'
3. *Heuchera* 'Beauty Colour'
4. Feather grass, *Stipa tenuissima*
5. *Persicaria microcephala* 'Red Dragon'
6. *Angelica archangelica*

1 MARK OUT YOUR PATTERN
Chose a sunny site and improve the soil with organic matter before planting, then use sand or string to mark out lines to create the formal, parallel-effect. Space out the plants to allow room for them to spread.

2 PLANT OUT
Plant the tall *Persicaria* at the back, and the *Heuchera* and *Salvia* at the front to form a neat carpet. Use accent plants, such as *Angelica*, to add interest to the pattern.

3 AFTERCARE
You may have to lift and replant every few years to keep the pattern strong. Experiment with rows of different plants until you find a combination that is happy in your conditions.

Lay a gravel bed

Drought-tolerant plants that originate from arid, rocky places look most at home in a gravel garden. Ideal for a hot, sunny spot, a gravel border is easy to make, and can create a mosaic of colours and textures in areas where other plants struggle to survive.

 WHEN TO START
Spring
AT ITS BEST
Summer

TIME TO COMPLETE
6 hours

YOU WILL NEED
 Drought-loving plants
Horticultural grit
Washed sand
Landscape fabric
Scissors
Galvanized staples
Watering can
Gravel
Boulders

1 PREPARE THE AREA
Dig over the area thoroughly and remove any weeds. You need a well-drained soil to keep drought-tolerant plants happy, so dig in washed sand and horticultural grit to make sure that yours drains freely, even in wet weather.

2 LAY MEMBRANE
Weed-suppressing membrane or landscape fabric allows rain to soak through to the roots, yet prevents weeds from growing. Lay it over the entire area, overlapping the edges, and pinning them down with galvanized staples as you go.

3 CUT CROSSES FOR PLANTS
Place your plants in their positions on the landscape fabric, and then arrange them to create a pleasing display. For each plant, cut a cross in the fabric, and fold back the flaps.

4 PLANT THROUGH FABRIC
Dig a hole and plant your plants at the same depth they were at in their pots. Add a little fertilizer to the back-filled soil, and firm it in. Replace the fabric to fit around the stems.

5 SPREAD GRAVEL MULCH
Once all of the plants have been watered in, spread a 5cm (2in) layer of gravel over the entire area. You may need to top this up occasionally to keep the garden looking its best. Water the plants in dry spells for the first year.

Self-seeded gravel garden

A slightly different style of gravel garden uses no landscape fabric. Plants are left to self-seed and create a wonderfully natural effect, but make sure you remove every scrap of perennial weed during the preparation.

ENCOURAGE SEEDING
Both weeds and seedlings of desired plants will spring up in a gravel bed, and it is important to learn the difference between them. You may have to allow weeds to grow larger than you would ideally like to identify them. In addition, take a relaxed approach to deadheading; seeds will never get the chance to form if the flowers are nipped off the moment they start to fade.

❶ *Eryngium giganteum*; ‡90cm (36in) ↔30cm (12in) ❷ *Meconopsis cambrica*; ‡45cm (18in) ↔25cm (10in) ❸ *Nigella damascena* Persian Jewel Group; ‡40cm (16in) ↔23cm (9in) ❹ Foxglove, *Digitalis purpurea*; ‡1.5m (5ft) ↔60cm (24in)

OTHER PLANTING OPTIONS

Alchemilla mollis	Nasturtiums
Alyssum	Shirley poppies
Aquilegias	Snapdragon
Eschscholzia	*Stipa tenuissima*
Feverfew	*Verbena bonariensis*

Mediterranean-style plants

Many of the plants that we associate with holidays abroad will grow well in cooler climates, particularly in a well-drained, sandy soil. Choose those with bold shapes and silvery foliage to evoke Mediterranean memories, and throw in a few with vivid flowers such as *Hibiscus,* to brighten things up. Keep plants with aromatic leaves, such as *Cistus*, close at hand; they release spicy oils as the sun warms them, and will transport you back to lazy days.

❄❄❄ fully hardy   ❄❄ hardy in mild regions/sheltered sites   ❄ protect from frost over winter
☼ full sun   ☀ partial sun   ☀ full shade   ◇ well-drained soil   ◗ moist soil   ● wet soil

1 Rock rose, *Cistus x dansereaui* 'Decumbens'; ‡40cm (16in) ↔60cm (24in) ☼ ◇ ❄❄❄   **2** Viper's bugloss, *Echium vulgare* 'Blue Bedder'; ‡50cm (20in) ↔30cm (12in) ☼ ◇ ❄❄   **3** *Phormium* 'Sundowner'; ‡2m (6ft) ↔2m (6ft) ☼ ◇ ❄❄❄   **4** Sea holly, *Eryngium x tripartitum*; ‡80cm (32in) ↔50cm (20in) ☼ ◇ ❄❄❄   **5** Spurge, *Euphorbia myrsinites*; ‡10cm (4in) ↔30cm (12in) ☼ ◇ ❄❄❄   **6** *Eriobotrya japonica*; ‡8m (25ft) ↔8m (25ft) ☼ ◇ ❄❄   **7** Oleander, *Nerium oleander*; ‡3m (10ft) ↔2m (6ft) ☼ ◇ ❄❄   **8** Cardoon, *Cynara cardunculus*; ‡1.5m (5ft) ↔1.2m (4ft) ☼ ◇ ❄❄❄   **9** *Anthemis punctata* subsp. *cupaniana*; ‡30cm (12in) ↔90cm (36in) ☼ ◇ ❄❄   **10** *Hibiscus syriacus* 'Boule de Feu'; ‡3m (10ft) ↔2m (6ft) ☼ ◇ ❄❄❄   **11** *Lavandula angustifolia* 'Nana Alba'; ‡30cm (12in) ↔30cm (12in) ☼ ◇ ❄❄❄

Plant by a hedge

Hedges make beautiful backdrops to beds and borders, as well as providing superb habitats for wildlife, but they present their own problems. The soil close to a hedge is usually dry and it can shade the planting in front, but choose carefully and both plants and hedge will thrive.

PLANTING IN A SUNNY SITE

In south-facing gardens, hedges can help to shade plants that receive the full force of the summer sun almost all day. However, for both the hedge and plants to succeed, they need sufficient water. When planting (*see pp.192–197 for methods*) dig plenty of organic matter, such as well-rotted farmyard manure, into the soil before you start, and mulch around the hedge annually with more organic matter. This should help keep the hedge happy. Select drought-tolerant plants for the beds, as a mature hedge will suck out much of the soil water. Plant about 45cm (18in) in front of the hedge, and again dig organic matter into the soil and mulch to help it retain moisture.

∧ > *Sun worship*
Cirsium rivulare *and* Geum rivale *are combined here in front of a mixed deciduous hedge, to produce an airy, informal effect* (above). *Lavender tolerates the dry conditions in front of this smooth yew hedge, creating an elegant line of purple flower spikes in summer* (right).

PLANNING FOR SHADY AREAS

Your choice of plants for borders in dense shade in front of a hedge will be limited, since only a few have adapted to the extremes of drought and darkness. When planning a hedge, try to site it where it will not shade the beds in front all day; if you have inherited a hedge that does this, select plants that can tolerate these difficult conditions (*see pp.58–59*).

You will have a wider choice of plants for areas that receive sun for part of the day, but moisture retention will still present a problem here, so dig plenty of organic matter into the soil. In addition, you could lay a trickle hose (a perforated hose pipe that seeps water into the soil) around the border. In these damper conditions, many woodland plants, such as *Geranium phaeum,* foxgloves (*Digitalis*), bleeding heart (*Dicentra*), and Japanese anemones (*Anemone* x *hybrida*) will thrive.

< *Flowery picture*
The hedge here provides a dark backdrop to the pale foxgloves and pink roses, which will tolerate some shade, and annual tobacco plants (Nicotiana). *The* Alchemilla mollis *in the foreground is happy almost anywhere.*

DESIGNER TRICKS

Where space allows, a wide margin between the hedge and border allows a much greater plant choice and less maintenance, as the plants will not require watering as frequently. Turf over the area between the hedge and the border, or opt for a paved, decked, or bark-chip walkway to separate them. Another designer trick is to make a "fedge", which is simply a chain-link or wooden fence covered with ivy or other evergreen climber. Ideal for smaller gardens where a deep hedge is not an option, a fedge will still draw moisture from the soil, but to a lesser extent.

∧ > *Simple solutions*
This "fedge" (above) is a chain-link fence with ivy growing through it, providing a super-slim screen to enhance the bright perennials in front. For larger gardens (right) a border set about a metre (3ft) from the hedge allows sun-loving shrubs and perennials to thrive.

Planting options

Unless your border faces south, and is sunny for most of the day, select shade-tolerant plants to grow in front of hedges.

CONTRAST COLOURS AND TEXTURES

Check plant labels before you buy and select those whose foliage is not exactly the same colour as your hedge, or they will simply disappear into the background. Pastels and white flowers show up best against a dark yew (*Taxus*) hedge, and large-leaved plants work well with hornbeam (*Carpinus*) or beech (*Fagus*) hedges that have a more textured look. Dark foliage creates a striking contrast when matched with golden privet (*Ligustrum ovalifolium* 'Aureum') or shrubby honeysuckle (*Lonicera nitida* 'Baggesen's Gold'). The following plants are all good choices to plant in beds in front of hedges:

❶ *Bergenia* x *schmidtii*; ‡30cm (12in) ↔ 60cm (24in)   ❷ *Hypericum calycinum*; ‡60cm (24in) ↔ indefinite   ❸ *Maianthemum racemosum*; ‡90cm (36in) ↔ 60cm (24in)   ❹ *Epimedium* x *versicolor*; ‡↔30cm (12in)   ❺ *Campanula poscharskyana*; ‡15cm (6in) ↔ 60cm (24in)   ❻ *Tricyrtis formosana*; ‡80cm (32in) ↔ 45cm (18in)

Create an easy-care border

This bold mix brings together rich colours and contrasting flowers and foliage to create an easy-care summer border. Ideal for free-draining soil and a sunny site, these plants rarely need watering once established.

>> **WHEN TO START**
Early spring

AT ITS BEST
Summer

TIME TO COMPLETE

 1 hour

YOU WILL NEED

 Horticultural grit
Well-rotted organic matter, such
 as farmyard manure
Spade
All-purpose granular fertilizer

1. Montbretia, *Crocosmia*
   'Bressingham Blaze'
2. *Heliopsis helianthoides*
   Loraine Sunshine
3. *Lavandula angustifolia*
   Blue Cushion
4. *Sedum telephium*
   (Atropurpureum Group)
   'Bressingham Purple'

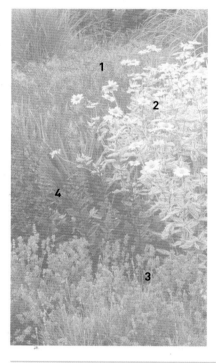

1 PREPARE THE SOIL
Choose a sunny, open position and, a week before planting, spread an 8cm (3in) layer of organic matter over the soil, and dig it into the top 15cm (6cm). Clay soils will also require horticultural grit to improve drainage.

2 PLANT THE PERENNIALS
Starting at the back of the border, plant the *Crocosmia*, with the *Heliopsis* and *Sedum* in front, (*see steps on pp.30–31*). Take care not to bury their stems, as this may cause them to rot.

3 PLANT THE LAVENDER
Plant a line of lavender at the front, (*see steps on pp.82–83*), ensuring that the stems are above the soil. Spread a gravel mulch. Water the plants regularly for the first year, until they are established. Apply a granular fertilizer each spring.

Easy-care shrubs

For a really low-maintenance border, try these hardy shrubs. They look after themselves once established, and tolerate periods of drought. Simply trim them annually to keep them in shape, removing dead, diseased or damaged stems.

❶ *Brachyglottis* (Dunedin Group) 'Sunshine' (evergreen, prefers sun); ↕1.5m (5ft) ↔2m (6ft) ❷ *Choisya* x *dewitteana* 'Aztec Pearl' (evergreen, prefers sun); ↕2.5m (8ft) ↔2.5m (8ft)
❸ *Mahonia* x *wagneri* cultivar (evergreen, prefers shade); ↕80cm (32in) ↔1m (3ft) ❹ *Viburnum sieboldii* (deciduous, prefers sun or partial shade); ↕4m (12ft) ↔4m (12ft)

Creative cubes

Originally used by the construction industry, galvanized wire mesh crates, known as "gabions", have been adopted by designers for modern garden landscapes. This exciting show garden is easy to recreate on a smaller scale; buy the gabions at a garden centre, or commission a specialist to make them for you.

WHEN TO START
Autumn
AT ITS BEST
Summer

TIME TO COMPLETE
3–4 days

YOU WILL NEED
Gabions
Flagstones or stones of your choice
Wooden box or foam cube
Spirit level
Thick nylon tights
Topsoil or soil-based compost
Well-rotted organic matter
All-purpose granular fertilizer

1. *Gunnera manicata*
2. *Astilboides tabularis*
3. *Hosta undulata* var. *albomarginata*
4. Mind-your-own-business, *Soleirolia soleirolii*
5. Silver birch, *Betula utilis* var. *jacquemontii*

< *Modular garden*
The gabions in this modern design are simply piled on top of one another to create a textured effect, with large leafy plants filling the gaps.

1 STACK THE CRATES
This garden is made from gabions stacked together to create the structure and surface. Simply fill them with flagstones and set them on the soil, checking that they are level with a spirit level – dig out or add soil beneath them as necessary. Leave spaces for planting. Fill more gabions and place them on the foundation level to create stepping stones and seats, and leave a few empty to produce an exciting layered effect.

2 MAKE LEAFY GABIONS
To make the planted crates, place a wooden box or block of foam in the centre of a gabion. Then fill up the legs of some thick nylon tights with moist compost, tie up the ends, and pack them around the sides and top of the gabion. Buy small plants of mind-your-own-business, cut holes in the tights, and plant into these. Keep well watered. The plants will soon spread to fill out the crates.

3 PLANT THE BEDS
In the gaps between the gabions, fill the planting beds with a soil-based compost. Mix in some well-rotted organic matter, such as farmyard manure or homemade garden compost, to increase water retention for these moisture-loving plants (make a mini bog garden for the *Gunnera*, see pp.330–331). Plant the birch trees in late autumn (*see pp.178–179*) and the other plants in early spring. Keep well watered for the first year, and during dry spells thereafter.

Crate fillers

You can fill your gabions with almost anything, from used bottles to wood offcuts. If you are building a new garden, look around the site for fillers, such as bricks, pebbles, and rocks.

Try these crate fillers: ❶ Used beer bottles; wine bottles would also work well ❷ Bricks and clay garden edging ❸ Layers of small logs, pebbles, and slate, which form this beautiful design.

Plant dahlia tubers

Once shunned by fashionable gardeners, these flashy, colourful jewels have staged something of a comeback, and are now considered an essential feature of the mid- to late-summer border, as well as injecting life into tired autumn gardens. They also provide lots of cut flowers for indoor displays.

>> **WHEN TO PLANT**
Late spring
AT THEIR BEST
Midsummer to autumn

TIME TO COMPLETE
30 minutes for planting

YOU WILL NEED
Dahlia tubers
Well-rotted organic matter, such as farmyard manure
Slug rings or organic pellets
Canes and twine for staking
Wooden boxes
Potting compost
Plant labels

1 PLANT THE TUBERS
Once the danger of frost has passed, dig a hole 30cm (12in) deep and add a layer of organic matter to the bottom. Place the tuber in with the buds pointing up, as well as a cane for support, and carefully refill with soil.

2 PINCH OUT SHOOT TIPS
Provide slug protection as young growth appears. When the stems are 30cm (12in) high, pinch out the top bud to encourage bushiness and lots of flowers.

3 FROST PROTECTION
As soon as the first light frost has blackened the leaves, cut off the foliage and dig up the tubers. Place them somewhere airy and frost free, so that the stems can dry out fully.

4 STORE OVERWINTER
When dry, brush the soil off the tubers, label them clearly and plant them in wooden boxes or large pots of dry potting compost. Keep them in a cool, dry, frost-free place until you can plant them out again the following spring.

Try tropical cannas

Cannas bring tropical colour to the late-summer garden, but are not entirely hardy. They are tougher than dahlias, though, and can survive outside in milder areas with the right care.

>> **WHEN TO PLANT**
Late spring
AT THEIR BEST
Midsummer to autumn

TIME TO COMPLETE
🕐 30 minutes for planting
YOU WILL NEED
ℹ️ Canna rhizomes
Well-rotted organic matter, such as farmyard manure
Mulch
Straw
Chicken wire or wooden box

1 SITING CANNAS
These plants need a hot and sunny spot to flower well; a south-facing, sheltered area is ideal. Also, make sure that your cannas are not shaded by neighbouring plants, or competing with them for moisture, which can affect flowering.

2 IMPROVE THE SOIL
Cannas are thirsty plants, so improve the soil with organic matter to help retain moisture. To plant, dig a hole about 20cm (8in) deep and lay a rhizome in it horizontally. Refill the hole with soil, water well, and apply a layer of mulch.

3 OVERWINTERING
In autumn, after the frost has blackened the leaves, cut down the stems. In mild regions, cover the rhizomes with straw, pinned down with chicken wire. In colder areas, lift and store them in dry potting compost, in a cool, dry, frost-free place, such as a shed.

Dramatic dahlias

The darlings of the gardening design world, dahlias are the glamour pusses of the mid- to late-summer border, providing sparkle and drama just as other stars are starting to fade. Choose from simple singles, neat pompons, star-shaped cactus-types, and dainty collerettes in a wide range of rich colours. Use them to colour up beds and borders, or to create eye-catching displays in large containers on a patio or terrace.

SELECTIONS >>

✻✻✻ fully hardy   ✻✻ hardy in mild regions/sheltered sites   ✻ protect from frost over winter
☼ full sun   ☀ partial sun   ☀ full shade   ◊ well-drained soil   ◖ moist soil   ● wet soil

1 'Gay Princess'; ‡1.5m (5ft) ↔75cm (30in) ☼ ◊ ✻   **2** 'Arabian Night'; ‡1.2m (4ft) ↔60cm (24in)
☼ ◊ ✻   **3** 'Easter Sunday'; ‡1m (3ft) ↔60cm (24in) ☼ ◊ ✻   **4** 'Kathryn's Cupid'; ‡1.2m (4ft) ↔60cm
(24in) ☼ ◊ ✻   **5** 'Ragged Robin'; ‡1m (3ft) ↔45cm (18in) ☼ ◊ ✻   **6** 'Yellow Hammer'; ‡60cm (24in)
↔45cm (18in) ☼ ◊ ✻   **7** 'Preston Park'; ‡45cm (18in) ↔45cm (18in) ☼ ◊ ✻   **8** 'Moonfire'; ‡1m (3ft)
↔60cm (24in) ☼ ◊ ✻   **9** 'Pink Giraffe'; ‡75cm (30in) ↔60cm (24in) ☼ ◊ ✻   **10** 'Polar Sight'; ‡1.2m
(4ft) ↔60cm (24in) ☼ ◊ ✻   **11** 'Zorro'; ‡1.2m (4ft) ↔60cm (24in) ☼ ◊ ✻

Contemporary urban mix

You don't need to rule out vegetables and herbs just because you live in the city. Here, the designer has created a stylish modern look with a mix of edibles and ornamental flowers in this chic urban garden. The box edging and cherry tree provide permanent structure to the ever-changing crops and flowers.

WHEN TO PLANT
Autumn to early spring

AT ITS BEST
Summer

TIME TO COMPLETE
2–3 days

YOU WILL NEED
Topsoil or soil-based compost
Well-rotted organic matter
All-purpose granular fertilizer

1. Fig, *Ficus carica*
2. Box, *Buxus sempervirens*
3. Sweet basil, chilli peppers and lettuces
4. Pot marjoram
5. Parsley
6. Daylily, *Hemerocallis*
7. *Rosa* 'Rose of Picardy'
8. Wild cherry, *Prunus avium*
9. Outdoor tomatoes

1 PREPARE TO PLANT
You can adapt this design to suit your own garden by creating four rectangular beds that fit your plot. The herbs, fig, vegetables, and rose prefer an open, sunny site, while the parsley and daylilies will be happy in the dappled shade beneath the tree. Enrich the soil with well-rotted organic matter, and on clay soils dig in grit too (*see pp.14–15*), as all the plants used here like moist but well-drained conditions.

2 PLANT THE BED
First, in early autumn, plant the box, rose, and tree, which form the structural backbone of the design (*see pp.178–179 for tree-planting; p.93 for roses; p.36 for planting a shrub*). Also plant the fig close to the house wall in early spring (*see p.316*). Clip the box into cube shapes. In late spring, plant the herbs, lettuces, and tomatoes in neat rows in the sunny areas, and the parsley and daylilies just beyond the tree canopy. They have been planted closer to the tree here than is recommended, as this is a show garden.

3 AFTERCARE
Water the tree regularly for the first two years after planting, and keep the area directly beneath it free from weeds. The tomatoes require staking and tying in (*see pp.272–273*). Water all the plants frequently in dry spells and throughout the summer. In autumn, buy plug plants of winter and early spring-cropping cabbages, kale, broccoli, and leeks, to replace the summer tomatoes, chillies, peppers, and sweet basil.

Plant a modern rose garden

Create a contemporary display using disease-resistant roses, such as 'Winchester Cathedral' (*below*), and pretty perennials for a modern mix of flowers and foliage. This classic white scheme is easy to plant and maintain; just follow the steps here for the rose, and on pages 30–31 for the other plants.

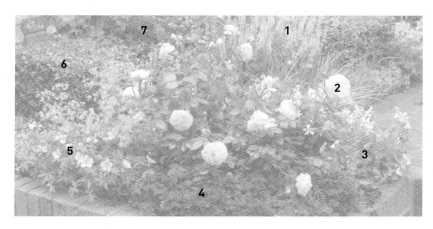

WHEN TO PLANT
Autumn or early spring

AT ITS BEST
Early to midsummer

TIME TO COMPLETE
🕐 3 hours

YOU WILL NEED
ℹ️ Spade
Heavy-duty gloves
Bamboo cane
Well-rotted organic matter

All-purpose granular fertilizer
Mycorrhizal fungi, eg, Rootgrow

1. *Veronica spicata* 'Alba'
2. *Rosa* Winchester Cathedral ('Auscat')
3. White violas
4. *Trifolium repens* 'Purpurascens Quadrifolium'
5. Hardy white geranium
6. *Alchemilla mollis*
7. *Actaea simplex* 'Brunette'

PREPARE TO PLANT
1 Dig a bucketful of organic matter into your proposed planting area, and mix it evenly with the soil. Then dig a hole a little deeper and twice as wide as the pot that contains the rose.

CHECK PLANTING DEPTH
2 Place the rose in its container into the hole, and using a bamboo cane, check that the graft union (the swelling at the base of the stems) will be below the soil surface when the rose is planted. Remove the rose and apply some general-purpose fertilizer to the base of the hole.

APPLY MYCORRHIZAL FUNGI
3 Water the rose and leave to drain. Apply mycorrhizal fungi to the base of the hole, following the directions on the packet. The roots must come into contact with the fungi granules after planting, as these help the rose's root system to establish. Wearing gloves, tip the rose from its container and plant in the hole.

FIRM IN SOIL
4 Backfill around the root ball with excavated soil. Firm the soil with your hands to remove any air pocket. Water the rose well, then apply a 5cm (2in) layer of well-rotted organic matter, making sure that it does not touch the stems. Water the rose regularly during its first year, and apply a rose fertilizer each spring.

Autumn impressions

Many borders fade as temperatures dip, but one packed with grasses, late flowers, and plants with strong, distinctive skeletons will solve the problem. It will look good throughout winter, too.

WHEN TO START
Autumn
AT ITS BEST
Autumn

TIME TO COMPLETE
3 hours to prepare; 3 hours to plant

YOU WILL NEED
Organic matter, such as well-rotted farmyard manure
Spade
Watering can

1. *Aster* x *frikartii*
2. *Sedum* 'Herbstfreude'
3. *Achillea* 'Walther Funcke'
4. *Miscanthus sinensis*
5. Feather grass, *Stipa tenuissima*

1 PREPARE THE SITE
The autumn, before you plan to start planting, carefully clear the border of all weeds, and then dig it over thoroughly. Incorporate plenty of organic matter as you dig (*see p.21*).

2 PLANT UP
In spring, buy plants and plant them in the border (*see pp.28–29*). Taller grasses, such as *Miscanthus*, can go towards the back, with sedums and asters at the front, and loose drifts of *Achillea* threaded throughout the middle.

3 AFTERCARE
Water the plants in thoroughly and apply a mulch of well-rotted organic matter. In spring, the asters and *Achillea* may require staking (*see p.67*). Leave the border to stand as it is over winter, then cut it to the ground in spring.

Jewel-like berries

Plants with fabulous autumn foliage tend to be on the large side, but there are many shrubs and perennials with colourful, glossy autumn berries that will fit into even the smallest of gardens. Plant a selection of these beauties and you will have plenty to look at once the glories of summer have faded. Many hang on to their fruits well into winter, providing birds and other wildlife with a ready supply of food at a lean time of the year.

SELECTIONS 《

✼✼✼ fully hardy   ✼✼ hardy in mild regions/sheltered sites   ✼ protect from frost over winter

☼ full sun   ☼ partial sun   ☀ full shade   ◊ well-drained soil   ◗ moist soil   ● wet soil

❶ Spindle tree, *Euonymus planipes*; ↕2m (6ft) ↔2m (6ft) ☼ ☼ ◗ ✼✼✼   ❷ *Clerodendrum trichotomum* var. *fargesii*; ↕5m (15ft) ↔5m (15ft) ☼ ☼ ◗ ✼✼✼   ❸ *Gaultheria mucronata* 'Wintertime'; ↕80cm (32in) ↔1.2m (4ft) ☼ ◗ ✼✼✼   ❹ *Viburnum tinus*; ↕2m (6ft) ↔2m (6ft) ☼ ☀ ◗ ✼✼✼   ❺ *Gaultheria tasmanica*; ↕7cm (3in) ↔25cm (10in) ☼ ◗ ✼✼✼   ❻ *Ophiopogon planiscapus* 'Nigrescens'; ↕20cm (8in) ↔30cm (12in) ☼ ◊ ✼✼✼   ❼ Silky dogwood, *Cornus amomum* 'Blue Cloud'; ↕3m (10ft) ↔ 4m (12ft) ☼ ☼ ◗ ✼✼✼   ❽ Beauty berry, *Callicarpa dichotoma*; ↕1.2m (4ft) ↔1.2m (4ft) ☼ ☼ ◗ ✼✼✼   ❾ Majorcan peony, *Paeonia cambessedesii*; ↕45cm (18in) ↔ 45cm (18in) ☼ ☼ ◗ ✼✼✼   ❿ *Leycesteria formosa*; ↕1.8m (6ft) ↔1.8m (6ft) ☼ ☼ ◗ ✼✼✼

Trim a simple topiary

Topiary lends structure and formality to any planting scheme, and makes a useful focal point, whether grown in a container or planted directly into the border. All you need to bring an overgrown specimen back into shape, or to make a cone from scratch, are some basic tools, patience, and a good eye.

≫ **WHEN TO START**
Early summer

AT ITS BEST
All year round

TIME TO COMPLETE
🕐 1 hour

YOU WILL NEED
ℹ One box plant, *Buxus sempervirens*
Household disinfectant
Sharp long-handled shears

1 SELECT A HEALTHY PLANT
When choosing a specimen to clip into topiary, look for one with dense, healthy growth, unblemished foliage, and a strong leading stem in the centre.

2 START TO TRIM BY EYE
Looking down on the plant, locate the central stem, which will form the top of the cone. With shears, trim around the stem to create the outline.

3 KEEP MOVING AROUND THE PLANT
Don't trim the topiary in "sides", as you risk over-clipping one area. Continually move around the plant, regularly taking a step back to look at the overall shape.

4 ASSESS SHAPE FROM TOP
When you have nearly finished, look down at the central stem to check that the outline of the cone is straight and even. Assess the shape all the way around, and trim accordingly.

5 ROUTINE CARE
Established topiary should be pruned once or twice a year in midsummer and early autumn. Never clip on hot, sunny days to prevent the newly exposed foliage from being scorched.

Tool choices

Creating topiary shapes is much easier if you have the right tools, and always keep the blades sharp and clean. Although you can use garden shears to trim cones and simple shapes, long-handled shears (*far left*) are a better choice as they offer greater control. For more intricate designs, use topiary shears (*below*).

TOP TIP: CLEAN CUTS

Box blight is a major disease affecting box (*Buxus sempervirens*), which is commonly used for topiary. Protect your specimens by cleaning your pruning shears between plants with a spray of household disinfectant.

< *Points of view*
Slim topiary cones provide structure in this small mixed border, as well some vertical emphasis.

Vibrant winter border

Flowers are few and far between in the winter garden, but devote an area to winter performers, such as bare-stemmed beauties and bright evergreens, and this season can be as colourful as any other.

 WHEN TO PLANT
Spring and late autumn (for trees)
AT ITS BEST
Winter

TIME TO COMPLETE
 6 hours

YOU WILL NEED
 Spade
Well-rotted organic matter
All-purpose granular fertilizer

1. *Salix alba* var. *vitellina* 'Britzensis'
2. *Cornus sericea* 'Flaviramea'
3. *Cornus alba* 'Sibirica'
4. Dwarf conifers
5. *Erica carnea*
6. Variegated ivies

1 START WITH STRUCTURE
Cornus and *Salix* grown for coloured bark can be pollarded, so their stems grow at head-height on a single trunk, or coppiced, where they grow up from the ground (*see pp.230–231*). Plant the taller pollards at the back of the border, and the coppiced shrubs nearer the front.

2 PLANT AROUND SHRUBS
Fill in the border around the structural plants with low-growing heathers in contrasting colours, dwarf conifers, and ivies. Position these plants so they help to enhance the colour of the naked stems.

3 AFTERCARE
Water plants regularly throughout the first year. Trim off dead growth from all plants, so that the area looks good for winter. Coppice or pollard *Cornus* and *Salix* every few years in spring and feed with all-purpose fertilizer.

Creative Containers

When choosing a container, check out the pros and cons of different materials and designs to find one that suits both your style and the plants you plan to pot up. You can then create exciting displays with easy-to-grow summer flower seeds, inexpensive plug plants, or mature shrubs and trees that will add height to your patio. Just remember that all plants in containers require regular watering and feeding to keep them in peak condition, especially during summer.

Choosing containers

Almost any vessel can be used as a planter, as long as it has holes for drainage, and will last one growing season, but take time to decide what type would best suit your design, and your plants.

SIZE MATTERS

When choosing a pot, remember that large containers hold more compost and water, and therefore dry out more slowly than small planters. So, if you can only tend to your pots a couple of times a week, avoid tiny terracotta pots that will need watering up to twice a day in summer. Also think about the shape of the pot. If you plant a shrub in an urn-like container with a slim neck, as the roots spread within the pot, the plant effectively becomes locked in. When the shrub needs repotting, you will almost certainly have to break the pot.

∨ *Vintage herb display*
A rustic set of metal pots of various sizes and shapes suit cottage garden schemes.

∨ > *Chic combinations*
These spiky succulents in galvanized metal containers of different sizes are real show stoppers, while three simple terracotta pots make an elegant group when filled with architectural palms.

GROUPING

To create a pleasing display using a selection of pots, consider each for its size, shape and the material it is made from. An easy rule of thumb is to opt for pots made from the same material. You can then either choose a number of identical planters for an elegant, modern display, or group a collection of pots of different shapes and sizes to create an informal but harmonious arrangement.

Selecting materials

From bright plastics to traditional clay and wood, containers come in a vast choice of colours and materials. Some may obviously suit your garden style and budget, but also be aware that the material a pot is made from affects its durability, and the maintenance it requires.

TERRACOTTA

Versatile and relatively inexpensive, terracotta pots come in a wide variety of shapes and sizes, and even colours, if you choose glazed containers. Terracotta is porous and allows air to pass through to plant roots, but this is also a disadvantage, since it absorbs water from the compost, drying it out. It is also prone to frost damage, unless fired to very high temperatures, which makes it much more expensive.

WOOD AND BASKETS

When buying wooden containers, check that the label carries the Forest Stewardship Council (FSC) logo, indicating that the timber has come from a sustainable forest. Although frost-proof, porous, and a good insulator for plant roots, wood decays, and must be painted or treated with a preservative to prolong its life. Baskets offer a similarly natural look, but are less durable, lasting just a few years before deteriorating.

METAL

This is a popular choice of material because it is so versatile. Metal containers come in a wide array of shapes and styles – choose from rustic utilitarian planters for a cottage-style garden, or try stylish modern galvanized or powder-coated metal containers in an urban, minimalist scheme. Beware that thin metal containers afford plant roots little insulation, making them prone to overheating and frost damage. Steel containers also corrode, and can leave rusty stains on light-coloured paving. Even galvanized and powder-coated metal containers will rust if their surfaces are damaged.

STONE AND CONCRETE

Strong, frost-proof, insulating and extremely durable, stone and concrete pots make perfect partners for plants. Both materials are less porous than terracotta, so will not dry out potting compost too quickly, but they are extremely heavy. While this makes them very stable, and suitable for growing tall, top-heavy plants like trees, they cannot be moved easily once planted up. While concrete pots tend to be inexpensive, you will pay a high price for stone. If you want the look of stone for a lower price, buy containers made from synthetic stone compounds.

SYNTHETICS

Plastics, polymers, fibreglass and resins all fall under the umbrella of synthetics. These man-made materials are used to produce pots large and small, plain and decorative, and they come in the widest range of colours, from natural shades to vibrant neon pinks and blues. Synthetic pots are frost-proof and not easily broken, so they are ideal if you have children or pets who may knock them over.

Create a spring medley

Pots brimming with spring bulbs lift the spirits after a long dark winter, but you need to plan ahead to create the most spectacular displays. As soon as temperatures dip in the autumn, look out for bulbs at garden centres or in mail order catalogues, and check flowering times for a synchronized display.

WHEN TO START
Mid-autumn

AT ITS BEST
Early to late spring

TIME TO COMPLETE

 1½ hours

YOU WILL NEED

Large frost-proof container
Broken clay pot pieces
All-purpose potting compost
Gravel

Selection of bulbs:
Tulips
Daffodils
Grape hyacinth, *Muscari*

1 PREPARE TO PLANT
Add pieces of clay pot or polystyrene to the base of the container to cover the drainage holes. Then add a 5cm (2in) layer of gravel.

2 PLANT IN LAYERS

Cover the gravel with good-quality potting compost, but leave sufficient space to cover your bulbs to the right depth (*see p.41*). Space the daffodil bulbs on the compost, ensuring the pointed ends are at the top, and cover with more compost so that the tips of the bulbs are just visible.

3 COVER BULBS

Now place the tulip bulbs between the daffodils and cover them with more compost. Finally, scatter the small *Muscari* bulbs on the top layer of compost and cover these, leaving a gap of about 5cm (2in) between the soil and rim of the pot to allow space for watering. Firm lightly.

4 FINISHING TOUCHES

Spread gravel on top of the compost, and water well. To aid drainage and prevent the bulbs from rotting, raise the pot off the ground on "feet" (*below*), and place it in a sheltered spot. Move the pot into the sun when the bulbs emerge.

Synchronize flowering

To create a display like this one, choose bulbs that flower at the same time to produce a dramatic show lasting a few weeks in mid-spring. Alternatively, in larger containers, you could opt for bulbs that flower in succession over some months, from early spring to early summer, deadheading blooms as they fade. Check labels for flowering periods.

TIMING TULIPS AND DAFFODILS

Different types of tulip and daffodil flower at different times; early daffodils can appear in late winter, while late tulips may still be in bloom at the beginning of summer. To help you synchronize flowering, choose from the following bulbs, which all bloom at about the same time in mid-spring, and last for several weeks.

TULIPS	DAFFODILS
'Abba' (tomato red)	'Geranium' (white and
'Abu Hassan' (mahogany)	orange)
'Apricot Beauty' (salmon	'Lemon Beauty' (lemon
rose)	and white)
Emperor series (various	'Lemon Drops' (white;
colours)	lemon cup)
'Mistress' (deep pink)	'Mount Hood' (white)
'Monte Carlo' (sulphur	'Red Devon' (yellow; red
yellow)	cup)
'Negrita' (purple)	'Salome' (white; pink cup)
'Prinses Irene' (orange)	'St Patrick's Day' (lemon)
'Ruby Red' (scarlet)	'Sweetness' (golden yellow)
	'Thalia' (white)

❶ *Tulipa* 'Madame Lefeber'; ↕30cm (12in) ❷ *Tulipa* 'Diana'; ↕35cm (14in) ❸ *Tulipa* 'Oriental Splendour'; ↕30cm (12in) ❹ *Narcissus* 'Tahiti'; ↕45cm (18in) ❺ *Narcissus* 'Dove Wings'; ↕30cm (12in) ❻ *Narcissus* 'Bartley'; ↕40cm (16in)

Sow easy summer seeds

Growing summer bedding plants from seed is both fun and cost-effective, especially if you have several pots to fill. The seeds used in this scheme are French marigolds (*Tagetes*), *Bidens*, nasturtiums, and annual dahlias, all of which germinate quickly, and make a colourful display from summer until the first frosts.

Sow seed

Sow half-hardy seeds indoors in seed trays, but check the packets first for any specific instructions.

>> **WHEN TO START**
Early spring
AT THEIR BEST
Summer

TIME TO COMPLETE
 A few hours over several weeks

YOU WILL NEED
Packets of seed
Seed compost
Clean seed trays
Modular seed trays
Selection of pots
Broken clay pot pieces
Slow-release fertilizer
All-purpose compost
Watering can with rose

1 FILL SEED TRAYS
Using seed compost, fill some clean seed trays to within 2cm (1in) of the top. Gently press another seed tray on top to level out and firm the surface.

2 SOW SEEDS
Water the compost with a can fitted with a fine rose and allow to drain. Pour some seeds into your hand and carefully space them out on the compost surface. Sprinkle some sieved compost over the seeds, but check the packet first to see what depth the seeds require.

3 COVER AND KEEP MOIST
Label the seed tray, and put the lid, or a clear plastic bag, over the top. Place in a light spot, and check the packet to see what temperature the seeds need. Keep moist, and remove the lid or plastic bag as soon as seedlings emerge.

Large seeds

Large seeds, such as nasturtiums (*Tropaeolum*), can be planted in small 8cm (3in) pots, and will not need to be potted on (*see right*).

1 FILL POTS WITH COMPOST
Fill pots with seed compost and press it down gently with your fingers, or the bottom of another clean pot. Use a blunt pencil or dibber to make three holes, 2cm (1in) deep.

2 PLANT SEEDS
Drop one seed into each hole and press the compost down lightly. Label and water the pots, then place in a clear plastic bag until the seedlings start to emerge.

1 REMOVE SEEDLINGS FROM TRAY
Half-fill modular trays with good quality all-purpose compost. Holding the seedlings gently by their first leaves, use a pencil or dibber to gently tease their roots from the seed compost.

2 PLANT IN MODULES
Place a seedling in the middle of each cell of the modular tray, and fill around the roots and lower stems with more compost. Firm the compost using your fingertips to secure the seedlings.

Pot on seedlings

Check your seedlings daily and keep them well watered. The most effective way to do this is to place the seed trays in a larger container (with no drainage holes), half-filled with water. Leave them until the water has seeped into the compost and the surface is damp, then remove the seed trays. When the seedlings have a few leaves, pot them on as shown here.

3 WATER IN
Repeat Steps 1 and 2 for each seedling, and water carefully. Keep the seedlings in a bright place, and at the right temperature. A few weeks before the last frost is forecast, set them outside during the day, bringing them in at night, to harden them off.

Plant up the pots

In late spring when all frosts have finally finished, plant your bedding outside in pots, window boxes or hanging baskets (*see pp.130–131*). The plants raised here from six packets of seed filled five pots, three window boxes and a hanging basket. Choose containers that suit your garden design.

1 SATURATE CLAY POTS
Before planting up terracotta pots, soak them with water. Terracotta is porous, and saturating it first helps to prevent the clay from drawing moisture out of the compost when the pot is planted up.

2 ADD DRAINAGE MATERIAL
Place a layer of broken clay pot pieces in the base of each pot to ensure good drainage. To reduce the amount of compost needed for larger pots, fill the bottom third of the container with pieces of polystyrene (old plant trays are ideal).

3 APPLY FERTILIZER
Fill each container to about 5cm (2in) from the rim with all-purpose compost. Mix slow-release fertilizer designed for container plants into the compost. You can also add water-retaining gel crystals, which help to keep the compost moist, and reduce the need to water as frequently.

4 LIFT THE PLANTS
Water the young plants in their modules and leave to drain. Then gently squeeze the bottom and sides of each cell to loosen the root balls, and remove the plants. Place them on the compost about 10cm (4in) apart.

5 PLANT UP
In this scheme the dahlias are the tallest, and should be planted at the back, while the dwarf French marigolds need to be at the front, with the other plants dotted in–between. Plant up, firm the plants in gently, and water them well.

TOP TIP: AFTERCARE

Place the pots in a sunny position and water the plants regularly. Deadhead frequently to keep them in bloom for longer, removing faded flowers with secateurs. Young plants are prone to attacks by snails and slugs, so apply a few slug pellets, use nematodes or fix a copper band around the pots to keep them at bay (*see pp.426–427*). A gritty mulch may also help to deter pests. To retain moisture in the compost, you can add a decorative mulch (*see p.405*), which will also help to set off the planting.

Pots of plenty >
Growing your own plants from seed is ideal if you have lots of pots to fill. The choice of varieties is also greater than the selection available as mature plants.

SELECTIONS»

Foolproof seeds

Some annual seeds are almost infallible, and guaranteed to provide you with a garden full of bright, summer flowers. Protect half-hardy types from frost by planting them indoors in spring; others, such as pot marigolds, cornflowers, and love-in-a-mist, are hardy and can be sown directly into the soil or a container where they are to flower. That said, results are usually better if you start them off in pots indoors, and plant them out later.

SELECTIONS 》》

✿✿✿ fully hardy   ✿✿ hardy in mild regions/sheltered sites   ✿ protect from frost over winter
☼ full sun   ☀ partial sun   ◉ full shade   ◊ well-drained soil   ◐ moist soil   ● wet soil

❶ Pot marigold, *Calendula officinalis*; ‡50cm (20in) ↔45cm (18in) ☼ ☀ ◊ ✿✿✿   ❷ *Cosmos bipinnatus* 'Sonata White'; ‡1.5m (5ft) ↔45cm (18in) ☼ ◊ ◐ ✿   ❸ Cornflower, *Centaurea cyanus*; ‡50cm (20in) ↔15cm (6in) ☼ ◊ ✿✿✿   ❹ Tobacco plant, *Nicotiana* 'Lime Green'; ‡50cm (20in) ↔20cm (8in) ☼ ☀ ◐ ✿   ❺ *Zinnia elegans* 'Peppermint Stick'; ‡60cm (24in) ↔40cm (16in) ☼ ◊ ✿   ❻ Corn poppy, *Papaver rhoeas* Shirley Group; ‡90cm (36in) ↔30cm (12in) ☼ ◊ ✿✿✿   ❼ Love-in-a mist, *Nigella damascena* Persian Jewel Series; ‡40cm (16in) ↔20cm (8in) ☼ ◊ ✿✿✿   ❽ Love-lies-bleeding, *Amaranthus caudatus*; ‡1.2m (4ft) ↔60cm (24in) ☼ ◐ ✿   ❾ *Callistephus chinensis* 'Pompon'; ‡60cm (24in) ↔45cm (18in) ☼ ◊ ◐ ✿   ❿ California poppy, *Eschscholzia californica*; ‡30cm (12in) ↔15cm (6in) ☼ ◊ ✿✿✿

Plant a pot of wallflowers

Wallflowers are biennial plants, which means they live for two years, producing leaves in the first, and flowers in the second. Buy them with bare roots and plant up in autumn, ready to bloom the following spring. These fragrant flowers come in many hot shades, and look stunning with violas and grasses.

>> **WHEN TO START**
Autumn

AT ITS BEST
Spring

TIME TO COMPLETE
30 minutes

YOU WILL NEED
Wallflowers, *Erysimum cheiri*
Winter-flowering violas
Feather grass, *Stipa tenuissima*
Frost-resistant container
Broken clay pot pieces
Multi-purpose compost
Bucket
Gravel

1 PREPARE WALLFLOWERS
Try to plant your bare-root wallflowers as soon as you get them home. If you have to store them for a few days, wrap the roots in damp newspaper and keep the plants in a cool garage or unheated greenhouse. Then, just before planting, plunge the roots in a bucket of water for about 15 minutes.

2 ADD THE PLANTS
Place clay pieces at the bottom of the pot and fill to within 5cm (2in) of the rim with compost. Plant the *Stipa* at the back and violas around the front. Gently unwrap and separate the wallflowers.

3 FIRM IN AND WATER
Plant the wallflowers between the *Stipa* and violas, making sure that they are upright. Firm in and water well. Place the container in a sunny position. Water during dry spells and remove spent flowers.

Sow grasses from seed

Über-fashionable and extremely versatile, annual grasses are easy to grow from seed, and can be used in wild, meadow-style plantings, as well as container schemes. If you have light, well-drained soil, and a sunny site, they may self-seed and recreate their beautiful, natural effect for free.

1 FILL MODULES AND SOW SEEDS
Fill a modular seed tray with seed compost to within 5mm (¼in) of the top. Tap the tray to settle the compost, top up if necessary, and sow about three or four seeds per cell on the surface. Each module will then produce a small clump of grass.

2 COVER SEEDLINGS
Sprinkle a thin layer of vermiculite over the seeds to keep the surface moist, while also allowing light through to aid germination. Water the tray, using a can fitted with a fine rose. The seeds will take up to three weeks to germinate, depending on the type of grass.

3 KEEP SEED TRAYS SHADED
Keep the newly-sown seed trays in a semi-shaded spot, and do not allow them to dry out. When the seedlings appear, move the trays out into the sun. Once they have several strong leaves, pot them up (*see p.110*) and set them outside. You can collect seed from your own ornamental grasses in late summer to sow the following spring.

WHEN TO START
Early spring
AT THEIR BEST
Summer to autumn

TIME TO COMPLETE
30 minutes to sow; 1 hour to plant

YOU WILL NEED

Modular seed trays
Seed compost
Vermiculite
Watering can
Small plastic pots
Multi-purpose compost

Seed suggestions:
Foxtail millet, *Setaria italica*
Hare's tail, *Lagurus ovatus*
Quaking grass, *Briza maxima* (*see above*)
Sorghum nigrum

Sculptural spikes

Plants with sword-like, spiky leaves have a natural drama and exuberance. If you want to create a subtropical look in your garden, or even just a bit of theatre, use these surprisingly easy foliage plants in large containers to form the architectural features within your planting scheme.

< ∧ Colourful cordylines
Variegated and purple cordylines add drama to container plantings, but they are not quite as tough as those with simple, plain green leaves.

Cordyline

Cordyline is commonly known as the cabbage palm. The coloured-leaved cultivars are great in pots, but if you want yours to grow into a large specimen, choose the hardiest, plain green *Cordyline australis*.

PLANTING AND AFTERCARE
Grow cordylines in sun or partial shade in a well-drained soil or multi-purpose compost if planting in a container. Feed them annually in spring with a granular slow-release fertilizer. Lower leaves turn yellow as the plant ages; cut these back to the trunk or leave them to fall off. In colder areas, leaves may suffer damage from winter winds and snow. Protect them by tying the foliage together loosely around the central leaves.

Yuccas

The best yuccas have striped, variegated foliage but also vicious spikes, so don't plant them where young children could be hurt.

PLANTING AND AFTERCARE
Yuccas will survive winter outdoors in all but the most exposed areas, but they do best in sheltered gardens in well-drained soil and full sun. Extremely drought tolerant, they thrive in containers, and are well suited to coastal gardens. They need little care, which is lucky, as their spikes make them difficult to get close to.

Make an architectural statement >
Yucca's arching shape suits a pot, but it will also grow well in the ground, as long as there is sufficient drainage and sunshine.

Phormiums

Commonly known as New Zealand flax, these striking plants come in many colours and sizes, from dainty, container-sized cultivars to vast, shrub-like specimens.

PLANTING AND AFTERCARE

Phormiums are easy and will grow well in all types of soil. They prefer full sun but will tolerate some shade. Although they are hardy, individual leaves may suffer frost damage, but these can be removed, and the plant will quickly recover in spring.

① *P. tenax* 'Variegatum'; ↕↔1.5m (5ft)
② *P. cookianum* subsp. *hookeri* 'Tricolor'; ↕↔1.5m (5ft) ③ *P.* 'Sundowner'; ↕↔2m (6ft)
④ *P.* 'Bronze Baby'; ↕↔80cm (32in)

< *Flexible flax*
This dwarf Phormium, 'Jester', only reaches 90cm (36in) in height and spread, and is ideal for pots.

Pot up climbers in containers

Many of the more compact climbers, such as jasmine and some clematis cultivars, are well suited to growing in pots, and add another layer of interest to areas such as patios or pathways where there is no soil. A good-sized container, suitable support, and regular watering and feeding is all they need.

>> **WHEN TO START**
Spring

AT THEIR BEST
Summer

TIME TO COMPLETE
1½ hours

YOU WILL NEED

- Jasmine or other climber
- A large frost-proof pot
- Broken clay pot pieces
- Soil-based compost, such as
  John Innes No.3
- Trellis
- Twine
- Gravel or pebbles to mulch
- Watering can

1 BEFORE YOU PLANT

Put pieces of broken clay pot into the base of the container to aid drainage, and then cover with a layer of compost. Position the support at the back of the container and then pack some compost around it to help hold it firmly in place. Make sure that there is enough room for the plant roots to spread out.

2 ANGLE PLANT TOWARDS TRELLIS

Part-fill the container with more compost. Set the climber on top to check that it will be at the same depth as it was in its pot when planted (*see p.219 for clematis*). Plant it with the stems angled towards the trellis. There should be a gap of 5cm (2in) between the compost surface and the rim of the pot.

3 TIE IN MAIN STEMS

Remove any supports the plant has been grown on. Tie the main stems loosely to the trellis with twine. When the stems have hardened, remove the ties and tie in new growth higher up the trellis.

4 WATER IN WELL

Water in well and place a layer of gravel or pebbles on top of the compost to minimize evaporation from the surface. This will also keep the roots cool, and improve the appearance of the pot.

TOP TIP: CHOOSING CLEMATIS FOR POTS

Many clematis are naturally compact and flower when still small, but take care to choose the right type. To keep clematis compact, cut back the stems of summer-flowering plants, such as *Clematis florida*, in late winter. Leave unpruned those that flower before late spring, such as *C. alpina* and *C. macropetala*, as they bloom on the previous year's growth (*see pp.218-219*).

∧ > *Spoilt for choice*
You can combine complementary coloured cultivars in the same pot (above), *or opt for just one flower-smothered plant* (right).

COMPACT CULTIVARS
'Arabella'
'Barbara Jackman'
'Bees' Jubilee'
'Comtesse de Bouchaud'
'Daniel Deronda'
florida var. *flore-pleno*
florida var. *sieboldiana*
'H.F. Young'
'Ice Blue' (*far left, white*)
'Kingfisher' (*far left, mauve*)
'Miss Bateman'
'Niobe'
'Ooh La La' (*left*)
'Perle d'Azur'
'Prince Charles'
'Royalty'

Grow plants from plugs

Quick, easy and cheap, "plugs" are basically well-developed seedlings that you pot on once before planting out. They are ideal if you do not have the space or time to sow seeds yourself, and they are the simplest option for plants that are difficult to germinate. Mail-order companies tend to offer the largest selection of bedding and tender perennial plugs, and they usually cost a fraction of the price of fully-grown plants.

WHEN TO START
Spring

AT THEIR BEST
Late spring to autumn

TIME TO COMPLETE

1½ hours

YOU WILL NEED

Plug plants – begonias have been used here
Dibber or pencil
Potting compost
Large modular trays or small 8cm (3cm) plastic pots
Watering can

1 ORDER YOUR PLUGS
When ordering plugs, make sure you will have time to pot them up soon after they arrive – most companies specify when they will be delivered. Plugs are also known as "miniplants" or "easiplants", and companies may offer them at different stages of development. The youngest plugs will be cheapest.

2 REMOVE PLUGS FROM CONTAINER
When the plugs arrive, water well and store them in a cool, frost-free place. Fill large modular trays, or small 8cm (3in) pots, with good-quality potting compost, designed for seedlings and young plants. Using the blunt end of a pencil or a dibber, gently push the plug plants out of their original containers.

3 PLANT UP IN MODULES
Make a hole with your finger or a pencil in the compost in the modules, and insert a plug plant in each. Firm the compost around the plug lightly with your fingers, taking care not to compact it or to damage the roots.

4 KEEP PLANTS WATERED
Water the plugs using a can fitted with a fine rose, and keep them in a cool, light, frost-free place. Water regularly, harden off (see p.109), and plant out in pots, or in the ground, when all risk of frost has passed.

Planting options

Most popular bedding plants, including pelargoniums, busy Lizzies, begonias, lobelia, snapdragons, dahlias and fuchsias are available as plug plants, although many companies also offer a selection of newer and more unusual varieties. Order in early spring for a late spring delivery.

❶ *Nicotiana* 'Nicki'; ‡45cm (18in)
❷ *Nemesia strumosa* 'KLM'; ‡25cm (10in)
❸ *Gazania* Chansonette Series; ‡30cm (12in)
❹ *Pelargonium* Horizon Series; ‡40cm (16in)

< *Shady treat*
This beautiful container, ideal for a partly shaded spot, is filled with Begonia *'Illumination Rose' and fragrant blue heliotropes, all grown from plugs, together with* Fuchsia *'Genii' and trailing* Lysimachia nummularia *'Aurea' (golden creeping Jenny).*

SELECTIONS»

Shade-loving container plants

Summer flower displays need not be limited by a shady garden as many pretty container plants prefer cooler conditions. A pot full of flowering begonias, fuchsias, violas or busy Lizzies will transform a sheltered patio, while plants grown for their foliage look particularly attractive in shade, where the sun will not bleach out their subtle colours. Leafy hostas, ferns, lamiums and heucheras also offer a wonderful variety of textures.

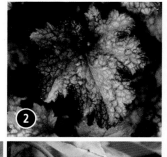

❄❄❄ fully hardy   ❄❄ hardy in mild regions/sheltered sites   ❄ protect from frost over winter

☼ full sun   ☼ partial sun   ☼ full shade   ◊ well-drained soil   ◐ moist soil   ● wet soil

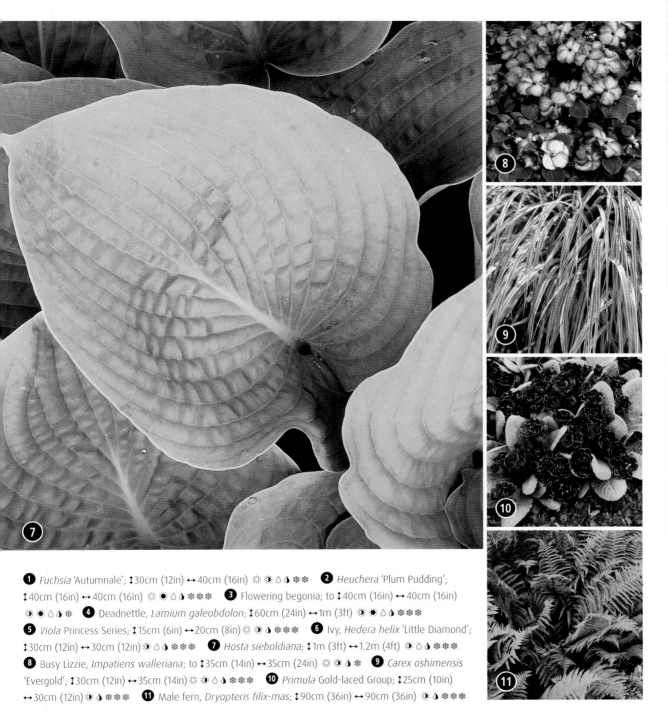

1 *Fuchsia* 'Autumnale'; ‡30cm (12in) ↔40cm (16in) ☼ ☼ ◊ ● ❄❄   **2** *Heuchera* 'Plum Pudding'; ‡40cm (16in) ↔40cm (16in) ☼ ☼ ◊ ● ❄❄❄   **3** Flowering begonia; to ‡40cm (16in) ↔40cm (16in) ☼ ☼ ◊ ● ❄   **4** Deadnettle, *Lamium galeobdolon*; ‡60cm (24in) ↔1m (3ft) ☼ ☼ ◊ ● ❄❄❄   **5** *Viola* Princess Series; ‡15cm (6in) ↔20cm (8in) ☼ ☼ ● ❄❄❄   **6** Ivy, *Hedera helix* 'Little Diamond'; ‡30cm (12in) ↔30cm (12in) ☼ ◊ ● ❄❄❄   **7** *Hosta sieboldiana*; ‡1m (3ft) ↔1.2m (4ft) ☼ ◊ ● ❄❄❄   **8** Busy Lizzie, *Impatiens walleriana*; to ‡35cm (14in) ↔35cm (24in) ☼ ☼ ◊ ● ❄   **9** *Carex oshimensis* 'Evergold'; ‡30cm (12in) ↔35cm (14in) ☼ ☼ ◊ ● ❄❄❄   **10** *Primula* Gold-laced Group; ‡25cm (10in) ↔30cm (12in) ☼ ● ❄❄❄   **11** Male fern, *Dryopteris filix-mas*; ‡90cm (36in) ↔90cm (36in) ☼ ● ❄❄❄

Plant pots of perfume

The epitome of high summer, sweetly scented lilies set by a front or back door will greet you with their perfume as you come and go, but keep your distance as their pollen stains clothing. The most cost-effective way to grow them is to plant fresh bulbs in early spring.

>> **WHEN TO PLANT**
Spring

AT THEIR BEST
Summer

TIME TO COMPLETE
🕐 30 minutes

YOU WILL NEED
ℹ️ Lily bulbs (*see Top Tip, right, for scented types*)
Deep container
Broken clay pot pieces
Multi-purpose compost
Horticultural grit

TOP TIP: LILY OPTIONS

Choose the following species for scent:

L. auratum
L. candidum
L. hansonii (below right)
L. regale, white
L. speciosum var. *rubrum* (below left)
Oriental hybrids, such as 'Star Gazer' (left), 'Tiger Woods', and 'Arabian Red'

1 PREPARE THE POT
In spring, buy fresh lily bulbs and choose a deep container; most lilies are planted at a depth of between 15–20cm (6–8in). Cover the drainage hole with broken pot pieces and then add a layer of multi-purpose compost.

2 PLANT THE BULBS
Add a 3cm (1½in) thick layer of horticultural grit over the compost and lay the bulbs on their sides on top. Positioning the bulbs like this allows water to drain out of the bulb scales, rather than collecting there and rotting the bulbs.

3 TOP UP THE CONTAINER
Cover the bulbs and top up the container to about 5cm (2in) below the rim with a 50:50 mix of compost and horticultural grit. Place your pots on "feet" in a sheltered spot and move them into the sun as soon as the shoots appear.

4 AFTERCARE
Water every couple of days, and apply a tomato feed to your lily pots every fortnight during the summer. Keep in a sheltered position over winter, and in spring, renew the top 5cm (2in) of compost. Lily beetle (*see pp.428–429*) is their main pest. Look out for these bright red beetles and pick them off as soon as you see them.

Elegant arrangement

Clear white lilies with a frilly skirt of *Diascia* and dramatic striped grasses make a chic windowbox display for the front of the house. The lily used here is *Lilium* 'Reinesse', and like all Asiatic lilies it is unscented, but you could easily substitute a perfumed-type, such as 'Muscadet', to produce a fragrant combination.

1 PREPARE THE BOX

If your windowbox has no drainage holes, make a few with an electric drill. In early spring, add a layer of broken clay pot pieces to the bottom of the box, and cover them with compost. Plant up bulbs as shown opposite. Plant the delicate *Diascia* at the front of the box and the stripy *Carex* at each end. Or, for an instant effect in summer, buy the lilies in flower and pot them up with mature *Diascia* and *Carex* plants.

2 CARING FOR THE DISPLAY

Feed your windowbox every two weeks with a tomato fertilizer, and keep it well watered from late spring and throughout the summer. The lilies will flower for a few weeks in summer, and can then be planted out in the garden in free-draining soil. The *Diascia* will bloom continuously all summer and can survive the winter outside in mild areas; the *Carex* is quite hardy too, and is effective in winter displays.

TIME TO COMPLETE

🕐 1 hour

YOU WILL NEED

- *Lilium* 'Reinesse'
- *Diascia*, white
- *Carex morrowii* cultivar
- Deep white windowbox
- Broken clay pot pieces
- Multi-purpose compost
- Horticultural grit

TOP TIP: DEADHEADING DIASCIA

To help prolong the display, regularly remove fading flowers on your *Diascia*. This stops the plants producing seeds and focuses their energy on making more flowers instead.

Make cottage-style containers

Even if you don't own a traditional garden with deep borders, you can still pull off the cottage garden look by planting in containers. Herbaceous perennials and annual climbers grow well in pots, which you can slot into existing planting schemes to add extra height and colour wherever you want it.

Morning glory tower

This annual climber, *Ipomoea*, can be easily grown from seed in spring, and will quickly romp over a container support, smothering it in trumpet-like flowers.

>> **WHEN TO START**
Spring

AT ITS BEST
Mid- to late summer

TIME TO COMPLETE
🕐 2 hours

YOU WILL NEED
ⓘ Morning glory, *Ipomoea*, seedlings
Large container
Multi-purpose compost and
 slow-release fertilizer
Broken clay pot pieces
Tall bamboo canes
Raffia or string

1 BEFORE YOU PLANT
Place broken clay pot pieces in the base of the pot, fill with compost, and mix in slow-release fertilizer granules.

2 TIE CANES TOGETHER
Arrange the canes around the edge of the pot and tie the tops together. Then stabilize the obelisk by tying each cane to the next with raffia to form a ring. Repeat this a few times up the canes.

3 PLANT SEEDLINGS
Take a pot or two of seedlings that you sowed indoors (*see pp.108–109*) in early spring. Carefully separate them out and plant one at the base of each cane. Firm in, and water the plants well.

4 AFTERCARE
The small plants will quickly start to climb of their own accord but may benefit from being tied in at first. Water the plants well all summer, and remove any spent flowers to keep them in bloom.

Pastel pot

Compact versions of cottage garden perennials grow well in pots, where they make a looser and more natural alternative to tender bedding plants.

WHEN TO START
Spring

AT ITS BEST
Summer

TIME TO COMPLETE
1 hour

YOU WILL NEED
Wide pot
Broken clay pot pieces
Soil-based compost, such as John Innes No.3
Slow-release fertilizer granules

Carex 'Ice Dance'
Delphinium grandiflorum
Stachys officinalis 'Hummelo'
Veronica spicata 'Rosenrot'

1 PREPARE AND PLANT
Place broken clay pot pieces over the holes in the base of the container, then half-fill it with compost. Plant the delphinium towards the back and arrange the other, lower-growing plants in front. Fill around them with more compost, and mix in slow-release fertilizer granules. Water the plants well.

2 AFTERCARE
With the correct care, this can be a long-lasting container that flowers year after year. In early spring, remove all dead growth to make way for the new spring shoots. At the same time, remove the top layer of compost, and replace with fresh compost mixed with fertilizer granules. The plants will also require regular division (*see right*).

TOP TIP: REPOTTING AND DIVIDING PERENNIALS

In the garden, herbaceous perennials need lifting, dividing and replanting every few years to keep them healthy. In a pot, this should be done more often, at least every two years. Lift the plants out of the pot and use your hands to tease sections apart. Discard any old or weak clumps, then replant the healthiest offsets into fresh compost with some fertilizer.

Inside out

Show-stopping plants with "wow" factor, tender Abyssinian bananas are ideal for terraces and patios, where they give welcome shade, and form a structural backdrop to other exotics. They must be kept in the warm during winter, so bear this in mind before you buy.

» **WHEN TO START**
Late spring
AT ITS BEST
Early summer to early autumn

TIME TO COMPLETE
🕐 1 hour

YOU WILL NEED
💧 Large pot
Broken clay pot pieces
Multi-purpose compost

1. Abyssinian banana, *Ensete ventricosum* 'Maurelii'
2. *Asparagus densiflorus* 'Myersii'
3. *Clerodendrum thomsoniae*
4. *Medinilla magnifica*

1 PLANT YOUR BANANAS
Widely available, *Ensete* are large perennials that grow very quickly in summer. They like a sunny spot, sheltered from strong winds that could tear their leaves. Line the base of a pot with broken clay pot pieces, and plant the *Ensete* in multi-purpose compost.

2 FEEDING AND CARE
To encourage the strongest, most luscious growth, water the plants regularly and feed every week using a liquid fertilizer. You can add to the display by underplanting your *Ensete* with ferns, trailing bedding plants, or other exotics with attractive foliage.

3 OVERWINTERING BANANAS
To make sure your *Ensete* survives the winter, bring the pots indoors before the first frosts. A plant mover (*right*) will make the task easier. Remove older leaves and keep the plant in a room, or heated greenhouse, at a minimum temperature of 7°C (45°F). Don't water in the colder months but start again in spring.

Exotic options

To complement your bananas, plant up pots of flowering exotics to inject spicy colours and scents into the mix. These summer-flowering plants enjoy a sunny site outside and can be brought into a heated conservatory for winter.

Grow these colourful exotic plants in large containers on a warm patio, and they will provide a beautiful, summer-long display. Plants will reach these dimensions when grown in a pot or container.

1 Glory lily, *Gloriosa superba* (climber); ↕2m (6ft) **2** *Brugmansia aurea*; ↕2m (6ft) ↔1m (3ft) **3** *Lantana camara*; ↕↔1m (3ft) **4** *Hibiscus rosa-sinensis*; ↕↔1m (3ft)

Plant a summer basket

Floating globes of flowers and foliage lend an exotic touch to patios and balconies throughout the summer. Plant up a large basket and hang it at head height, where you can focus on the colours, shapes and textures. To prolong your flowery display, water and deadhead daily.

 WHEN TO START
Late spring

AT ITS BEST
Early to late summer

TIME TO COMPLETE
 2 hours

YOU WILL NEED
Sturdy wall bracket
Pencil
Electric drill with masonry bit
Spirit level
Rawlplugs and coach bolts
Spanner
Large hanging basket and liner
Scissors
Multi-purpose compost
Slow-release granular fertilizer

Plants in this basket:
Trailing blue lobelia
Dichondra argentea 'Silver Falls'
Lotus berthelotii
Diascia Flying Colours Coral
Verbena 'Peaches 'n' Cream'
Verbena 'Derby'

1 POSITION WALL BRACKET
The most successful hanging baskets are the largest, because they hold greater quantities of compost and water and are less prone to drying out. However, big baskets require sturdy brackets fixed securely to the wall. Place the bracket on the wall and check it is vertical with a spirit level. Use a pencil to mark the positions of the screw holes.

2 DRILL HOLES
Remove the bracket, and using an electric drill with a masonry bit, drill holes through the pencil marks. You will find this easier if you drill the holes into the mortar rather than the bricks. Push a Rawlplug into each hole.

3 ATTACH BRACKET
Place the bracket back on the wall and line up the holes. Insert a washer and coach bolt and screw it into the wall using a spanner, as shown. A ratchet-style spanner makes this job easier. Repeat for the second hole. Tighten up both bolts fully to secure the bracket to the wall.

4 LINE BASKET
Line the basket with a suitable liner and trim to fit. Over the bottom third of the basket, lay a sheet of polythene punched with a few small drainage holes – a piece of bin liner is perfect. Add a layer of gravel and cover this with compost. Then, cut crosses at regular intervals around the sides just above the polythene.

5 THREAD PLANTS THROUGH HOLES

Water all the plants thoroughly and remove the lobelia plants from their cell pack. Wrap a little polythene around the leaves to protect them, and thread each plant through the crosses from the inside.

6 PLANT THE BASKET

Cover the lobelia with more compost and then start planting up the rest of the basket. Work from the centre out, with the tallest *Verbena* in the middle and the trailing *Dichondra* and *Lotus* around the edges.

7 FINISHING TOUCHES

Fill in around the plants with compost and some fertilizer. Water in well, and add a layer of gravel over the compost to help retain moisture. Water daily, even if it has rained, and deadhead regularly for a longer show of blooms.

SELECTIONS>>

Summer basket choices

In spring, garden centres are packed with plants for windowboxes and hanging baskets that will provide you with colour all summer long. Baskets crammed with flowers alone can look a little overwhelming, so choose a few foliage plants, such as red-leaved coleus, or silvery *Glechoma* and *Festuca*, to act as foils. Trailing plants, including lobelia and *Lotus (see pp.130-131)*, soften lines and continue the display below the main plants.

❀❀❀ fully hardy   ❀❀ hardy in mild regions/sheltered sites   ❀ protect from frost over winter
☀ full sun   ◑ partial sun   ☀ full shade   ◊ well-drained soil   ◔ moist soil   ● wet soil

1 *Osteospermum* cultivar; ‡40cm (16in) ↔60cm (24in) ☀ ◊ ❀❀❀   **2** *Ageratum houstonianum* 'Hawaii White'; ‡15cm (6in) ↔15cm (6in) ☀ ◊ ● ❀   **3** Coleus, *Solenostemon scutellarioides*; ‡20cm (8in) ↔20cm (8in) ☀ ◑ ◊ ● ❀   **4** *Festuca glauca*; ‡30cm (12in) ↔25cm (10in) ☀ ◊ ❀❀❀
5 Busy Lizzie, *Impatiens walleriana* Super Elfin Series; ‡60cm (24in) ↔60cm (24in) ☀ ◑ ◊ ● ❀
6 Ground ivy, *Glechoma hederacea* 'Variegata'; ‡15cm (6in) ↔2m (6ft) ☀ ◑ ◊ ● ❀❀❀   **7** Swan river daisy, *Brachyscome* 'Blue Mist'; ‡35cm (14in) ↔45cm (18in) ☀ ◊ ❀   **8** *Petunia* Shockwave Series Pink; ‡25cm (10in) ↔60cm (24in) ☀ ◊ ❀   **9** *Convolvulus cneorum*; ‡60cm (24in) ↔90cm (36in) ☀ ◊ ❀❀   **10** *Nemesia strumosa* 'KLM'; ‡30cm (12in) ↔15cm (6in) ☀ ◊ ● ❀

Make containers from cast-offs

It's easy to create plant pots for free from old household objects, such as pans, kettles, and colanders. Here, tin cans have been transformed into stylish containers for grasses and summer flowers. If you want larger displays, ask at local restaurants for their empty bumper trade-sized cans.

WHEN TO START
Spring

AT THEIR BEST
Summer to early autumn

TIME TO COMPLETE
30 minutes

YOU WILL NEED
Old tin cans
Gloves
Screwdriver with metal drill bit
Broken clay pot or polystyrene
 pieces
Multi-purpose compost

Brachyscome, lilac
Calibrachoa 'Million Bells Purple'
Festuca glauca 'Elijah Blue'
Festuca glauca 'Golden Toupee'

Recycling ideas

You will find more ideas for containers made from recycled materials at national flower shows and open gardens in your area, while charity shops and car boot sales offer good sources of planters, such as old handbags and bread bins.

1 DRILL DRAINAGE HOLES
Soak off the labels from the cans in hot soapy water. Wearing stout gloves, drill a few drainage holes in the bottom of each can.

2 FIRM PLANTS IN WELL
Add pieces of clay pot to the bottom of the cans and plant up the grasses and flowers, leaving a 2cm (1in) gap between the surface of the compost and the rim. Water well.

∧ Creative containers
Old wheelbarrows make excellent containers for summer bedding, such as marigolds. Drill holes in the bottom of the barrow to provide drainage.

FUNKY JUNK
Large plant pots can be expensive but you can get one for nothing at your local recycling centre. Old oil drums are perfect for trees or large shrubs (*above*), while worn tyres can be used singly and filled with turf to make stepping stones (*below*) or piled on top of each other to create taller containers.

Use tiny but tough succulents

Alpines are a group of plants that really allow you to be creative. Tolerant of drought and low winter temperatures, they flourish in thin, poor soils, and will grow in nooks and crannies that are too small for other plants. All they need is a free-draining soil and shelter from heavy winter rain.

Alpine shells

Little shells planted with houseleeks make an interesting garden feature. The fleshy rosettes have a wonderful, textured appearance; some types are covered with a gossamer webbing too.

 WHEN TO PLANT
Spring
AT THEIR BEST
Spring to autumn

 TIME TO COMPLETE
30 minutes

 YOU WILL NEED
Houseleeks, *Sempervivum* species
Soil-based compost,
 such as John Innes No.1
Horticultural sand
Spoon
Bowl for mixing compost
Large sea shells

1 MIX SOIL AND SAND

First wash out the shells you plan to use with hot soapy water, or soak them for an hour in baby-bottle sterilizing solution. In the bowl, mix together equal parts of soil-based compost and horticultural sand.

2 PACK SHELLS WITH COMPOST

Using a spoon, fill the shells with the compost mix and tap it down. Water the houseleeks well before planting them. To do this, stand them in their pots in a bowl of water for 15 minutes, take them out, then allow them to drain.

3 PLANT THE HOUSELEEKS

Remove the houseleeks from their pots and plant them carefully in the shells. Use the spoon handle to push more compost between the plants, and to cover the roots. Water well, and set the shells on their sides so that rain will drain away.

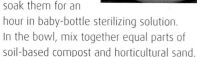

Canny idea

Decorate a tree or shrub with little watering cans brimming with sedums. Given a sunny position, the plants will become covered with tiny, starry yellow flowers in summer.

TIME TO COMPLETE

🕐 30 minutes

YOU WILL NEED

🛈 *Sedum spathulifolium* 'Purpureum'
Electric drill and metal bit
Soil-based compost
Small watering cans
Gravel
Horticultural sand
Strong raffia or garden twine

1 DRILL DRAINAGE HOLES
Using an electric drill and metal bit, make several drainage holes in the base of each watering can. Cover the holes with gravel, add a mix of compost and sand, and water the sedums before planting (*see Steps 1 and 2 opposite*).

2 FIRM PLANTS IN WELL
Remove the sedums from their pots and plant them in the watering cans, filling in around them with more compost and sand mix. Water the plants well and tie the watering cans, via their handles, to a tree or shrub using raffia or string.

Slate trough

Topped with slate chips, this trough mirrors a natural mountain scree. Plant *in situ* in a sunny site, as it will be heavy once filled, and use specialist nurseries (*see pp.446–447*) for a wide plant choice.

TIME TO COMPLETE

🕐 1½ hours

YOU WILL NEED

🛈 Trough
Broken clay pot pieces
Gravel
Soil-based compost
Horticultural sand
Slate chips

Delosperma harazianum
Draba hispanica
Erigeron compositus var. *discoideus*
Limonium bellidifolium
Polemonium viscosum
Saxifraga juniperifolia
Silene acaulis
Townsendia jonesii

1 PREPARE THE TROUGH
Cover the drainage holes at the bottom of the trough with clay pieces, then add a 5cm (2in) layer of gravel. Top up the trough, using a free-draining mixture of compost and sand (*see Step 1, opposite*). Leave 5cm (2in) between the rim and the surface of the compost.

2 ADD SLATE AND PLANTS
Top off the trough with slate chips, pushing them into the compost for stability, and leave spaces for the plants. Water the plants (*see Step 2, opposite*) and plant them in the gaps, making sure that their roots are covered with sand and compost mix. Water the plants thoroughly.

Plant up patio roses

Modern patio roses bloom for many months, and offer those with limited space the chance to enjoy their colour and fragrance. Not all roses thrive in cramped conditions, so look out for plants labelled "patio" or "miniature", and place your containers in a sunny position for the best blooms.

WHEN TO PLANT
Autumn or early spring

AT THEIR BEST
Early to midsummer

TIME TO COMPLETE
30 minutes

YOU WILL NEED
Large container, at least 45cm
 (18in) deep
Broken clay pot pieces
Gravel
Soil-based compost
Well-rotted farmyard manure
Slow-release fertilizer
Mycorrhizal fungi, such as
 Rootgrow rose fertilizer
Patio rose, such as *Rosa*
 'Regensberg'
Bedding plants, such as
 Sutera cordata (syn. *Bacopa*)

1 PREPARE THE CONTAINER

Plant your pot *in situ*, since it will be heavy and difficult to move once planted. Place a layer of broken pots or polystyrene pieces at the bottom of the container. Add a layer of gravel to aid drainage, and then some compost mixed with well-rotted farmyard manure (one part manure to ten parts compost).

2 CHECK PLANTING DEPTH

Place the rose, in its pot, on the compost and check that the graft union (swelling at base of stems) will be below the soil after planting. Remove or add compost to adjust the planting level, and mix in slow-release fertilizer and mycorrhizal fungi. Then remove the rose from its container and set it in the pot.

TOP TIP: FEEDING YOUR ROSES

3 PLANT UP ANNUALS

Fill around the root ball with the compost and manure mixture. Wearing gloves, firm it in gently with your hands. Leave a gap of 5cm (2in) between the compost and the rim of the pot to allow space for watering. For added summer colour, after the frosts in late spring, plant trailing bedding plants, such as *Sutera*, around the edge.

4 FINISHING TOUCHES

Water the plants well after planting; you may have to add a little more compost after watering if it exposes the roots. A mulch of well-rotted manure over the top of the compost will help to retain moisture. Keep the container moist during the growing season, and stand it on "feet" during winter to ensure excess water drains away easily.

In spring, remove the top layer of soil and add some fresh compost mixed with a granular rose fertilizer, applying it according to the manufacturers' instructions. You may need to top up with a liquid feed in the summer, but avoid doing so in late summer as this will encourage soft growth that is vulnerable to frost.

Create a modern patio mix

Green is the only colour used in this contemporary display, the subtle hues helping to emphasize the wonderful forms and textures of the plants. A slim vase-shaped container balances the tall spiky cabbage palm and pendent ferny foliage, while pineapple-like flowers lend an exotic touch.

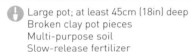

WHEN TO START
Late spring

AT ITS BEST
Early summer to early autumn

TIME TO COMPLETE
🕐 1½ hours

YOU WILL NEED
 Large pot; at least 45cm (18in) deep
Broken clay pot pieces
Multi-purpose soil
Slow-release fertilizer

1. Cabbage palm,
   Cordyline australis
2. Tobacco plant,
   Nicotiana 'Lime Green'
3. Maidenhair fern,
   Adiantum capillus-veneris
4. Pineapple lily,
   Eucomis bicolor

1 PREPARE TO PLANT
Prepare the pot as described in Steps 1 and 2 on page 110, but use only a thin layer of crocks at the base, because this display requires more soii to sustain it. Half-fill the container with compost, and then add some slow-release fertilizer. Water the plants well, and slip them out of their pots.

2 PLANT UP
Plant the palm at the back, and the pineapple lilies at intervals in front. Set the tobacco plants between the lilies, and squeeze in the ferns around the edge. Leave about a 5cm (2in) gap between the surface of the compost and rim of the pot, to make watering the container easier.

3 SUMMER CARE
Position your container in a sunny site but make sure it is shaded from the midday sun, which will scorch the fern. Water every other day in summer. Deadhead the tobacco plant regularly, and occasionally trim off leaves that look untidy.

4 WINTER CARE
These plants are borderline hardy, and will need some protection from very hard frosts; cover them with fleece or bring them indoors when bad weather is forecast. The pineapple lily will die back in the autumn, then re-emerge in spring. Only the tobacco plant is an annual, and will therefore need to be replaced each year.

Cool greens

The following plants would work equally well planted together in a container. All but the *Aeonium* are hardy enough to overwinter outside.

❶ *Phormium tenax* 'Variegatum'; ↕1m (3ft) ↔60cm (2ft) in a pot ❷ *Heuchera* variegated cultivar; ↕40cm (16in) ↔30cm (12in) ❸ *Aeonium arboreum*; ↕↔60cm (24in) in a pot

Contemporary containers

Glamorous and chic, contemporary containers transform a terrace into a catwalk for stylish plants. Seek out those with bold shapes and made from modern materials for a fashionable look, but don't be tempted to mix colours and styles or the effect will be lost. Give your patio a stunning makeover by employing tricks used by top landscape designers, such as lining up large identical containers or grouping them in threes.

1 These simple aluminium pots of different sizes are filled with clipped *Cryptomeria* and a golden dwarf juniper. **2** Rusted metal is at the height of fashion, and carries off this mop-head of love grass, *Eragrostis curvula* 'Totnes Burgundy', to perfection. **3** A black stainless steel container provides a great contrast to pastel summer bedding. **4** Modular square pots, hand-made from cement boards bracketed together, sprayed with metallic bronze Plasti-Kote and sealed with a waterproof sealant, create a funky group of box balls and bright marigolds. **5** This trio of glazed earthenware containers provides a chic, understated home for the bold green textured foliage plants. **6** This metal pot is set on a stabilizing plate which can be camouflaged with gravel to give the illusion of a gravity-defying cone. **7** Perfect for a deck or natural stone patio, these tall clay pots have been fired to a high temperature to make them frostproof. **8** Coated copper retains its subtle colour and this elegant bowl mirrors the metallic shades of the cannas, while creating a foil for the ferns.

Eastern promise

Graceful clumps of bamboos and grasses, carefully placed pebbles, and wooden railings combine to give this garden an Oriental look. Add dwarf bamboos in attractive pots, and bring a hint of Asia to your patio.

WHEN TO PLANT
Autumn or spring
AT THEIR BEST
All year round

TIME TO COMPLETE

🕐 3 hours

YOU WILL NEED

Matching containers
Soil-based compost, such as
 John Innes No.3
Slow-release fertilizer granules
Broken clay pot pieces

1. *Phyllostachys bambusoides*
  'Holochrysa'
2. *Pleioblastus variegatus*
3. *Indocalamus tessellatus*
4. *Pleioblastus variegatus*
  'Tsuboii'
5. *Fargesia murielae*

1 SELECT YOUR PLANTS
Low-growing bamboos are the best choice for pots, and there is a wide variety with coloured canes and brightly striped leaves. Arrange several close together to create a small, dense jungle.

2 PLANT THE BAMBOOS
Place broken clay pot pieces in the base of a pot and add a layer of compost. Water the bamboo, remove it from its pot, and set in the centre of the container. Fill in around it with compost and some fertilizer. Firm in and water. Bamboos are thirsty, so water often. As they grow very strongly, lift, divide, and repot them in new compost every three or four years (*see p.416*).

Style emerald topiary

Topiary adds real style to a patio or terrace, and although you can buy expensive pre-shaped shrubs, making your own is quite easy and very rewarding. Pot up your box plant first in a large container, and then choose between an elegant spiral (*below*) or go a step further and add a finial on top (*right*).

>> **WHEN TO START**
Early summer

AT ITS BEST
All year round

TIME TO COMPLETE
🕐 3 hours

YOU WILL NEED
💧 Large box, *Buxus sempervirens*
Topiary shears
Secateurs
Wire
Large container
Soil-based compost, such as
  John Innes No.3

< *Get into shape*
Topiary shapes, such as pyramids and spirals, are easy to make. Once you have mastered the basics, try developing your own designs.

1 CLIP INTO ROUGH OUTLINE
Plant up your box into a large container filled with soil-based compost (*see p.151*). To create a spiral shape with a ball on top, start off by roughly trimming your plant into a cone (*see pp.98–99 for method*). If you want to create a ball finial on top, leave the upper portion unclipped at this stage.

2 SHAPE WITH TOPIARY SHEARS
You may be able to create the outline by eye, but if you want a guide, place a loose spiral of wire around the cone, and use shears to clip in between, cutting back to the central stem. Use secateurs for woodier stems. Do not rush, and stand back regularly to check how the shape is developing.

3 ROUND OFF THE EDGES
Once you have a rough spiral, start creating the final shape. Use your shears to gradually round off the edges to give the appearance of a tube winding around the central stem. To keep the shape in proportion, and to make it look solid and stable, taper the spiral so that it is thinner at the top and thicker at the base. Regularly inspect your work as you go, tweaking as necessary.

4 SHAPE THE LOLLIPOP TOP
Either leave the spiral as it is, or trim a ball on top. When clipping a ball, try using a wire template (*see Top Tip, right*) to create a regular shape. Move the template around the ball to check that it is spherical. If you make a mistake, leave the area to re-grow then try again.

TOP TIP: CIRCULAR TEMPLATE

To make a circular template, wrap a piece of thick wire around something round and solid, and about the same size as the ball you wish to create; a paint can would be ideal. Then twist the ends together to keep the shape.

Autumn stars

Patio planters need not fade away as summer comes to a close. There are lots of plants that will leap into action as the days shorten, filling your patio with colourful foliage and plenty of flowers.

>> **WHEN TO PLANT**
Late summer or autumn
AT THEIR BEST
Autumn

TIME TO COMPLETE
🕐 4 hours

YOU WILL NEED
🛈 Planters
Broken clay pot or polystyrene
 pieces
All-purpose potting compost

1. *Salvia officinalis* 'Tricolor'
2. *Lamium galeobdolon*
3. *Carex conica* 'Snowline'
4. *Sedum* 'Lemon Coral'
5. *Aster dumosus*, purple hybrid
6. *Heuchera* 'Amber Waves'

1 PREPARE THE POTS
Add clay pieces to the base of each pot. If you are using tall planters such as these, half-fill with polystyrene pieces (*see p.110*), then fill with compost to within 10cm (4in) of the rim.

2 POSITION THE PLANTS
In autumn, plants don't grow very much, so avoid leaving gaps as you would when planting summer bedding. Pack your plants in closely to make the planters look "finished".

3 AFTERCARE
Densely planted containers can get very dry, even in wet weather, so water them regularly. These plants will not need feeding, as they will soon become dormant, and growth will halt over winter.

Create a year-round shrub display

Containers are not just for summer flowers; displays for autumn and winter often last longer and help to brighten up these cold, dark months when viewed from the warmth of your kitchen or living room. Make sure that the pot you buy can withstand low winter temperatures – frostproof clay pots tend to be more expensive but should come with a guarantee and last for many years.

›› **WHEN TO START**
Early autumn
AT ITS BEST
All year round

TIME TO COMPLETE
1½ hours

YOU WILL NEED
Large frostproof container, at least
  45cm (18in) deep and wide
Broken clay pot or polystyrene
  pieces
Soil-based compost, such as
  John Innes No.3
Mulching material
All-purpose granular fertilizer

Plants used in shrub display (left):
Skimmia japonica 'Rubella'
Juniperus 'Grey Owl'
Osmanthus heterophyllus 'Goshiki'
Erica arborea var. *alpina*
  'Albert's Gold'

1 PREPARE THE POT
Add some broken clay pot or polystyrene pieces to the bottom of the container, and cover them with a layer of soil-based compost. Set the plants, still in their original pots, on the compost and check that they will sit about 5cm (2in) below the rim when planted. Keep them in the container, and start to fill in around them with compost.

2 SLIDE THE PLANTS OUT
Pack damp compost around all the pots up to their rims – only one is shown here, but the method works equally well with a few plants. Carefully slide out the plants in their pots to leave spaces for planting.

3 TIP PLANTS OUT OF THEIR POTS
Water all the plants well before tipping them out of their plastic pots. If the roots are congested, gently tease them out (*see p.31*). Carefully replace them in their positions in the container, and then firm more compost into any remaining gaps.

4 ADD A MULCH
Add a layer of gravel, slate chips or other decorative mulch over the soil. Water the container well, and set it on "feet" to allow the winter rains to drain through easily. Place it where you can see it easily from the house, and continue to water it during the autumn and winter if the soil under the mulch feels dry.

TOP TIP: ANNUAL CARE

The container will need watering frequently in the spring and summer. Each year in early spring, remove the mulch and top few centimetres of compost and replace it with fresh compost mixed with some all-purpose granular fertilizer. Water immediately after this, and then renew the mulch. When the plants become congested, plant them out in the garden or move to larger containers.

Shrubs for pots

Offering great value with their decorative foliage, sculptural forms and seasonal flowers, shrubs in containers are also fairly easy to look after, if you choose both container and plant carefully – a large pot will afford a greater choice of shrub and require watering less frequently than a small one. The plants here will all be happy in a container for a few years if you replace the top layer of compost and feed them annually each spring.

SELECTIONS》

✿✿✿ fully hardy   ✿✿ hardy in mild regions/sheltered sites   ✿ protect from frost over winter

☼ full sun   ◐ partial sun   ● full shade   ◊ well-drained soil   ◐ moist soil   ● wet soil

1 *Rhododendron* 'Hydon Dawn'; ‡1m (3ft) ↔1m (3ft) ☼ ◐ (acid soil)◐ ✿✿✿   **2** Rock rose, *Helianthemum apenninum*; ‡40cm (16in) ↔ 60cm (24in) ☼ ◊ ✿✿✿   **3** *Pieris japonica* 'Flamingo'; ‡1.2m (4ft) ↔1m (3ft) ☼ ◐ (acid soil)◐ ✿✿✿   **4** Bay, *Laurus nobilis*; ‡1.2m (4ft) ↔ 45cm (18in) if clipped ☼ ◐ (acid soil)◐ ✿✿   **5** *Hebe* 'Silver Queen'; ‡60cm (2ft) ↔60cm (2ft) ☼ ◐ ◊ ✿✿   **6** *Fatsia japonica*; ‡1.2m (4ft) ↔1m (3ft) ☼ ● ◐ ✿✿   **7** *Hydrangea serrata* 'Bluebird'; ‡1m (3ft) ↔1m (3ft) ☼ ◐ (acid soil)◐ ✿✿   **8** Mock orange, *Philadelphus microphyllus*; ‡80cm (32in) ↔80cm (32in) ☼ ◐ ◊ ✿✿✿   **9** *Viburnum tinus* 'Variegatum'; ‡1m (3ft) ↔1m (3ft) ☼ ◐ ◐ ✿✿✿   **10** *Lavandula* 'Willow Vale'; ‡60cm (24in) ↔ 60cm (24in) ☼ ◊ ✿✿✿

Tiered courtyard

The perfect solution for a plant-lover with a tiny plot, the designer of this dramatic show garden has used tiered raised beds bursting with colour to make the most of a small patio.

WHEN TO PLANT
Early spring

AT ITS BEST
All year round

TIME TO COMPLETE

🕐 1 day to plant

YOU WILL NEED

💧 Soil-based compost,
   such as John Innes No.3
Well-rotted organic matter
All-purpose granular fertilizer
Rubble to aid drainage

1. *Rudbeckia hirta* 'Prairie Sun'
2. *Fatsia japonica*
3. *Euonymus fortunei* 'Emerald Gaiety'
4. *Euphorbia characias* Silver Swan
5. *Agapathus*, white form
6. *Carex oshimensis* 'Evergold'
7. *Coreopsis verticillata* 'Moonbeam'

1 FILL THE BEDS
Unless you are a skilled DIYer, you will need a professional to build these beds, made from medium-density blocks, as they must be safe and drain freely. Once built, line them with 10cm (4in) of rubble and fill with compost.

2 PLANT UP
Set out the plants in their pots to check that you are happy with the display. They have been packed tightly here to give an instant effect, but in reality, they will need more space to grow.

3 AFTERCARE
Plant them up at the same depth as they were in their original pots, adding some granular fertilizer to the planting holes as you go. Water well, and feed the beds annually in spring. The shrubs here are evergreens, but the flowers will die down in winter.

Plant a winter hanging basket

Seasonal hanging baskets add a splash of colour to the garden throughout the coldest months. This one includes a few cyclamens, winter-flowering violas, and a range of evergreens. You could also push into the compost some miniature daffodil bulbs to extend the interest through spring.

>> **WHEN TO PLANT**
Early autumn
AT ITS BEST
Autumn to early spring

TIME TO COMPLETE
 1½ hours

YOU WILL NEED
 Hanging basket
Liner
Polythene bag
Wide low pot
Scissors
Container compost
Newspaper
Small plastic pot
Watering can
Skimmia japonica 'Rubella'
Heathers, *Erica*
Cyclamen
Winter-flowering violas
Small ivies, *Hedera helix*

1 BEFORE YOU PLANT
Stand the basket on a wide pot to keep it stable during preparation. Then add a proprietary basket liner.

2 **CUT OUT PLANTING HOLES**
Lay a circle of polythene over the bottom of the liner to act as a reservoir. Cut out a few evenly spaced crosses around the sides of the liner.

3 **ADD IVY AROUND THE EDGE**
Add a layer of potting compost to the bottom. Wrap paper around the root ball of each ivy and push them through the holes in the sides.

4 **PLANT THE TOP AND WATER**
Add the plants and fill in around them with more compost. Firm them in. Place a small plastic pot near the centre to act as a watering reservoir. Water into this pot to make sure it reaches the plants' roots.

Woven basket mix

This basket is easier to plant up than an open-sided one because it already has a liner inside, but remember to make a few drainage holes in the plastic before planting. You can use a range of foliage plants, including those like this yellow-leaved *Choisya* that can grow quite large, since plants put on little growth in winter. Violas also flower reliably in cooler months, if kept in a sheltered spot.

》 **WHEN TO PLANT**
Early autumn
AT ITS BEST
Autumn to early spring

TIME TO COMPLETE
1 hour
YOU WILL NEED
Woven hanging basket
Scissors
Wide low pot
Container compost
Watering can
Choisya ternata Sundance
Deadnettle, *Lamium
    maculatum* 'Aureum'
Small ivies, *Hedera helix*
Winter-flowering violas
Gaultheria procumbens

1 **PREPARE THE BASKET**
Place the basket on a low pot to stabilize it and punch a few drainage holes in the plastic liner. Half fill the basket with compost, then arrange your plants on top.

2 **FINISHING TOUCHES**
Remove the plants from their pots, place them in the basket and then firm them in with compost, as described in step 4 (*left*), and water well. Water baskets during dry spells.

TOP TIP: ORGANIC BASKET LINER

For a natural, organic alternative to a plastic liner, use conifer clippings from a hedge or tree. These also help to insulate the plants and will decompose over time and create an acidic soil environment, ideal for *Gaultheria* to thrive.

Keep a tree for life

Recycle your Christmas tree by potting it on and enjoying it on your patio throughout summer. Then bring it back inside for a second or even third season before planting it outside in the ground.

Tree choices

If you want to keep your tree after Christmas, it is important to buy one that has been grown in a container. To check that a tree is suitable for growing on, carefully slide it out of its pot and check that it has lots of small feeder roots, just like any other container-grown plant you would buy.

These are the most commonly available container-grown trees:

1 Norway spruce, *Picea abies* (also main picture) **2** Fraser fir, *Abies fraseri*
3 Nordmann fir, *Abies nordmanniana*

Caring for your tree

To ensure a wide choice, buy your tree early in the season. Water it every day, and prevent needle loss by storing it in a shed, garage, or greenhouse with good natural light for a few weeks before bringing it inside. Display your tree in a cool place indoors, keeping it well watered, and repot it in the New Year.

 WHEN TO START
Late winter to early spring

AT ITS BEST
All year round

 TIME TO COMPLETE
🕐 1 hour

YOU WILL NEED
- Large plastic pot
- Broken clay pot pieces
- Soil-based ericaceous compost, eg, John Innes ericaceous No.3
- Sturdy gloves
- Well-rotted organic matter, such as farmyard manure
- All-purpose granular fertilizer (eg, Growmore)
- Secateurs

1 WATER WELL
When the festive season is over, store your tree for a few weeks in a shed, as you did before bringing it into the house for Christmas. Water it frequently, and don't allow the compost to dry out.

2 PREPARE A NEW CONTAINER
Buy a plastic pot, which will be light and easy to move around, one size larger than the original container. Put some broken clay pot pieces over the drainage holes at the bottom and add a layer of compost on top.

3 REMOVE THE TREE
Wearing heavy-duty gloves, squeeze the tree's pot around the sides to dislodge the root ball, and then slide it out. Place the tree in its new pot.

4 ADD FERTILIZER
Check that there is 5cm (2in) between the top of the root ball and the pot rim. Fill in around the roots with compost mixed with some fertilizer, and firm in well.

5 SHAPE UP
Water the tree well. Trim back the stems lightly with secateurs to create a cone shape. If there are two stems at the top, cut one back to a bud to leave a single "leader".

TOP TIP: TRIMMING FIRS

Fir stems end with a three-pronged fork – to trim, cut out the middle prong, which will stimulate bushy growth along the stem. Do not cut the single, main "leader" stem at the top.

Luscious leaves

With their bold foliage and wide colour range, hostas are the darlings of the designer world. Grow a few in pots on a shady patio for a lush, sophisticated display that will last from early summer until the autumn.

WHEN TO START
Spring
AT THEIR BEST
Early summer to early autumn

TIME TO COMPLETE
2 hours

YOU WILL NEED
4 pots of different sizes
Soil-based potting compost
Broken clay pot pieces
Slow-release granular fertilizer
Horticultural grit

1. *Hosta* 'Francee'
2. *Hosta* 'Krossa Regal'
3. *Hosta fortunei* var. *albopicta* f. *aurea*
4. *Hosta* 'August Moon'

1 CHOOSING POTS
First choose suitable containers. *Hosta* 'Francee' and *H.* 'August Moon' have spreading habits and suit wide pots, while *H.* 'Krossa Regal' is more upright and looks best in a taller container. *H. fortunei* f. *aurea* is small in stature, so select a little pot for this diminutive plant. Buy frostproof containers for your hostas; they are perennial plants and will pop up year after year.

2 PLANTING UP
Prepare your pots according to the instructions on page 111, and water the hostas well before planting. Add slow-release fertilizer to the compost and plant the hostas slightly deeper than they were in their original pots. Water them, and apply a gritty mulch to deter slugs and snails (*see Top Tip, below*).

3 AFTERCARE
Hostas like damp conditions and need frequent watering, especially in summer. Use about half a full watering can on each plant, so that the moisture reaches the bottom of the pot. Take precautions against slugs and snails, and feed annually.

TOP TIP: SLUG AND SNAIL REPELLENTS

To keep your hostas free from slug and snail damage, sprinkle a few slug pellets sparingly around young plants after planting. Organic controls include pouring used coffee grounds around the plants, applying a mulch of eggshells or grit, or fixing a copper strip around each pot (*right*). Alternatively, see pages 426–427 for biological controls.

Create a winter windowbox

When your summer flowers are spent, and window displays are looking bedraggled and dull, give them a quick makeover with colourful evergreens that will last the course through the coldest winter. This combination of conifers, shrubs, grasses and herbs is guaranteed to perform for many months.

 WHEN TO START
Early autumn

AT ITS BEST
Early autumn to spring

TIME TO COMPLETE
1½ hours

YOU WILL NEED

Large windowbox
Ericaceous compost
Broken polystyrene pieces
Bucket
Carex oshimensis 'Evergold'
Cupressus macrocarpa 'Goldcrest'
Golden thyme, *Thymus pulegioides* 'Archer's Gold'
Leucothoe Scarletta
Gaultheria mucronata

1 BEFORE PLANTING
Buy a frost-resistant windowbox – this one is made from terracotta, but a plastic imitation would be best if you live in a cold, exposed area that is prone to frosts. Check that your plants fit comfortably in the container.

2 SOAK THE PLANTS
Water each plant well, either with a watering can without a rose, or by dunking the plants in a bucket of water. Allow the bubbles to dissipate, then remove the pots and allow them to drain.

3 PROVIDE GOOD DRAINAGE
Break up a polystyrene plant tray and add the pieces to the bottom of the windowbox. Then add a layer of ericaceous compost – the *Leucothoe* and *Gaultheria* are both acid-loving plants and do best in this type of soil.

Extend the season

This colourful windowbox makes a bright winter display with a mixture of pansies and textured evergreens. Then, as the weather starts to warm up, blue grape hyacinths and dainty daffodils (not in flower here) appear in succession to keep the interest going throughout spring.

4 PLACE PLANTS IN POSITION
Place the plants in their original pots in the windowbox and make sure that they will sit about 2cm (1in) below the rim when planted to allow sufficient space for watering.

5 PLANT UP AND FIRM IN
Plant up and fill in around each plant with compost, firming it in with your fingers as you go. Water well. Water your box once or twice a week in winter, and more frequently in spring.

YOU WILL NEED
- Large windowbox
- Multi-purpose compost
- Broken polystyrene pieces
- Bucket
- *Stipa tenuissima*
- Japanese tassel fern, *Polystichum polyblepharum*
- Winter-flowering pansies, Imperial Antique Shades
- *Cupressus macrocarpa* 'Goldcrest'
- Grape hyacinth, *Muscari*
- *Narcissus* 'Topolino'

1 PLANT UP BULBS
Follow Steps 1 to 3 opposite. Evenly space the narcissi bulbs on the layer of compost, and plant the rest of the plants carefully between them.

2 FINISHING TOUCHES
Fill in around the plants and cover the bulbs with compost, up to about 8cm (3in) from the rim. Add a few grape hyacinth bulbs between the plants and then cover with compost to about 2cm (1in) from the rim. Firm gently and water.

TOP TIP: CARING FOR PANSIES

Winter-flowering pansies will bloom throughout the cold winter months, although they put on their best performance in spring. Remove the dying flowers as you see them, and if plants become straggly in spring, renovate them by cutting the stems back to 8cm (3in). Then apply an all-purpose fertilizer and water in well.

Plants for winter patios

There are many bedding plants that provide welcome colour throughout the winter months in frost-proof containers on a patio or terrace. Pansies and primulas will flower during all but the coldest spells, and the foliage of ornamental cabbage intensifies as the weather cools. You can also use small specimens of evergreen shrubs, such as *Euonymus*, *Skimmia*, and *Choisya*, and plants with bright berries, including *Gaultheria*.

❄❄❄ fully hardy ❄❄ hardy in mild regions/sheltered sites ❄ protect from frost over winter
☼ full sun ◐ partial sun ● full shade ◊ well-drained soil ◔ moist soil ◆ wet soil

❶ Ornamental cabbage, *Brassica oleracea*; ‡45cm (18in) ↔ 45cm (18in) ☼ ◊ ❄❄❄ ❷ *Viola* x *wittrockiana* purple cultivar; ‡20cm (8in) ↔ 25cm (10in) ☼ ◐ ◊ ◔ ❄❄❄ ❸ *Euonymus fortunei* 'Emerald 'n' Gold'; ‡60cm (24in) ↔ 90cm (36in) ☼ ◊ ◔ ❄❄❄ ❹ *Asplenium scolopendrium*; ‡50cm (20in) ↔ 60cm (24in) ◐ ◊ ◔ ❄❄❄ ❺ *Gaultheria procumbens*; ‡15cm (6in) ↔ 1m (3ft) ◐ ◆ ❄❄❄ ❻ *Helictotrichon sempervirens*; ‡1.4m (4½ft) ↔ 60cm (24in) ☼ ◊ ❄❄❄ ❼ *Skimmia japonica* 'Rubella'; ‡75cm (30in) ↔ 75cm (30in) ☼ ◐ ◊ ◆ ❄❄❄ ❽ Ivy, *Hedera helix* 'Eva'; ‡1.2m (4ft) ↔ 30cm (12in) ☼ ◐ ◊ ◆ ❄❄ ❾ Mexican orange blossom, *Choisya ternata* Sundance; ‡2.5m (8ft) ↔ 2.5m (8ft) ☼ ◐ ❄❄❄ ❿ *Primula* (Polyanthus Group) Crescendo Series; ‡15cm (6in) ↔ 20cm (8in) ☼ ◐ ◊ ◔ ❄❄❄ ⓫ *Senecio cineraria* 'Silver Dust'; ‡30cm (12in) ↔ 30cm (12in) ☼ ◊ ❄❄

Cool combinations

Summer patio displays often lack height and structure, but this simple idea solves both problems. Stack pots of annuals on the steps of an old wooden ladder and use tall cosmos in containers on the ground to create a tower of flowers and foliage. Choose bright sunny colours or select elegant cool notes, like the blues and whites used here. Remember that the tiny pots will need watering every day in summer.

WHEN TO START
Spring
AT THEIR BEST
Summer to early autumn

TIME TO COMPLETE
3–4 hours

YOU WILL NEED
Blue and white containers
Broken clay pot pieces
Multi-purpose compost
Slow-release granular fertilizer
Grey slate pebbles

1. *Salvia farinacea*, blue
2. *Cosmos bipinnatus* 'Purity'
3. Chives
4. *Antirrhinum majus*, white
5. *Ophiopogon planiscapus* 'Nigrescens'
6. *Lobelia erinus*, white

1 PREPARE THE LADDER
Rub down the ladder with sandpaper to remove dirt and grease, and either paint it with a clear preservative or a wood stain. Collect together your plants and pots, and decide how you would like to pair them up. Make sure all the pots have drainage holes in the bottom – drill some if they don't – and put a few pieces of broken clay pot or polystyrene plant trays over the holes.

2 PLANT THE CONTAINERS
Cover the clay or polystyrene pieces with a layer of multi-purpose compost. Then arrange the plants, still in their pots, in the containers and check that you are happy with your collective display. Also make sure that the plants will be about 3–4cm (1¼–1½ins) below the rims when planted. Water the plants well, remove them from their pots and plant them up, firming in compost around them.

3 AFTERCARE
Add some fertilizer to the compost, and water the plants in well. Place decorative pebbles over the surface to finish the pots off and to help minimize moisture loss. Then arrange the pots on the ladder, wedging the smaller ones between the steps, if necessary, to keep them in place. Water the containers every day, and remove the fading blooms regularly. If plants start to flag later in the season, apply a dose of tomato fertilizer.

TOP TIP: SOW COSMOS SEEDS

Cosmos are tall airy plants with feathery foliage and a continuous display of white or pink summer flowers. Despite their delicate appearance they are very easy to grow from seed, and one packet will give you sufficient plants to fill five or six containers. Simply follow the instructions for sowing large seeds (*see p.108*), and the seedlings should appear within a few days. Cosmos are not hardy, and must be kept inside until the risk of frost has passed. Deadhead spent flowers

Create a table-top display

Just as you might place a vase of flowers on a dining-room table, why not decorate your garden furniture as well? This pot, planted with scented alpine pinks and pretty sea heath, *Frankenia*, makes a drought-tolerant table centrepiece that will provide colour and interest throughout the summer months.

WHEN TO PLANT
Early spring

AT ITS BEST
Spring to autumn

TIME TO COMPLETE
🕐 1 hour

YOU WILL NEED
Shallow bowl
Broken clay pot pieces
Soil-based compost and grit
Pink, *Dianthus* 'Devon Flores'
Sea heath, *Frankenia thymifolia*

1 PREPARE THE POT
Choose a pot that is slightly deeper than the plants' root balls. Place a piece of broken pot over the drainage hole, and add a layer of gravel. Mix two parts of soil-based compost to one part of horticultural grit in a bowl.

2 PLANT UP
Water the plants well. Add a thin layer of compost over the gravel and position the plants on top, with the pinks in the middle. Use the compost and grit mixture to fill in around the plants.

3 CARING FOR YOUR DISPLAY
Place your display on a table that is in full sun for at least half the day. Water and feed it regularly, and the plants will perform well in the same pot for a number of years after planting.

Decorative and fun ideas

Evergreen alpines and other drought-tolerant plants are ideal for table displays. You can also try low-growing herbs, such as thyme, or for a more seasonal scheme, plant bulbs and spring flowers. For the best overall effect, use containers that complement your garden furniture and tableware.

❶ Use a cup and saucer, and a milk jug, topped with pots of mind-your-own-business *(Soleirolia soleirolii)* to make this fun centrepiece. ❷ Garden succulents, including houseleeks, need little soil and water to thrive, and come in a range of colours and forms. Plant them in a shallow tray for a textured design. ❸ Fresh herbs are a must for any garden, and this line of thymes in tiny terracotta pots is a fresh way to grow and display them. ❹ Lily-of-the-valley *(Convallaria majalis)* is unmatched for spring scent. Line a basket with perforated plastic, and plant up a number to welcome in the season.

Up on the roof

Perfect for a modern patio or roof terrace, this contemporary scheme combines drought-tolerant grasses and spiky irises to enclose a stylish dining area. The smooth lightweight metal containers complement the textured foliage plants and gravel floor, and create a barrier that shields diners from wind and prying eyes.

》 **WHEN TO START**
Spring
AT ITS BEST
Late spring to early autumn

TIME TO COMPLETE
🕐 1 day

YOU WILL NEED
ℹ️ Large lightweight containers
Gravel
Broken clay pot pieces
Multi-purpose compost
Slow-release granular fertilizer

1. *Calamagrostis x acutiflora*
2. Bearded iris (not in flower)
3. Box, *Buxus sempervirens*
4. *Panicum virgatum*
5. *Stipa tenuissima*

1 SITE YOUR CONTAINERS

Select large zinc, galvanized, or powder-coated metal containers that will not rust. Position rectangular pots close together to form a wall around your seating area, and use round ones to create focal points. Apply a thin coat of baby oil to zinc pots to clean off any marks and maintain their finish.

2 ADD PLANTING

All plants here enjoy full sun and free-draining soil, conditions that suit containers on a roof terrace. Ensure pots have drainage holes, or drill some if not, and cover these with clay pieces. Then add compost, half-filling the containers. Add some fertilizer, and plant the grasses and box (*see p.151*). Add more compost to the iris containers and plant them so that the rhizomes (bulb-like structures) lie on top of the compost (*see p.31*).

3 LONG-TERM CARE

Water in the plants well, and lay 5cm (2in) of gravel on the floor. Water the containers regularly during spring and summer. The following spring, remove the top layer of compost and replace it with fresh compost, mixed with some slow-release fertilizer. The *Calamagrostis* and *Panicum* are deciduous but their dried stems add interest in winter; the iris dies down completely, but reappears in spring.

Plait a bay tree

Bay trees can be kept trimmed to make classic evergreen lollipop-shaped topiary. Straight stems look smart, but for extra texture you can plait or twist several stems around each other. It is an expensive look that you can achieve yourself; all you need are young plants and time for them to grow.

 WHEN TO PLANT
Late spring or early summer
AT ITS BEST
All year round

TIME TO COMPLETE
4 hours

YOU WILL NEED
Two or three young bay plants,
  or a plant with suckering stems
Sharp spade
Secateurs
Large container
Broken clay pot pieces
Soil-based compost, such as
  John Innes No.3
Slow-release granular fertilizer

1 SELECT STRAIGHT STEMS
If you have a multi-stemmed bay, dig it up and select the longest and straightest stems. Alternatively, buy a plant with lots of stems. Sever the root ball between the stems with a sharp spade.

2 PLANT STEMS TOGETHER
Place some clay pot pieces in the base of a large container, at least 30cm (12in) wide. Add soil-based compost and some fertilizer, and plant two or three stems as close together as possible.

3 REMOVE LEAVES
Make sure that the bay stems are planted at the same depth as they were in the ground or pot. Use secateurs to remove the leaves from the lower two-thirds of the stems. Rub off any new leaf buds with your fingers.

4 PLAIT STEMS TOGETHER
In spring and summer, when the wood is sappy, the stems should be pliable enough to be loosely plaited, repeatedly passing the stems left over right, right over left. It may look forced at first, but will even out as the stems grow.

5 TRIM OFF UNEVEN GROWTH
Once you have finished plaiting, secure the stems temporarily with strong garden twine, then trim off any uneven growth to leave a compact head (*see right*). As the tree grows, prune lightly to encourage bushier growth.

Structural Features

Trees are wonderful features, adding height, colour, and shade to beds and borders. They also provide striking focal points in lawns. Follow the advice in this chapter to ensure you plant correctly, and remember to water your trees regularly for the first two years. Hedges and climbers also make beautiful vertical features; include a selection of different types for flowers and foliage throughout the year, and lay a carpet of lawn to create a natural green foil for your plants.

Choosing a tree

Every tree brings a range of benefits to the garden. As well as flowers and fruit, some offer sculptural shapes, coloured bark, vibrant autumn colour, and differing degrees of shade, or a combination of these qualities. The choice is wide, so decide what you want most from a tree before you buy one.

ASSESS YOUR NEEDS

Trees are an investment in time, money and space, so it is important to pick one that suits your garden. Soil type and aspect are important considerations, but so too is the amount of space you have available, bearing in mind how large the tree will grow. Also remember that trees cast shade, and draw large quantities of moisture and nutrients from the soil, affecting other plants growing nearby. They can also undermine foundations with their roots, so be careful to site your tree at a distance from buildings. You should also prioritize the qualities you want from your tree, whether it's aesthetic beauty, structure, privacy, or wildlife habitat.

Silver stems >
Grouping several trees of the same species, such as the Himalayan birch, Betula utilis var. jacquemontii, *makes a strong visual impact.*

SEASONAL INTEREST

Some trees have several seasons of interest, and offer great garden value. *Prunus serrula* has spring blossom and copper bark for winter appeal. Both *Malus* x *moerlandsii* 'Liset' and *Sorbus vilmorinii* have spring flowers and autumn fruits; the *Sorbus* also has attractive foliage. With spring flowers, summer berries and rich autumnal tints, *Amelanchier lamarkii* has a lot to offer, and is ideal for smaller plots.

① *Prunus serrula;* ↕↔10m (30ft)
② *Malus* x *moerlandsii* 'Liset'; ↕↔6m (20ft)
③ *Sorbus vilmorinii;* ↕↔5m (15ft)
④ *Amelanchier lamarckii;* ↕↔10m (30ft)

∧ *Welcome shade*
With its broad leaves, the Indian bean tree, Catalpa bignonioides, *acts like a living parasol, providing relief from the sun.*

DESIGN EFFECTS

Trees play a number of useful and decorative roles in the garden. Where there is space and a clear line of sight, consider a tree with a strong structure, such as a birch or decorative cherry, to act as a stand-alone focal point. A tree with a good canopy, such as the Indian bean tree, *Catalpa bignonioides*, provides shade from hot summer sun when planted close to a south-facing seating area. Large-leaved trees can also help create a tropical effect in the garden. Try the fragrant snowbell, *Styrax obassia*, with its scented white flowers, or the evergreen loquat, *Eriobotrya japonica,* an ideal choice for year-round privacy.

❶ Yellow birch, *Betula alleghaniensis*; ↕25m (80ft) ↔10m (30ft)   ❷ Crab apple, *Malus* x *magdeburgensis*; ↕↔6m (20ft)   ❸ Loquat, *Eriobotrya japonica*; ↕↔8m (25ft)

How to plant a tree

An investment in time and money, a tree will eventually become a striking presence in your garden and make a beautiful year-round feature. Plant it well and take care of it afterwards, and your tree will soon pay dividends, providing you with colour, shade, and structure for many years to come.

WHEN TO START
Late autumn
AT ITS BEST
All year round

TIME TO COMPLETE
 2 hours

YOU WILL NEED
 Tree
Spade
Fork
Cane
Stake
Tree tie
Mulch
Gardening gloves

1 PREPARE THE GROUND
Dig a circular hole twice the width and the same depth as the root ball. Do not dig over the base, as this may cause the tree to sink once planted. Instead, puncture the base and sides with a garden fork to allow roots to penetrate.

2 CHECK PLANTING DEPTH
Most trees are planted with their root ball slightly proud of the soil surface, which helps them to establish a strong root system. Place the tree in the hole, lay a cane across the top to check the level, and add or remove soil as required.

3 TEASE OUT ROOTS
Lift the tree from the hole and use your fingers to gently tease the outer roots away from the root ball. This will encourage them to root into the surrounding soil, helping the tree to establish, and is particularly important if the tree is "root-bound" (*see p.20*).

4 PLANT THE TREE
Place the tree in the hole and turn it round until its best side is facing the right direction. Then fill around the root ball with the excavated soil. Do this in three stages; add soil and gently firm it down with your foot each time to remove any air pockets around the roots.

5 GENTLY FIRM IN
Make sure the root ball is just above the soil surface. As a guide, look for the "nursery line", where the trunk darkens at the base, showing the level the tree was grown at in the nursery. This must not be buried. Then add a thin layer of soil over the root ball so that no roots are exposed.

6 ATTACH TREE TO WOODEN STAKE

Choose a stake that will reach a third of the way up the trunk. Use a mallet to hammer it into the ground at an angle of about 45 degrees, with the top facing the prevailing wind. Attach a tree tie at the point where tree and stake meet, using a spacer to prevent them rubbing together.

7 AFTERCARE

Water the tree well, and then apply a thick mulch, such as composted bark chippings, to suppress competing weeds and seal in moisture. Keep it clear of the stem. Water the tree regularly for two years, and check and loosen ties frequently. The ties can be removed after two or three years when the tree has fully established.

< *Woodland scene*
The delicate pink blossom of this hawthorn, Crataegus, is followed in autumn by masses of scarlet berries, which make a tempting feast for birds. Ferns, hazel, and bleeding hearts, Dicentra, enhance the texture and colour of the border.

Grow a sculptural fern

Tree ferns have huge, arching fronds, a unique trunk, and a shape reminiscent of their tropical rainforest origins. Although expensive to buy, they pay their way by adding drama and an exotic element to a garden, and they flourish in awkward, damp, dark corners where most other plants struggle to grow.

WHEN TO PLANT
Spring
AT THEIR BEST
Summer

TIME TO COMPLETE
🕐 1½ hours

YOU WILL NEED
🔧 Pot-grown tree fern,
   Dicksonia antarctica
Spade
All-purpose granular fertilizer
Garden cane
Watering can

1 CHECK PLANTING DEPTH
Dig a hole twice as wide as the trunk and as deep as the height of the container, then loosen the earth at the base. Position the fern in the hole and, with a cane, check that the final soil level will be the same as it is in the pot. Add or remove soil as necessary.

2 ADD FERTILIZER
Lift the tree fern from its hole and add a small amount of a general fertilizer, such as blood, fish and bone meal, to the base. Mix this into the soil so that it does not touch the roots directly. Tree ferns rarely need feeding after this initial application.

TOP TIP: OVERWINTERING

The crowns of tree ferns need protecting from the wet and cold during winter. Make a chicken wire frame around the plant and pack it loosely with straw. Then cover with a waterproof hat made from polythene sheeting. Tie it on securely. This will insulate the plant and keep it dry, but still allow essential ventilation.

3 FIRM IN AROUND BASE
Remove the tree fern from its pot and place it in the hole. Check that it is upright, then backfill with soil, using your foot to carefully press all round the edge of the plant, to ensure it is held firmly in place. Take care not to compact the soil, as this may hinder drainage.

< Fern friends
Tree ferns make textural focal points in shady corners, where they can be underplanted with low-growing plants, such as ferns and hostas, that enjoy similar conditions.

4 WATER THOROUGHLY
Tree ferns are unusual because, rather than their roots, it is their leafy crowns that need to be kept moist. However, you should water them at the base as well when first planting them, as it helps to settle the soil, and hold the trunk upright.

Multi-stemmed trees

Some trees have particularly beautiful bark, and you can create a dazzling effect by encouraging them to develop multiple stems. This involves some drastic pruning, but the end result is well worth it.

⟫ **WHEN TO PLANT**
Late autumn

AT THEIR BEST
Winter

TIME TO COMPLETE
🕐 3 hours

YOU WILL NEED
One tree (see options)
Spade
Fork
Organic matter
Pruning saw
Stake
Tree tie

TOP TIP: PLANTING OPTIONS

Some trees are better suited than others to growing as multi-stemmed specimens, so if you are unsure, ask before you buy. The following species can all be grown in this way:

Eucalyptus
Himalayan birch, *Betula utilis* var.
 jacquemontii
Snake-bark maple, *Acer davidii*
Tibetan cherry, *Prunus serrula*
Hazel, *Corylus*
Willow, *Salix*

 PREPARE THE GROUND
Dig out a planting hole, as deep as the root ball, and at least twice as wide. Puncture the base and sides of the hole with a fork, and mix a little organic matter into the excavated soil. Plant your tree so that the root ball is slightly proud of the surrounding soil surface, using a cane to check the planting level. Backfill with soil, stake, then secure firmly with a tree tie (*see pp.178–179*). Water well.

 PLANTING AND STAKING
You can buy multi-stemmed trees, which require no further pruning, but it is cheaper to buy a single-stemmed tree and prune it yourself. Ideally you should give it a full growing season first, then the following winter, cut the trunk to the ground, and remove the stake.

 AFTERCARE
New stems will appear from the base in spring, and become the new framework of branches. If there are lots, prune them selectively to promote a good shape. Water the tree freely the first year after planting, and also the year after pruning to help it recover. Feed with a tree and shrub fertilizer in early spring.

Snowy structure >
The peeling white bark of these Himalayan birches provide a beautiful contrast to the understorey of ferns and astilbes.

Trees for small spaces

Many gardeners are wary of planting trees in confined areas, but because they take up very little space on the ground, it's possible to squeeze a tree into the smallest of gardens. All growth is at canopy level, providing privacy and structure, but leaving plenty of space for planting underneath. Choose compact, more manageable trees; there are many available, sporting spring flowers, autumn berries, or simply beautiful foliage.

❋❋❋ fully hardy   ❋❋ hardy in mild regions/sheltered sites   ❋ protect from frost over winter
☼ full sun   ☀ partial sun   ☀ full shade   ◊ well-drained soil   ◖ moist soil   ◕ wet soil

❶ Crab apple, *Malus* 'John Downie'; ‡6m (20ft) ↔4.5m (14ft) ☼ ☀ ◖ ❋❋❋   ❷ Winter cherry, *Prunus* x *subhirtella* 'Autumnalis Rosea'; ‡8m (25ft) ↔8m (25ft) ☼ ☀ ◖ ❋❋❋   ❸ Japanese maple, *Acer palmatum* 'Sango-kaku'; ‡6m (20ft) ↔5m (15ft) ☼ ☀ ◖ ❋❋❋   ❹ *Magnolia liliiflora* 'Nigra'; ‡3m (10ft) ↔2.5m (8ft) ☼ ☀ ◖ ❋❋❋   ❺ Cornelian cherry, *Cornus mas*; ‡5m (15ft) ↔5m (15ft) ☼ ☀ ◊ ❋❋❋   ❻ Dogwood, *Cornus kousa* 'Miss Satomi'; ‡5m (15ft) ↔5m (15ft) ☼ ◖ ❋❋❋   ❼ *Laburnum* x *watereri*; ‡8m (25ft) ↔8m (25ft) ☼ ◖ ❋❋❋   ❽ Hawthorn, *Crataegus laevigata* 'Rosea'; ‡4.5m (14ft) ↔5m (15ft) ☼ ☀ ◖ ❋❋❋   ❾ Strawberry tree, *Arbutus unedo*; ‡6m (20ft) ↔6m (20ft) ☼ ◊ ❋❋❋   ❿ Judas tree, *Cercis siliquastrum*; ‡10m (30ft) ↔10m (30ft) ☼ ◊ ❋❋❋

Golden arch

A traditional laburnum walkway makes a spectacular feature in early summer, and can be created in most gardens. Enjoy its blast of seasonal colour, and plant around it to double the display.

 WHEN TO PLANT
Late autumn
AT ITS BEST
Early summer

TIME TO COMPLETE
 4 days

YOU WILL NEED
 4 laburnum trees (or more
for a longer walk)
Metal-framed fruit tree arch
Spade
Fork
Tree ties
Wire

1 INSTALL THE ARCH SUPPORTS
You can buy sturdy fruit tree or vine arches in a variety of sizes to suit your needs. Select two that will span your walkway, or ask a blacksmith to make a set to fit your scheme. Most metal arches are simply set into the soil.

2 PLANT AND TRAIN
Plant one tree next to each arch upright, water well and secure with a tree tie (*see pp.178–179 for more planting instructions*). Train the branches over the arch as they grow, tying them in with tree or tube ties. Over time, you may find it necessary to link the arches with coated wires to support new stems.

3 AFTERCARE
Water the trees regularly for the first two years until they are established, and check and loosen tree ties every few months. Feed each spring with a shrub and tree fertilizer to promote the best possible display. Prune any wayward branches in winter, and regularly remove thicker, woodier growth to make space for young flowering stems. Plant other shrubs and climbers below, and nearby, for additional colour. All parts of a laburnum are poisonous if ingested, so do not plant where children or pets play.

< *Golden veil*
You need just four trees to create this spectacular spring display. Underplant with Alchemilla mollis *to complete the effect.*

TOP TIP: UNDERPLANTING

Bulbs are ideal for planting beneath your arch. Early bulbs, such as daffodils, will flower before the trees, while tulips and alliums (*below*) bloom at the same time. Shade-loving ferns will provide long-lasting interest.

Grow trees from seeds

Even large trees can be kept to a manageable size when planted in a container, and they are easy to grow from seeds you can find for free when walking in the park. In autumn, look out for conkers from horse chestnuts, acorns from oaks, and sycamore seeds, all of which will germinate after a few months.

 WHEN TO PLANT
Autumn

AT THEIR BEST
Spring to autumn

TIME TO COMPLETE
 30 minutes

YOU WILL NEED
Tree seeds (here, we used a conker
  from a horse chestnut tree)
Plant pot
Broken clay pot pieces
Soil-based compost, such as
  John Innes No.3
Trowel

1 PREPARE TO PLANT
Check your seeds are firm and have no holes or other signs of insect larvae inside. Place some clay pieces at the bottom of the pot, and nearly fill it with compost.

2 PLANT YOUR SEEDS
Plant the conker about 2cm (1in) deep, and cover with compost. Water, and place in a shady spot outside. Check that the soil doesn't dry out. Your seed will sprout in spring.

∧ *Diminutive chestnut*
If grown in the ground this chestnut would be a large tree, but after ten years in a container, it is still a small specimen, ideal for an urban garden or patio.

Other seeds to try

It's worth planting a range of tree seeds, just in case some do not germinate. Collect seeds when they are ripe – undamaged seeds that have fallen to the ground will be at the right stage – and plant them immediately, since they dehydrate quickly if they are stored.

EASY TO GROW
Collect ripe acorns, hazelnuts, crab apples, eating apples and cherries, either from the park or from your own or a friend's garden. Remove the flesh from the fruits and wash the seeds first before sowing. Many tree seeds require a period of cold, or even frost, before they will germinate, so leave your pots outside where they won't get blown over.

Miniature woodland

Trees such as oaks, hollies, and rowans will grow large with time, but you can restrict their size by planting them in containers or raised beds, as shown here. Surround them with shade-loving plants to create a tiny woodland.

WHEN TO START
Autumn
AT ITS BEST
Spring to autumn

TIME TO COMPLETE
3 hours to plant

YOU WILL NEED
Well-rotted organic matter
Drainage material
Soil-based compost, such as
 John Innes No.3
Young trees grown from seed
Male ferns, *Dryopteris filix-mas*
Woodruff, *Asperula*
Ivy, *Hedera helix*

1 PREPARE THE BED
Buy or build a raised bed (*see pp.254–255*), or hire a landscaper to construct a rendered brick bed like this one. Add drainage materials, such as broken bricks, rocks, etc, to the base and fill the bed with garden soil or compost and some well-rotted organic matter.

2 PLANT UP
First plant your young trees, staking them if required (*see Top Tip, right*). Position the woodland plants about 45cm (18in) from the trees. Water well and mulch. Keep the bed watered, even after the plants have established.

TOP TIP: STAKING AND FEEDING

When your seedlings have grown, you can either plant them in large pots (*see opposite*), in raised beds (*above*), or in the ground. In windy sites, those planted in beds or the soil may require staking (*see p.179*). Check your trees regularly and loosen the ties as the trunks expand. Remove the stakes after a couple of years. In spring, apply a shrub and tree fertilizer to the soil. For those in pots, replace the top 5cm (2in) of compost with new compost mixed with some fertilizer.

Blossoming beauties

There is no more spectacular harbinger of spring than an ornamental cherry tree bursting into bloom. After a winter of bare branches come clouds of fluffy, pastel blossoms. Some produce fruits that attract birds to the garden, and many also have good autumn colour to end the year with a bang.

WHEN TO PLANT
Late autumn

AT ITS BEST
Spring

TIME TO COMPLETE
2 hours

YOU WILL NEED
Cherry tree
Stake
Tree tie
Spade

< *Colour match*
Ornamental cherries flower before they are in full leaf, which gives enough time, and sunlight, for spring-flowering bulbs to add their own splash of colour beneath.

1 CHOOSE A SITE
Ornamental cherries grow best in moist, fertile, but well-drained soil, in full sun, although they tolerate partial shade and a drier soil once they are established. Make sure there is ample room for the tree to grow, as some mature into large trees.

2 PLANTING AND STAKING
Dig a hole the same depth as the root ball and twice as wide. Plant the tree so that the root ball is slightly proud of the surrounding soil surface. Hammer in a stake angled into the prevailing wind, and attach it to the tree using a flexible, adjustable tree tie (*see pp.178–179 for more planting advice*).

3 AFTERCARE
Water the tree thoroughly after planting, and apply a mulch, keeping it away from the trunk. Water for the first two years. Check the tie often, and loosen it if need be. After a couple of years, you can remove the stake as the tree will be fully established.

TOP TIP: PRUNING

If you choose the right-sized cherry for your garden, the only pruning required will be to remove dead, diseased, or damaged growth. If you need to shape your tree, do so after flowering in early summer, as there are fewer diseases then, and you will not remove the flower buds.

Planting choices

Cherry trees come in a wide variety of shapes, sizes, and colours to suit all gardens. *Prunus* 'Spire' has a slender, upright habit, ideal for smaller gardens. *P.* x *subhirtella* and *P. incisa* are both compact trees with pale pink flowers and attractive autumnal colour. *P.* 'Shizuka' is medium-sized, and has large, scented, white, semi-double flowers.

❶ *P.* 'Spire'; ↕10m (30ft) ↔ 6m (20ft)
❷ *P.* x *subhirtella*; ↕↔8m (25ft)
❸ *P. incisa*; ↕↔8m (25ft)
❹ *P.* 'Shizuka'; ↕↔4m (12ft)

Plant an informal hedge

If you prefer a relaxed, rustic style of garden, avoid formal hedges, and opt instead for one that contains a mix of species. This style of hedge is good for wildlife, as it provides food and somewhere to live. It is also relatively easy to look after, needing just one trim per year in late autumn.

 WHEN TO START
Autumn
AT ITS BEST
All year round

 TIME TO COMPLETE
 3 hours, or more for long hedges

YOU WILL NEED
Wildlife hedging plants (blackthorn, dog rose, hawthorn, hazel, holly)
Spade
Fork
String and pegs
Well-rotted organic matter, such as farmyard manure

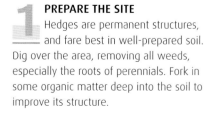 **1 PREPARE THE SITE**
Hedges are permanent structures, and fare best in well-prepared soil. Dig over the area, removing all weeds, especially the roots of perennials. Fork in some organic matter deep into the soil to improve its structure.

2 COMPRESS SOIL
Use your weight to compress the soil, shuffling slowly over the entire area. Then repeat this at a right angle. If planted immediately after it has been dug over, the soil will settle, and plants will not be anchored properly.

3 MARK GUIDE LINES
For a deep hedge, set out two lines of string, held taut by pegs, 35–40cm (14–16in) apart. These form the planting guides for your two rows of hedging. For a slimmer hedge, you will need just one line of plants.

4 PLANT IN TRENCHES
To ensure a really straight hedge, dig out a long trench, rather than individual holes. Plant one line at a time and position the plants along its length, about 35cm (14in) apart. Alternate the different plant species for a mosaic effect.

5 CHECK PLANTING DEPTHS
Hedging plants suffer when planted too deeply or shallowly, so take care to ensure that they are at the same depth as they were in the nursery, or in their pots. The stems will be darker where they previously touched the soil.

6 STAGGER PLANTING
If planting a double row, stagger the second line, so that the plants grow in the gaps between those in the first row. Water in all plants well, and mulch with organic matter, keeping it clear of the stems. Water the hedge regularly throughout the first year.

Thorny barriers

An informal wildlife hedge can also double as a barrier to deter intruders, as many wildlife-friendly plants are covered in vicious spikes and thorns. Burglars will avoid barriers that look tricky or painful to negotiate, and are more likely to go elsewhere for easier pickings. Alongside the classic native plants, there are also many roses that make beautiful but fearsome hedges.

1 SITE AND SOIL
Ideally most hedging plants, including roses and the other plants used here, prefer a sunny site, with well-drained and fertile soil. If your soil is not perfect, spend some time preparing the ground by digging in plenty of organic matter down to a spade's depth.

2 PLANT SPECIES ROSES
Follow the advice for planting roses (see p.93). However, species roses, which are ideal for hedges, do not have a graft union, and are planted at the same depth they were growing at in their pots, or in the field (see Step 5, left).

3 AFTERCARE
Once plants have started growing in spring, cut them back by about a third to encourage bushy growth from the base. Keep them watered throughout their first year and regularly remove any weeds around their base. This will prevent your roses having to compete for nutrients and water while they are in the process of becoming established.

PLANT OPTIONS

Berberis darwinii
Blackthorn, *Prunus spinosa*
Dog rose, *Rosa canina*
Field maple, *Acer campestre*
Guelder rose, *Viburnum opulus*
Hawthorn, *Crataegus*
Hazel, *Corylus avellana*
Holly, *Ilex aquifolium*
Rosa glauca

Hedging plants

Tiny or tall, hedges make beautiful natural screens and borders, providing colour and texture throughout the year. Choose an evergreen plant, such as yew, box, or lavender, and clip it closely for a smooth barrier, or try a deciduous type with flowers and berries for a more seasonal effect. If you want to create a home for wildlife, mix a few of each and trim just once a year in late summer when the birds have flown their nests.

SELECTIONS 》

❀❀❀ fully hardy   ❀❀ hardy in mild regions/sheltered sites   ❀ protect from frost over winter
☼ full sun   ☼ partial sun   ☀ full shade   ◊ well-drained soil   ◖ moist soil   ● wet soil

❶ *Berberis thunbergii* f. *atropurpurea* 'Golden Ring'; ↕1m (3ft) ↔2.5m (8ft) ☼ ☼ ◊ ❀❀❀   ❷ Box, *Buxus sempervirens* 'Elegantissima'; ↕↔1.5m (5ft) ☼ ☼ ◊ ❀❀❀   ❸ *Forsythia* x *intermedia*; ↕↔1.5m (5ft) ☼ ☼ ◖ ❀❀❀   ❹ *Lavandula angustifolia* 'Twickel Purple'; ↕60cm (24in) ↔1m (3ft) ☼ ◊ ❀❀❀
❺ Yew, *Taxus baccata*; ↕10m (30ft) ↔8m (25ft) ☼ ☀ ◊ ❀❀❀   ❻ Privet, *Ligustrum obtusifolium*; ↕3m (10ft) ↔4m (12ft) ☼ ☼ ◊ ❀❀❀   ❼ *Potentilla fruticosa* 'Goldfinger'; ↕1m (3ft) ↔1.5m (5ft) ☼ ◊ ❀❀❀   ❽ Holly, *Ilex aquifolium* 'Madame Briot'; ↕10m (30ft) ↔5m (15ft) ☼ ◖ ❀❀❀   ❾ Silk-tassel bush, *Garrya elliptica*; ↕↔4m (12ft) ☼ ☼ ◊ ❀❀   ❿ Firethorn, *Pyracantha* 'Mohave'; ↕4m (12ft) ↔5m (15ft) ☼ ☼ ◊ ❀❀   ⓫ Hornbeam, *Carpinus betulus*; ↕15m (50ft) ↔12m (40ft) ☼ ☼ ◊ ❀❀❀

Plant a formal hedge

Yew, hornbeam, and beech make excellent closely-clipped hedges, and you can reduce the cost by buying young bare-rooted plants from late winter to early spring from specialist nurseries and growing them on yourself. Prepare your soil in advance and plant immediately, unless the soil is frozen or waterlogged.

 WHEN TO PLANT
Late autumn to early spring
AT ITS BEST
All year round

TIME TO COMPLETE

 4 hours or more depending on hedge size

YOU WILL NEED

 Young bare-rooted hedging plants
(yew, *Taxus baccata*, shown here)
Well-rotted organic matter, such as
farmyard manure
Spade
Fork
Canes
Garden string
Watering can or hose
All-purpose granular fertilizer

1 PREPARE THE SITE
Six weeks before planting, remove all weeds from the site and dig a trench the length of the hedge and 1m (3ft) wide. Fork in organic matter, and refill the trench. Set out a line to mark the edge of the hedge.

2 MARK PLANTING INTERVALS
Dig a trench twice as wide and as deep as the plants' root balls. Using a ruler or guide, lay canes at 45–60cm (18–24in) intervals along the string line to mark the planting distances.

3 CHECK PLANTING DEPTHS
Check that the plants will be at the same depth as they were in the field when planted – you will see the soil line just above the roots. Place one plant by each cane, and backfill around the roots with soil, removing any air gaps with your fingers.

4 FIRM IN WELL
When in place, check that the plants are upright and then firm in around them with your foot. Create a slight dip around each plant to act as a reservoir, and water well. Add a thick mulch of compost or manure, keeping it clear of the plant stems. Water for the first year and feed plants annually in spring.

Using pot-grown plants

Some plants, such as lavender, box, holly, and privet, are not generally available in bare-root form and are grown and sold in pots. The planting technique is similar to that for bare-root types but pot-grown hedging can be planted at any time of year, as long as the soil is not frozen or very dry.

WHEN TO START
Any time; early autumn or spring is best

AT ITS BEST
All year (evergreen)
Spring to autumn (deciduous)

 TIME TO COMPLETE
3 hours or longer depending on hedge size

YOU WILL NEED
Pot-grown holly plants, *Ilex aquifolium*
Well-rotted organic matter, such as farmyard manure
All-purpose granular fertilizer
Spade
Fork
Canes
Garden string
Watering can or hose

1 DIG PLANTING HOLES
Prepare the soil and mark out the area as in Steps 1 and 2 opposite. Either dig a long trench or individual holes for each plant – holes need to be twice as wide and as deep as the root ball.

2 TEASE OUT ROOTS
If planting in spring, add some fertilizer to the excavated soil. Tease out any congested roots before planting at the same depth as the plant was in its original pot. Firm in with your foot and water well. (*See Step 4 opposite for aftercare.*)

Create a lavender hedge

The perfume from a lavender hedge is without equal, while the beautiful purple flowers attract scores of bees and butterflies in summer. The strongest scent is released when the flowers are brushed, so plant your hedge where you can run your fingers through the stems as you pass.

 WHEN TO PLANT
Spring

AT ITS BEST
Summer

TIME TO COMPLETE

 2 hours

YOU WILL NEED

 Small lavender plants
Well-rotted organic matter, such as
 farmyard manure
Horticultural grit
Trowel or small spade
All-purpose liquid fertilizer

1 PREPARE THE GROUND

A month or two before planting your hedge, dig plenty of well-rotted organic matter into the soil to improve drainage. Also dig horticultural grit into heavy clay soils, as lavender will rot in wet conditions.

2 SPACE PLANTS EVENLY
In spring, buy small plants and make holes at 30cm (12in) intervals, or dig out a long trench. The plants will not require additional fertilizer at this stage. Plant the lavenders so they are at the same level as they were in their pots.

3 FIRM IN SOIL
In heavier, clay-rich soil, plant the lavenders slightly above the soil surface, and draw up soil around the root ball, to encourage water to drain away from the base of the plant. Firm in around all the plants with your fingers.

4 WATER IN
Water the plants well. Although lavenders are very drought-tolerant, they will need to be watered for the first growing season until they are fully established. In spring, apply an all-purpose liquid fertilizer to the plants and cut them back twice a year (*see right*).

Shear your lavender

Although lavenders are generally easy plants, requiring little or no additional watering once established, they do need annual care. Leave small, young plants unpruned for the first 12 months after planting to allow them to put on some growth, but in subsequent years cut your hedge twice a year to prevent it becoming leggy.

 WHEN TO START
Late summer, after flowering, and early spring

 YOU WILL NEED
Garden shears
Household disinfectant
Secateurs
All-purpose liquid fertilizer

 TIME TO COMPLETE
1 hour or longer depending on hedge size

1 PRUNE INTO SHAPE
To keep your lavender plants young, bushy and healthy, cut them back in late winter or early spring. Clean your tools thoroughly and spray them with a household disinfectant before you begin work. Then, using sharp shears, cut the stems back as close as possible to the old wood.

2 THE CORRECT CUT
Take care not to cut into old brown wood, since the plants will not reshoot from this. Shear to a few healthy leaves above the brown stems (*right*), and work systematically along the hedge, keeping it as level as possible.

3 AFTER FLOWERING
In late spring or early summer, the sheared plants will grow an abundance of side shoots to create a compact, bushy hedge. To keep it neat, cut it back again after flowering in late summer: remove all the old flowerheads to prevent the plants putting their energy into making unwanted seed.

Make a wall of fiery geraniums

Wander down any residential street in the Mediterranean region and you will find houses ablaze with fiery geraniums. These drought-loving plants bask happily in the burning sun in their tiny terracotta pots, creating a dazzling display that requires very little care. If you have a sunny wall, buy young plants in late spring to create your own summer holiday effect at home.

»» WHEN TO PLANT
Late spring

AT THEIR BEST
Early summer to early autumn

TIME TO COMPLETE
2 hours

YOU WILL NEED

Bedding geraniums, *Pelargonium*
Small terracotta wall pots
Broken clay pot pieces and gravel
Multi-purpose compost
Slow-release all-purpose fertilizer
Masonry nails or Rawlplugs
 and coach bolts
Hammer or electric drill

1 PREPARE THE WALL POTS
Buy at least five wall pots and make sure that each has a drainage hole – if not, make one with an electric drill. Cover the hole with a piece of clay pot. Add 2cm (1in) of gravel and then a layer of compost to the base of each container.

2 PLANT THE GERANIUMS
Water the plants. Put one geranium (*Pelargonium*), still in its original container, into the wall pot and check that it will sit at least 2cm (1in) below the rim when planted. Remove it from its pot and plant up, firming in around it with multi-purpose compost mixed with a little slow-release fertilizer. Water well.

3 FIX POTS TO WALL
For a more dramatic effect, paint the wall white or a pale colour. Hammer in a masonry nail at a slight angle; alternatively, if you can't drive in a nail, drill a hole with an electric drill, push in a Rawlplug, and screw in a coach bolt. Fit the pots on to the wall.

TOP TIP: WATERING YOUR POTS

Geraniums require watering every few days in summer, so make sure you can reach them easily or use a long-handled hose. As the plants grow and their roots develop, it is best to water them from below by placing the wall pots in a bowl of water for 30 minutes.

< Colourful combinations
Choose either a single colour theme, or try geraniums in a combination of matching shades, as shown here.

Create a checkerboard

This simple scheme of square pavers and plants could be used to create a dramatic courtyard or a fun space for children's playground games. Plant it up with turf, chamomile, mind-your-own-business (*Soleirolia soleirolii*) or low-growing herbs, such as thyme or Corsican mint (*Mentha requienii*).

 WHEN TO START
Spring
AT ITS BEST
All year round

TIME TO COMPLETE
1 day

 YOU WILL NEED
Turf or low-growing plants
Rake
Timber boards
Tape measure
String and sticks
Sand and mortar mix
Mallet
Spirit level
Square paving stones

1 COMPACT THE SOIL
Clear the area of stones, weeds and grass, and rake it to create a flat surface. Lay down a wooden board and walk across it, moving it along systematically to level the whole area.

2 MARK OUT THE SQUARES
Measure the paving stones, and using string and some sticks mark out the area into squares of equal size, as shown. Cover the squares that will be used for pavers with a 5cm (2in) layer of sand.

3 LEVEL THE SAND
Using the back of a rake, tamp down the sand to compact and level it. Don't worry if some sand spills out into the surrounding squares; any surplus can be mixed with the soil for the plants or turf.

4 APPLY MORTAR
Mix up a wet mortar mix of four parts sand (half-and-half sharp sand and builder's sand) to one part cement, or use a ready mix. Place a trowel-full in the corners and in the centre of a square allocated to a paver.

5 BED IN PAVERS
Position the paver on the mortar and use the wooden end of a mallet to gently tap it into place. Use a spirit level to check that it is level. Mortar in each of the pavers in the same way and leave them to set for a day or two.

6 PLANT UP
Fill between the pavers with topsoil and plant up the herbs or turf. If using turf, lay it slightly proud of the paving so you can run a mower over the whole area. Water in. Keep plants watered until they are established.

Plant a rockery wall

Dry stone walls make perfect homes for alpines, such as this aubretia, which creates a mass of evergreen foliage and cascades of pretty flowers in spring. Choose small plants and use this planting method to secure them in the wall.

WHEN TO START
Early autumn

AT ITS BEST
Spring

TIME TO COMPLETE
30 minutes

YOU WILL NEED
Bucket
Piece of dried turf
Alpines, such as:
Aubretia
Campanula poscharskyana
Houseleek, *Sempervivum*
Gold dust, *Aurinia saxatilis*
Saxifrage, *Saxifraga*

1 PREPARE TO PLANT
Take the dried turf and dunk it in a bucket of water to drench it. Remove and allow to drain. Water the plant and remove it from its pot. Wrap the damp turf around the plant roots.

2 EASE PLANTS INTO CREVICES
Carefully wedge the turf-wrapped plant into a crevice. Fill around it with a half-and-half mix of horticultural sand and soil-based compost, such as John Innes No.1. Mist the plant regularly.

Plants for crevices

These little gems are never happier than when squeezed into tight spaces between paving, or in a dry-stone wall, softening the hard edges with their delicate blooms. Most are evergreen, with the exception of the *Alchemilla*, *Campanula* and *Erigeron*, and all are hardy, withstanding both hot sun and low temperatures. Also ideal for tiny containers, you can use them to dress up a dining table, or to grow in a line of small pots along a wall.

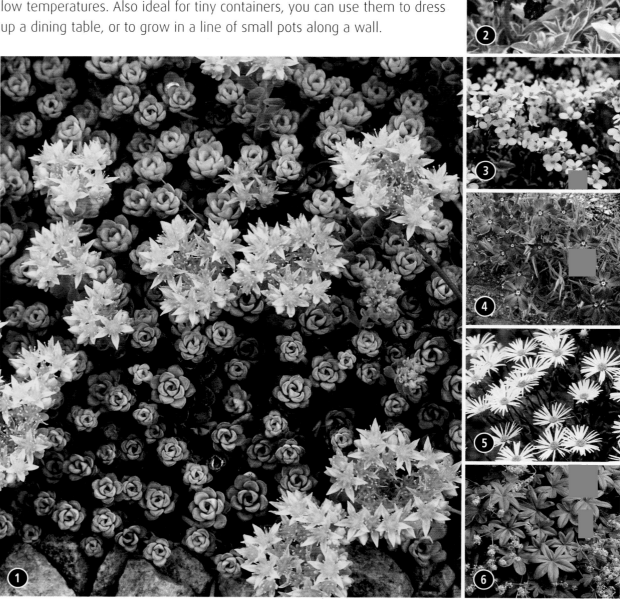

❀❀❀ fully hardy ❀❀ hardy in mild regions/sheltered sites ❀ protect from frost over winter
☼ full sun ☼ partial sun ☀ full shade ◊ well-drained soil ◐ moist soil ● wet soil

1 *Sedum spathulifolium* 'Cape Blanco'; ‡10cm (4in) ↔ 60cm (2ft) ☼ ◊ ❀❀❀ **2** *Aubrieta* 'Argenteovariegata'; ‡5cm (2in) ↔ 60cm (24in) ☼ ◊ ❀❀❀ **3** *Arabis* subsp. *caucasica* 'Variegata'; ‡15cm (6in) ↔ 50cm (20in) ☼ ◊ ❀❀❀ **4** *Phlox nana*; ‡20cm (8in) ↔ 30cm (12in) ☼ ◊ ❀❀❀ **5** *Celmisia walkeri*; ‡30cm (12in) ↔ 30cm (12in) ☼ ☼ ◊ ◐ ❀❀❀ (best for paving) **6** *Alchemilla alpina*; ‡8cm (3in) ↔ 50cm (20in) ☼ ☼ ◐ ❀❀❀ (best for paving) **7** *Androsace sarmentosa*; ‡8cm (3in) ↔ 30cm (12in) ☼ ◊ ❀❀❀ **8** *Erigeron karvinskianus*; ‡15cm (6in) ↔ 1m (3ft) ☼ ◊ ❀❀❀ **9** *Dianthus* 'Little Jock'; ‡10cm (4in) ↔ 20cm (8in) ☼ ◊ ❀❀❀ **10** *Alyssum wulfenianum*; ‡10cm (4in) ↔ 50cm (20in) ☼ ☼ ◊ ❀❀❀ **11** *Campanula carpatica* var. *turbinata* 'Jewel'; ‡10cm (4in) ↔ 60cm (2ft) ☼ ☼ ◊ ❀❀❀

Turf a lawn

The quickest, if not cheapest, way to achieve a beautiful lawn is to lay turf, but if your money is to be well spent, take time to prepare your site a month or two beforehand.

TURF OPTIONS

Buy your turf from a specialist supplier, and if possible, inspect it before purchasing to ensure that it is weed- and disease-free. Reject turf with patches of yellow or dying grass. Your choice of turf will generally be limited to high-quality ornamental grass for formal lawns, and hardwearing utility turf for walkways and play areas.

Grass choices >
Price may be an issue, but good-quality turf from a reputable supplier may prove the best value for money in the long term.

Lay turf

Turf should not be stored for long, so agree a delivery date with your supplier that allows you to lay it immediately.

>> **WHEN TO START**
Early autumn or early spring
AT ITS BEST
All year round

TIME TO COMPLETE
 1 day to prepare; 1 day to lay turf

YOU WILL NEED
 Turf
Well-rotted organic matter, such as farmyard manure
Horticultural grit
All-purpose granular fertilizer
Rake and broom
Sharp knife
Top soil and horticultural sand

1 PREPARE THE SITE
Two months before the turf arrives, weed the site thoroughly (*see pp.402–403*). Dig 10cm (4in) of organic matter into the soil, and plenty of grit into heavy clay to increase drainage. Level with a rake. Tread over the soil on your heels in one direction, and repeat at right angles in the other direction.

2 LAY THE FIRST ROW
Remove stones and debris from the site, and leave for five weeks for the soil to settle. Weed the site again and apply an all-purpose granular fertilizer at the recommended rate. Make sure the soil is moist, not wet, before laying. Place the first piece of turf at one edge, and tamp it down with the back of a rake.

TOP TIP: SHAPING A LAWN

Use a hosepipe or rope to create a guide for a curved lawn, and with a half-moon grass cutter or sharp spade cut around your template. For a straight edge, stretch some string between two pegs pushed into the soil at each end.

3 STAGGER THE JOINTS
Create a tight seam between turves by butting them together so they almost overlap and then pressing the crease down firmly with your thumbs. Continue to lay the turves in rows, and stagger the joints, like a brick wall. Stand on a plank of wood to protect the turf you have already laid.

4 APPLY A TOP DRESSING
Do not use small pieces at the edge of the lawn as they will dry out quickly and shrink – instead, lay them in the middle of the site. Scatter sandy loam, made from topsoil mixed with horticultural sand, into the joins and brush it into the turf to fill any gaps. Water well, and water the lawn in dry spells during the first growing season.

Seed a lawn

Sowing lawn seed is much cheaper than turfing, but you will have to wait a few months before it is ready for use. The best time to seed a lawn is in early autumn when the soil is warm and germination quick; sowing in early spring is an option but the colder soil conditions may prolong germination.

» **WHEN TO START**
Early autumn or early spring
AT ITS BEST
All year round

TIME TO COMPLETE
3 hours or more for larger lawns

YOU WILL NEED
Lawn seed
Well-rotted organic matter
Horticultural grit
All-purpose granular fertilizer
Canes or string
Pen and plastic cup
Bird-proof netting

1 CHOOSE YOUR SEED

Unlike turf, where you have a choice of just two or three types, lawn seed is available in many forms, including seed for shady spots or dry areas and clover lawns. Prepare the soil as for turf (see p.206). Mark out a square metre (yard) with canes or string, and weigh the right quantity of seed for that area. Pour the seed into a plastic cup and mark the top level with a pen. You can then use it as a measuring cup.

2 SOW SYSTEMATICALLY

Cover the soil evenly by scattering half the seed in the cup over the square metre (yard) in one direction, and then the other half at right angles. Set out the next square and fill the cup to the marked level; repeat the sowing process. Continue in this way until you have sown the whole area. If you have to walk over soil you have already seeded, stand on planks of wood to prevent your feet creating hollows in your new lawn.

3 PROTECT FROM BIRDS

Rake the seed into the soil to just cover it. Water with a can fitted with a rose, or spray lightly with a hose. Cover the seed with bird-proof netting, raised off the ground by about 30cm (12in). The seedlings should appear within 14 days; continue to water regularly. When the grass reaches 5cm (2in), make the first cut with your mower on a high setting. For autumn-sown lawns, maintain this height until spring, then lower the blades.

Lay a chamomile lawn

Sweet, soothing, scented chamomile has long been a desirable alternative to grass, and with the availability of turf, it is quick and easy to lay. Chamomile likes free-draining soil and, because it will not tolerate heavy wear and tear, is most suitable for decorative lawns, and fragrant seats.

 WHEN TO START
Early autumn or early spring
AT ITS BEST
All year round

TIME TO COMPLETE
2 hours or more for larger lawns

YOU WILL NEED
Chamomile turf
Well-rotted organic matter, such as farmyard manure
Horticultural grit
All-purpose granular fertilizer
Topsoil and horticultural sand

1 LAY THE TURF
Prepare your site as for turf (*see p.206*), and if you have heavy clay, dig in lots of grit to ensure your soil drains freely; waterlogged soil will kill chamomile. Turf will consist of *Chamaemelum nobile* 'Treneague', a non-flowering, compact chamomile that spreads to form a dense mat. Lay the turf in the same way as grass (*see pp.206–207*).

2 CARING FOR CHAMOMILE
There's no need to mow chamomile because it naturally grows to just 6cm (2½in) in height. Trim it occasionally during summer, using garden shears to remove straggly growth and sideways spread. Pull out any weeds by hand before they have time to establish – do not use lawn weedkiller, as this will kill the chamomile. Each spring, apply a slow-release granular fertilizer and sprinkle a top dressing of sieved soil and horticultural sand over the lawn. Tread in the dressing to crush the stems, which promotes strong root growth.

Carpets of colour

Create spectacular effects, even on a small scale, by naturalizing bulbs in a lawn or under trees. Choose robust plants able to compete with roots and grass: snowdrops, daffodils, or crocuses (*shown here*) are ideal. Leave them to their own devices and they will gradually spread, year after year, to form a beautiful flowering carpet.

WHEN TO PLANT
Autumn

AT ITS BEST
Early spring

TIME TO COMPLETE
1–2 hours

YOU WILL NEED
Spring bulbs – between 15–25 bulbs per 30cm (12in) square
Slim trowel or bulb planter
Spade
All-purpose granular fertilizer

1 PREPARE THE GROUND
In autumn, remove any perennial weeds, such as dandelions and daisies, and mow the grass. Since bulbs dry out quite quickly, aim to plant them as soon as possible after buying them. When planting, choose a fine day when the soil is not waterlogged or frozen.

2 PLANTING RANDOM GROUPS
To achieve a random, natural effect, toss the bulbs into the air and plant them individually where they fall. For each bulb, dig out a small plug of soil and turf, 2–3 times the depth of the bulb, with a slim trowel or bulb planter. Add a little fertilizer, plant the bulb, and replace the soil plug.

3 PLANTING IN SMALLER GROUPS
For smaller groups of bulbs, cut an H-shape into the grass with a sharp spade. Holding the spade horizontally, slice under the turf and fold it back to reveal the soil. Remove more soil for larger bulbs, such as daffodils (*see p.41*). Add a little fertilizer and plant the bulbs. Cover with excavated soil and gently fold back the flaps. Water well.

Plant a climber

Create a wall of flowers and foliage by clothing your boundaries and other vertical surfaces with beautiful climbers. The planting method shown here is ideal for twining climbers (*see opposite*) and roses that need some support; ivy and other self-clinging plants will not require wires.

 WHEN TO START
Autumn or early spring
AT ITS BEST
Summer, for honeysuckle shown

TIME TO COMPLETE
2 hours

YOU WILL NEED

 Climber – honeysuckle, *Lonicera periclymenum* used here
Screwdriver
Plastic-coated wire
Vine eyes
Well-rotted organic matter
All-purpose granular fertilizer
Bamboo canes
Garden twine
Bark chipping mulch
Spade and trowel

1 WIRE UP YOUR SURFACE
Screw parallel rows of vine eyes, 45cm (18in) apart, into wooden fence posts (use a drill and Rawlplugs in concrete posts). Fix horizontal wires between each row, and turn the vine eyes a few more times to tighten the wires.

2 DIG A PLANTING HOLE
Prepare the soil (*see pp.14–15*). Dig a hole twice as wide and a little deeper than the plant pot, about 45cm (18in) from the fence or screen. Place the plant in its pot in the hole to check the planting depth.

3 INSERT CANES
Place the bamboo canes in the hole at the edge closest to the fence or screen. Arrange the canes into a fan shape and attach them to the horizontal wires. These will provide the climbing plant with a temporary support until it reaches the wires. The canes can then be removed but take care not to break any stems that have wrapped themselves around them.

POSITION THE PLANT
Water the plant, then remove it from its pot. Place it in the hole and lean it towards the fence; ensure the root ball is not above the soil surface. Add fertilizer to the excavated soil and backfill.

CREATE A RESERVOIR
Using some of the surrounding soil, form a circular ridge around the base of the climber to create a saucer-shaped depression. This acts as a water reservoir, and guides moisture to the roots.

FINAL TOUCHES
Tie the stems loosely to the bamboo canes with garden twine. Water the plant and mulch with organic matter or chipped bark, keeping it clear of the stems. Water regularly throughout the first year, especially during dry spells.

Choosing climbers

Climbers have developed a variety of means to adhere to vertical surfaces, and understanding what method your chosen plant uses will help you to provide the right support. Use the examples below as a guide.

HOW CLIMBERS CLIMB

Some climbers attach themselves to surfaces without requiring additional support. These include ivy (*Hedera*), which clings using aerial roots, and Virginia creeper and Boston ivy (*Parthenocissus* species), which use adhesive pads. Plant self-clingers with caution, as they can damage old or weak brickwork. Roses climb using their thorns to hook onto taller plants, and unless you grow them through a host plant, they need support from horizontal wires or trellis. Clematis, sweet peas, passion flower (*Passiflora*), and honeysuckle (*Lonicera*), among others, use twining stems or tendrils to climb, and are best supported by canes or wires thin enough for them to wrap around, or by growing them through a host plant.

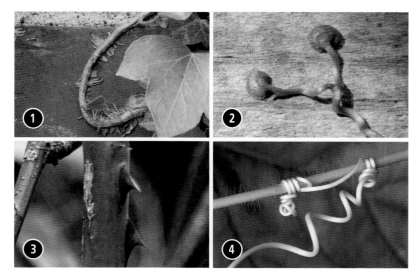

❶ Ivy climbs via aerial roots ❷ Virginia creeper grips with adhesive pads ❸ Roses hook their thorns onto supports ❹ Passion flower tendrils grasp whatever is in reach.

SELECT THE RIGHT SUPPORT

Check the final height of your chosen climber, and select a support that will be large and strong enough for a mature plant. As an alternative to wires (*see left*), you can tie smaller climbers directly to trellis, or a bought, or home-made obelisk (*see pp.216–218*). Threading climbers through shrubs or trees takes up no extra space, but offers a dual effect – perfect for small plots.

Clematis for all seasons

Thread these climbers through trees and shrubs or grow them over arches and pergolas for colour from spring to autumn. Their fluffy seedheads then steal the show in winter, making clematis a must for any garden. Choose a selection, starting with spring-flowering, scented *armandii* and *montana*, followed by 'Vyvyan Pennell' and 'Bees' Jubilee' in early summer, with the remainder providing dazzling colour from midsummer to autumn.

SELECTIONS》

✳✳✳ fully hardy   ✳✳ hardy in mild regions/sheltered sites   ✳ protect from frost over winter
☼ full sun   ☀ partial sun   ☀ full shade   ◊ well-drained soil   ◖ moist soil   ◗ wet soil

1 *Clematis* 'Ville de Lyon'; ↕2–3m (6–10ft) ☼ ☀ ◖ ✳✳✳   **2** *Clematis* 'Etoile Rose'; ↕2.5m (8ft)
☼ ☀ ◖ ✳✳✳   **3** *Clematis* 'Vyvyan Pennell'; ↕2–3m (6–10ft) ☼ ☀ ◖ ✳✳✳   **4** *Clematis* 'Bill
MacKenzie'; ↕7m (22ft) ☼ ☀ ◖ ✳✳✳   **5** *Clematis henryi*; ↕3m (10ft) ☼ ☀ ◖ ✳✳✳   **6** *Clematis
montana* var. *rubens* 'Tetrarose'; ↕5m (15ft) ☼ ☀ ◖ ✳✳✳   **7** *Clematis* 'Bees' Jubilee'; ↕2.5m (8ft)
☼ ☀ ◖ ✳✳✳   **8** *Clematis* x *diversifolia*; ↕2–3m (6–10ft) ☼ ☀ ◖ ✳✳✳   **9** *Clematis armandii*;
↕3–5m (10–15ft) ☼ ☀ ◖ ✳✳   **10** *Clematis* 'Purpurea Plena Elegans'; ↕3m (10ft) ☼ ☀ ◖ ✳✳✳
11 *Clematis* 'Ascotiensis'; ↕3–4m (10–12ft) ☼ ☀ ◖ ✳✳✳

Make an obelisk for climbers

Timber obelisks suit almost any garden design, be it formal or a relaxed country-cottage style. Use them draped with clematis or other flowering climbers to add height to a border, as a feature to flank an entrance, or to create a focal point at the end of a walkway. Top-quality wooden types are expensive to buy, but you can make one yourself for a fraction of the cost, if you have reasonable DIY skills.

 WHEN TO START
Any time

AT ITS BEST
Depends according to planting

TIME TO COMPLETE

 1½ hours

YOU WILL NEED

 4 x 2.5m pieces of 34mm x 34mm
  timber for uprights
  2 x small offcuts of timber for
  template
  25m of 34mm x 9mm batten,
  cut into short lengths for
  horizontal struts
  Offcuts of 75mm x 25mm timber
  for top plinth
  1 x decorative finial
  Galvanized 34mm screws
  Drill with countersinking bit
  Screwdriver
  Saw
  Non-toxic wood stain or timber
  preservative

1 MAKE A TEMPLATE
First, make templates for the sides. Drive two screws halfway into a timber offcut, 12cm (5in) apart, for the top of the obelisk. Drive two more screws halfway into a second offcut, 50cm (20in) apart, for the bottom. Lay both offcuts parallel to one another, 2.4m (8ft) apart. Place two upright timbers between them to create a quadrangle shape.

2 CREATE THE SHAPE
Bring the top ends of the upright timbers up against the screws in the top offcut template, as shown. Repeat at the other end of the timbers, butting these up against the screws in the bottom offcut template.

3 SCREW IN A BATTEN
The uprights now form a fat triangular shape. Take a piece of batten and lay it across the uprights, 30cm (12in) from the bottom ends. Using the drill with the countersinking bit, make holes in the batten and uprights, and screw them together.

4 ATTACH A PLINTH
In the same way, place a small offcut for the plinth at the top of the two uprights (narrow end). Make four holes, two in each upright, and screw the plinth into place to secure the top.

Clematis cladding >
To help clematis climb this obelisk, tie garden twine between the struts for the tendrils to cling to.

continued...

5 FINISH THE BATTENS

Following the instructions in step 3, screw more battens in place at 15cm (6in) intervals, from the base to the plinth, to create a triangular, ladder-like structure.

6 TRIM THE ENDS

Using a saw, trim the battens flush with the sides of the uprights. Repeat Steps 2 to 5 to create a second ladder-like structure and trim the battens. Treat both with a wood stain or preservative.

7 FIX SIDES TOGETHER

Fit the two sides of the obelisk into the two templates, as shown here. Then, screw in a piece of batten between the two sides to start forming the third side, lining it up with the existing battens. You may find this easier if someone holds the structure to keep it stable.

8 FINISH THE SIDES

Work your way up the third side, screwing the battens carefully into place, and then repeat the steps for the fourth and final side. Trim all the battens as described in Step 6.

9 CUT THE CAP

Screw in offcuts to complete all four sides of the plinth. Measure the top and cut a square to fit. Stain it and, when dry, screw it into place in each corner to form a cap

11 FINISHING TOUCHES

To complete the project, stain the remaining battens and touch up any missed areas. The stain or wood preservative will prevent decay and prolong the life of the obelisk. Reapply it every couple of years in early spring before clematis and other deciduous climbers come into growth. Secure the obelisk in place, either by burying the bottom 10cm (4in) of the structure in soil, or by using proprietary fence post supports.

10 FIX ON FINIAL

Wooden finials are available in various styles. Here, we have used an acorn. Stain the finial and screw it to the centre of the cap.

Plant a clematis

Their elegance, colour, variety and exquisite flower shapes have catapulted clematis to the top of the climbers' charts. Plant them with care and you will enjoy these superstars for many years to come.

∧ *Shade the roots*
Choose a site where the clematis roots will be shaded, and the flowers can reach the sun.

WHEN TO START
Early autumn
AT ITS BEST
Depends on variety, see pp.214–215

TIME TO COMPLETE
🕐 1½ hours

YOU WILL NEED
➕ Clematis plant
Well-rotted organic matter, such
  as farmyard manure.
Spade and fork
All-purpose granular fertilizer
Bamboo cane
Wires and vine eyes (if planting
  next to a wall or fence)
Garden twine

1 PREPARE THE GROUND
First, dig plenty of organic matter into the soil. If growing clematis up a wall or fence, position the plant 45cm (18in) away from it. Dig a hole about 30cm (12in) deep, fork over the base, and add some fertilizer to the excavated soil.

2 CHECK THE DEPTH
Clematis are best planted deeply, so that if clematis wilt strikes, the plant will survive (*see p.432*). Place the clematis in its pot in the hole, and lay a cane over it to check that the lower stems will be 5cm (2in) beneath the soil surface when it is planted.

3 PLANT AND BACKFILL
After watering thoroughly, remove the clematis from its pot and plant it in the hole. Carefully backfill with the fertilized soil, pushing it gently between the brittle stems with your fingers and making sure there are no air pockets as you go.

4 AFTERCARE
Gently firm the soil with your foot, and tie stems to an obelisk or other support (*see pp.212–213*). Water in well. Add a thick mulch of well-rotted organic matter, keeping it clear of the stems. Continue to water regularly until the plant is established.

Decorative vines

Vigorous climbing vines, such as grapes and Boston ivy, excel at clambering up and over solid structures, blurring their lines with soft, leafy growth. The best have attractively shaped foliage that displays vibrant shades in autumn, adding an extra dimension to the garden.

>> **WHEN TO START**
Autumn
AT ITS BEST
Autumn

TIME TO COMPLETE
 1 hour

YOU WILL NEED
 Vine, such as *Vitis vinifera* 'Purpurea' or *V. coignetiae*
Spade
Well-rotted organic matter
Twine

1 SELECT A SUPPORT
Vines are commonly grown over pergolas and up walls, but they look equally good when allowed to scramble through large shrubs, trees, and conifers. Look around your garden for structures that require softening, or for large plants that need brightening up. Vine stems twine around their supports, and will require wire or trellis attached to pergolas or walls (*see pp.212–213*).

2 PLANT YOUR VINE
Large solid structures cast rain shadows, and mature shrubs suck lots of moisture from the soil. To ensure your vine gets plenty of water, plant about 45cm (18in) away from your chosen support, and lean the climber towards it. Dig a large hole, incorporate well-rotted organic matter, plant, and water the vine in well (*see also pp.212–213*).

3 AFTERCARE
Regularly tie in new growth to the wires or trellis to help secure the stems to the support. Water the vine well throughout the first year, and feed in spring with a tree and shrub fertilizer.

< *Colourful coat*
While vines are useful for solid structures, they can add extra interest to any large, well-established shrub or tree that is strong enough to support them.

Cling-ons

Self-clinging climbers have no need for wires or trellis. Once attached, they will romp away up your chosen structure without any need for tying in, and are great for time-poor gardeners.

The following are all self-clinging, and develop bright red foliage in autumn:
❶ Boston ivy, *Parthenocissus tricuspidata*; ↕20m (70ft) ❷ Virginia creeper, *Parthenocissus henryana*; ↕10m (30ft)
❸ *Parthenocissus tricuspidata* 'Lowii'; ↕20m (70ft)

< *Vine-draped pergola*
Decorative vines are vigorous and attractive climbers that can produce large amounts of tasty fruit for birds to enjoy. They also develop fiery autumnal shades of red, purple, or orange.

Make a rose arch

Add height and colour to your garden with a classic timber arch, framed with climbing roses and clematis. Available in kit form, arches are quite easy to assemble and the steps outlined here show the basic method, although some types may differ slightly in design.

 WHEN TO START
Any time
AT ITS BEST
Spring to summer

TIME TO COMPLETE
 1 day

YOU WILL NEED
 Rose arch kit
Tape measure
Galvanized screws
Electric screwdriver
Spade
Hard core (broken bricks, stones, etc)
Spirit level
Ready-mixed post-mix concrete

1 LAY OUT THE PIECES
Lay out all the pieces in the kit on the ground. Starting with the roof of the arch, align the short horizontal pieces so that they slot into the two long crossbeams that make up the roof. Use a tape measure to check that they are evenly spaced.

2 JOIN THE SECTIONS
Using galvanized screws and an electric screwdriver, join the horizontal pieces to the beams. Then, attach the two vertical sides of the arch onto the roof, as directed by the kit instructions. The trellis sides in this arch came in two complete sections that slotted into the roof.

Summer >
sparkles
This arch is planted with
Rosa 'Seagull', *Clematis* armandii *and golden hop,* Humulus lupulus 'Aureus'.

DIG OUT FOOTINGS

To secure the arch in the ground, stand it in its final site, and mark out the positions of the four vertical legs. Dig holes for the legs, 45cm (18in) deep and 30cm (12in) wide. Add a 5cm (2in) layer of hard core to the base of each hole.

POSITION THE ARCH

Tamp down the hard core with a pole. With help, lift the arch and lower its legs into the holes. Make sure each leg is standing on the hard core base, and add or remove material until all four are solidly supported.

CHECK THE UPRIGHTS

Use a spirit level to make sure that all the verticals are correctly aligned, and that the horizontal pieces are level. If necessary, manoeuvre the arch until it is perfectly upright; when you are satisfied that it is, pack more hard core around the legs.

MORTAR IN THE LEGS

Pour the ready-mixed concrete into each hole, up to ground level, ensuring that it completely surrounds the legs. Slowly add water to the holes to soak the concrete, and allow it to dry and harden for a day or two. Now stain the arch in your chosen colour, and plant around it.

Climbers for arches

There are climbing plants to suit every taste. For a showy display, go for the weird and wonderful *Eccremocarpus* or the vivid flame nasturtium, and for simple but colourful foliage try golden hop. Climbing roses lend a more traditional look, and for delicious fragrance try the scented chocolate vine, honeysuckle, or star jasmine. Many of these plants mingle together beautifully; there is no need to confine yourself to just one.

SELECTIONS》

✳✳✳ fully hardy　✳✳ hardy in mild regions/sheltered sites　✳ protect from frost over winter
☼ full sun　☼ partial sun　☀ full shade　◌ well-drained soil　◗ moist soil　◖ wet soil

❶ Late Dutch Honeysuckle, *Lonicera periclymenum* 'Serotina'; ↕7m (22ft) ☼ ◗ ✳✳✳　**❷** Chilean glory flower, *Eccremocarpus scaber*; ↕3m (10ft) ☼ ◌ ✳✳　**❸** Chocolate vine, *Akebia quinata*; ↕10m (30ft) ☼ ☼ ◗ ✳✳✳　**❹** Golden hop, *Humulus lupulus* 'Aureus'; ↕6m (20ft) ☼ ◗ ✳✳✳　**❺** Morning glory, *Ipomoea purpurea*; ↕3m (10ft) ☼ ◌ ✳　**❻** *Rhodochiton atrosanguineus*; ↕3m (10ft) ☼ ◗ ✳　**❼** Flame nasturtium, *Tropaeolum speciosum*; ↕3m (10ft) ☼ ◗ ✳✳　**❽** Star jasmine, *Trachelospermum jasminoides*; ↕6m (20ft) ☼ ☼ ◌ ◗ ✳✳　**❾** Chilean potato tree, *Solanum crispum* 'Glasnevin'; ↕6m (20ft) ☼ ◌ ◗ ✳✳　**❿** *Rosa* 'Compassion'; ↕3m (10ft) ☼ ◗ ✳✳✳

Perfumed pendants

Big and beautiful, wisteria is the queen of climbers. Some would consider growing it for its gnarled, twining growth and graceful, green foliage alone, but then in early summer, it tops all this by producing a truly breathtaking display of long, pendant, scented flowers. All it needs is a little annual care.

CHOOSING PLANTS

Wisteria is notorious for being slow to flower, but this is only if it is grown on its own roots. Whereas plants grown from seed may take over ten years to start flowering, grafted ones can bloom within three or four years. The nursery or garden centre should be able to reassure you about this, and you can see the graft yourself at the base of the stem, but the best way to be sure is to buy a plant in flower. The open flowers also give you the chance to decide exactly which colour you prefer.

PLANTING AND SUPPORT

Wisterias are big, heavy climbers, so only plant them where you have a large, sturdy support in place such as heavy-duty wires or a pergola. Prepare the soil well before planting, digging it over and mixing in plenty of organic matter (*see pp.212–213 for planting advice*). At first you may need to tie the stems loosely to their supports, but this task won't be necessary for long as they begin to twine (*see right*).

Pruning care

Wisterias should be pruned twice a year to encourage them to flower well.

1 SUMMER PRUNING
The best time to assess the overall shape of your plant is after flowering. If there are any gaps, fill these by training new stems along the support in that direction. Tie this new growth in loosely to the framework using twine.

2 REDUCE NEW SHOOTS
Once stems are tied in, cut back all other growth to about 30cm (12in) from where it sprouts. Restricting growth, and allowing sunlight and air to ripen the young stems helps to promote flowering the following year.

3 WINTER PRUNING
For best results, prune again in late winter. First identify any long, sappy stems that sprouted after pruning in summer, and prune them back to about five buds away from the main branch, cutting just above a bud.

4 SPUR PRUNE
Then, shorten the shoots that were pruned in the summer even further, back to two or three buds. Look carefully for the fat, round flower buds, and avoid cutting these off. Foliage buds, which can be removed, are slimmer and pointed.

5 KEEP PLANTS IN CHECK
Wisteria is a vigorous plant, and its stems can become thick and woody with age. These can cause problems if they grow where they are not wanted, so cut stems away from gutters, windows and behind pipes when you are pruning.

Grow scented sweet peas

The scent of sweet peas is like no other, and a vase of cut blooms filling a room with fragrance is reason enough to grow these cottage-garden favourites. In warm areas, sow seeds in the autumn; in colder parts sow in spring in a warm greenhouse or on a windowsill. Grow them on in an open, sunny area.

1 CHIP THE SEED
Sweet pea seeds have a hard shell, and unless water can penetrate it, the seeds will not germinate. To ensure the seed absorbs water, use a sharp penknife or nail clippers to carefully nick it opposite the "eye" (small, round scar) and remove a small piece of the seed coat.

2 SOW SEED
In autumn, fill trays or pots with seed compost and sow the seeds 1cm (½in) deep. Keep the seedlings in a cool greenhouse or cold frame until the following spring, only providing extra heat during severe frosts. In mid-spring, remove the tip of the main shoot from each seedling.

≫ **WHEN TO PLANT**
Autumn or early spring
AT THEIR BEST
Summer

TIME TO COMPLETE
2–3 hours over several months

YOU WILL NEED
- Sweet pea seeds
- Sharp penknife or nail clippers
- Deep seed trays or root trainers
- Seed compost
- Well-rotted organic matter
- Obelisk or canes
- Garden twine
- All-purpose liquid feed

3 SEEDLING CARE
If you sow sweet peas in early spring, grow the seedlings indoors, or in a warm greenhouse, at 14–17°C (58–62°F). When they reach 10–15cm (4–6in) high, remove the tips down to the first set of leaves. Pinching out the tips like this encourages sideshoots to form.

Sweet pea supports

Sweet peas climb using their twining tendrils, which cling to slim supports, such as canes or sticks. These bushy plants reach up to 1.8m (6ft) high, so make sure your support is tall enough to accommodate them.

4 HARDEN OFF AND PLANT OUT
Autumn-sown seedlings can be planted out directly into the ground in mid-spring. Spring-sown seedlings will have tender shoots that need to be hardened off for a few weeks by bringing them outside by day, and inside at night. Plant hardened seedlings out in late spring.

5 PLANT CARE
Enrich the soil with well-rotted organic matter and plant one or two seedlings close to the base of a suitable support (*see right*) and tie them in loosely. The tendrils will soon take hold of the support as the plants grow. Water during dry spells, and apply a liquid feed every two weeks from midsummer. Pick the flowers regularly to encourage more.

TOP TIP: HOME-MADE SEED POTS

Roll folded newspaper around a glass and tuck the top ends into it. Remove, then flatten the tucked-in ends to form the base. Plant seedlings *and* their pots into the soil – the pots will just rot away.

BUYING SUPPORTS
Wooden or metal obelisks and tripods are ideal for sweet peas, and make decorative additions to flower borders or to vegetable beds, where you can plant them alongside runner or French beans. (Do not confuse the pods when harvesting, as sweet peas are poisonous). You may find that young plants struggle to take hold of smooth materials, such as metal, or do not cover the whole support evenly. To remedy this problem, wind some string around the poles and tie it horizontally across the legs of the support to provide the plants with more grip.

Elegant additions >
Stylish pyramids look stunning when dressed with a mix of sweet peas and runner beans.

MAKE YOUR OWN
It's easy to make your own sweet pea supports by setting out canes to form a wigwam and tying them securely at the top. Alternatively, grow them up pea sticks (*see p.307*), or create a support with plastic mesh wrapped around a circle of sturdy canes driven into the ground, securing the trellis with garden twine or wire. As the plants grow, these supports quickly disappear beneath the flowers and foliage.

< Tunnel vision
This fragrant garden arch is made from metal poles and wire mesh, available from DIY stores, fixed at the top with wire. The sweet peas are scrambling over it to create a tunnel of flowers.

Striking stems

Many dogwood and willow varieties have brightly coloured stems that are a boon in the winter garden. The young growth is the most impressive, so prune hard to encourage bright new shoots.

Willow wands

Willows (*Salix*) look great grown as pollards. Let a single stem grow to about 1.5m (5ft) tall, and prune so that new growth develops at the top, creating a head of colourful young stems.

>> **WHEN TO START**
Late winter or early spring
AT ITS BEST
Winter

TIME TO COMPLETE
 1 hour

YOU WILL NEED
 Willow plant
Secateurs
Loppers or pruning saw
All-purpose granular fertilizer

2 **PRUNE TO ONE OR TWO BUDS**
Before new growth appears in spring, use secateurs to cut back every stem to one or two buds. Use a pruning saw to remove larger material.

3 **AFTER PRUNING**
The shrub will look strange after pruning but don't panic; it will quickly re-grow. Give it an annual feed of all-purpose granular fertilizer, worked into the soil around the base of the plant. Use the cut stems to support perennials in spring and summer.

1 **REMOVE WEAK GROWTH**
When the leaves fall in autumn, tidy the plant by carefully pruning out weak and damaged stems, and remove any shoots from the main trunk.

Dramatic dogwoods

Dogwoods (*Cornus* species) are grown for their bare winter stems, which can be green, red, orange, or bright yellow. The youngest growth is the most vibrant, so prune them almost to the ground every year to encourage new stems.

1 ANNUAL PRUNING
In late winter or early spring, prune dogwoods back by cutting all stems to one or two buds above the ground. Use secateurs for the thinner stems, and loppers or a pruning saw for larger ones.

2 LEAVE AN OPEN STRUCTURE
New stems will grow from the top buds left behind. If there are several buds, remove those facing into the centre of the plant by rubbing them off with your fingers. This stops the new stems becoming too congested, which will weaken the winter display.

3 ALTERNATIVE APPROACH
Instead of pruning your dogwoods entirely to the ground, you can prune out every third stem. The plant will look less scalped through the summer, although the winter show will not be as dramatic as a result.

< *Bare essentials*
Plant spring-flowering bulbs beneath your dogwoods and willows to give an extra splash of colour.

Weave a living willow screen

Slimmer than a hedge and just as easy to create, willow screens are ideal for partitioning small gardens or as boundaries in rural settings where you want a barrier that mirrors the natural landscape beyond. Once established, they also make good windbreaks for a vegetable plot or flower garden.

>> **WHEN TO START**
Winter, when willow is dormant
AT ITS BEST
All year round

TIME TO COMPLETE
4–5 hours over a few months

YOU WILL NEED
Willow setts
Well-rotted organic matter,
 such as farmyard manure
Spade
Garden tarred twine
Rubber plant ties

TOP TIP: BUYING AND CARING FOR WILLOW

1 GROW OR BUY WILLOW
The most common willow for weaving is *Salix alba*, which has colourful stems in winter. Buy your cuttings or "setts" in winter and plant as soon as possible. Do not plant near buildings or drainage pipes, as the roots are invasive.

2 PLANT SETTS
Dig plenty of organic matter into the soil and remove weeds. Push a spade into the soil 20cm (8in) deep, insert a willow sett into the slit and firm in. Space setts 20cm (8in) apart. Water well. Wait until new growth appears before weaving.

3 WEAVE THE WILLOW
Criss-cross the stems over and under one another to form a rigid diamond-shaped structure. Tie stems where they cross with twine, and use rubber plant ties to secure the top of the screen. This allows some movement and prevents stems from snapping in the wind.

The easiest way to buy willow cuttings is from a specialist willow nursery – most now have online and mail-order shops. The cuttings are harvested when dormant in winter, and will only be available at this time. They are normally 20–30cm (10–12in) long and take a season to grow to a suitable length for weaving. Rods for tunnels are longer. Keep the growing area free of weeds (*see p.76 to lay a weed-suppressing membrane*) and water the cuttings well after planting and until they are fully established.

Make a tunnel

Natural and inexpensive, this willow tunnel takes no longer to make than a screen, and can be used for children's play areas or in a cottage or informal design. To create a living tunnel, buy longer "rods" instead of setts or cuttings.

1 MARK OUT THE SITE
Prepare the site and soil as for screens (*see opposite*). Measure the length of the tunnel and calculate the number of rods you will need: they are planted in pairs 30cm (12in) apart, or closer if you want a dense effect. You will also need a few spares. When the rods arrive, plant as for setts (*see opposite*), but in slits that are 30cm (12in) deep.

2 FORM THE ARCH
Plant rods in matching pairs on either side of your marked-out tunnel. Bend each pair over to form an arch and twist them together. Secure with rubber plant ties. Plant some rods between the other stems and weave them across the structure to help strengthen it. Tie these rods on either side of the arch stems, as shown above.

3 FINAL TOUCHES
Water well and apply a mulch each spring. Keep the arch well watered for the first year and weed regularly.

TOP TIP: PRUNING AND AFTERCARE

To top up moisture levels, consider installing a leaky hose beside the arch (*see pp.406–407*), which can be attached to an automatic timer. Remove any dead plants as you see them and replant with fresh ones. Do not trim your hedge or arch until the end of the first year when the leaves have dropped. Once well established, willow structures will produce long shoots, which you can cut back and chip for use as a mulch or as fuel for a woodburner. Alternatively, you can plant these "cuttings" to make more willow structures.

Plant a wall of berries

Wall shrubs, such as firethorn, are easy to grow and provide a rich tapestry of evergreen foliage, spring flowers, and vibrant autumn berries that add texture and colour to the garden. On a boundary, their sharp thorns also deter intruders, and the fruits provide a feast for hungry birds.

 WHEN TO START
Autumn

AT ITS BEST
All year round

TIME TO COMPLETE
 2 hours

YOU WILL NEED
 Firethorn, *Pyracantha*
Well-rotted organic matter,
  such as farmyard manure
Granular shrub fertilizer
Coated wire and vine eyes
Garden twine
Secateurs

1 PREPARE THE GROUND
Plant your firethorn about 50cm (20in) from the wall or fence, and dig a bucketful of organic matter and some general purpose fertilizer into the soil within the planting area. Do not add extra organic matter to the planting hole.

2 PLANT AND TIE STEMS IN
Fix horizontal wires across the wall or fence (*see pp.212–213*). Dig a planting hole twice the width and as deep as the plant pot. Place the firethorn in the hole and lay a cane across the top to check that the plant will be at the same depth as it is in its pot once planted. Remove from its pot, and plant. Backfill with excavated soil and firm in with the ball of your foot. Remove stems from the supporting canes supplied with the plant and tie to the wires with twine.

3 TRIM STEMS

With clean, sharp secateurs, prune wayward stems that are growing away from the wall or fence. Cut them back to the main stem or a bud close to a stem that is growing along the fence. Shorten other side shoots to encourage bushier growth.

4 WATER AND MULCH

Water the plant well, and apply a thick mulch of well-rotted organic matter, keeping it clear of the stems. Water regularly for a year or two, until the plant is well established. Only water during prolonged dry spells thereafter.

5 PRUNING PYRACANTHA

In spring, when flower buds appear, cut back outward-growing stems or those growing towards the fence, and shorten others to keep the plant compact, making sure that you retain as many buds as possible. Wear heavy-duty gardening gloves to protect yourself from the thorns. In late summer, cut the stems back to within a few buds of the berries so that the fruits are more visible.

Wall shrub options

For flowers, rather than berries, try one of these beautiful wall shrubs. Each has its individual charms: both the Californian lilac and the silk-tassel bush are evergreen, while the flowering quince and flannel bush have bright, colourful blooms.

MAKING A CHOICE

Heralding spring, the bare branches of the flowering quince, *Chaenomeles*, are laced with bright pink or red flowers, and are followed by the blue pom-poms of Californian lilacs, *Ceanothus*, which open at the end of the season. The flannel bush, *Fremontodendron*, has large waxy yellow flowers that appear from late spring to early autumn, and to close the year, the silk-tassel bush, *Garrya*, displays its long cream catkins while the rest of the garden sleeps.

PLANTING SHRUBS

Plant the Californian lilac and flannel bush in a sunny spot. The silk-tassel bush and quince will grow well in partial shade or full sun. None of these plants, apart from the quince, tolerate hard frosts so select a sheltered area, and follow the same planting method as for firethorn (*see left*). You can train the plants onto a trellis instead of wires, if you prefer, but make sure that it is fixed securely to the wall or fence.

AFTERCARE

Although these shrubs tolerate quite dry conditions, water them frequently for the first year until they are established. Trim back the quince and lilac annually after flowering in early summer. Prune the silk-tassel and flannel bushes in mid-spring. Prune out wayward stems that are growing away from their supports, and trim other stems to create a neat framework. Tie in long stems to the wires or trellis. The plants will also benefit from an application of granular shrub fertilizer in early spring.

❶ Flowering quince, *Chaenomeles* x *superba*; ↕1.5m (5ft) ↔1.8m (6ft)
❷ Californian lilac, *Ceanothus* 'Concha'; ↕↔1.5–3m (5–10ft) ❸ Silk-tassel bush, *Garrya elliptica*; ↕↔4m (12ft) ❹ Flannel bush, *Fremontodendron californicum*; ↕6m (20ft) ↔4m (12ft)

Decorative catkins

Whether soft and furry, or long and dangling, catkins never fail to delight. Those of the silver birch are perhaps the most familiar, and add a strong, vertical accent hanging from the bare, twiggy branches. But there are also many other types of catkin, equally attractive, that are often overlooked. They add a tactile and surprising dimension to the spring garden, at a time of year when positive change is most welcome.

SELECTIONS>>

❋❋❋ fully hardy   ❋❋ hardy in mild regions/sheltered sites   ❋ protect from frost over winter
☼ full sun   ☼ partial sun   ☀ full shade   ◊ well-drained soil   ◐ moist soil   ● wet soil

1 *Salix hastata* 'Wehrhahnii'; ‡1.2m (4ft) ↔1.2m (4ft) ☼ ◐ ❋❋❋   **2** *Alnus incana*; ‡20m (70ft)
↔10m (30ft) ☼ ◐ ❋❋❋   **3** *Betula nana*; ‡60cm (24in) ↔1.2m (4ft) ☼ ☼ ◊ ◐ ❋❋❋
4 *Itea ilicifolia*; ‡↔3m (10ft) ☼ ◊ ◐ ❋❋❋   **5** *Salix lanata*; ‡1m (3ft) ↔1.5m (5ft) ☼ ◐ ❋❋❋
6 *Itea virginica*; ‡2m (6ft) ↔1.5m (5ft) ☼ ◊ ◐ ❋❋❋   **7** *Betula papyrifera*; ‡20m (70ft)
↔10m (30ft) ☼ ☼ ◊ ◐ ❋❋❋   **8** *Salix caprea*/'Kilmarnock'; ‡1.5m (5ft) ↔2m (6ft) ☼ ◐ ❋❋❋
9 *Salix reticulata*; ‡8cm (3in) ↔30cm (12in) ☼ ◐ ❋❋❋   **10** *Salix hastata*; ‡↔1m (39in) ☼ ◐ ❋❋❋

Cover up for winter

Cold, dark winter days can be depressing, but with a few well-chosen climbers to dress up your screens, boundaries, and bare-stemmed trees, this can be an exciting and beautiful season. Bright, variegated foliage, sunny yellow flowers, and sweetly scented blooms are among the delights in store.

Ivy arch

Often overlooked or dismissed as too common, ivy comes into its own in winter, with beautiful leaf shapes and bright colours. Grow it over an arch for a spectacular foliage effect.

 WHEN TO START
Autumn
AT ITS BEST
All year, especially winter

TIME TO COMPLETE
 1 day to make arch; 1 day to plant

YOU WILL NEED
 Garden arch (kits are available)
Well-rotted organic matter, such
   as farmyard manure
Garden twine
Secateurs
Ivy plants, good choices include:
   Hedera helix 'Cavendishii',
   'Glacier', 'Oro di Bogliasco', and
   Hedera colchica

∧ *Winter greens*
This beautiful arch, covered with variegated ivy and flanked by evergreen Euonymus and bay, creates a show-stopping winter focal point.

1 ERECT AN ARCH
When bold foliage is at a premium, ivy has plenty to offer, with plain or variegated, and large or small leaves. Select a tall cultivar of *Hedera helix* or the large-leaved *Hedera colchica* for an arch. Either buy a pre-assembled arch, or make one from a kit (*see pp.222–223 for instructions*) and erect it close to a screen, over a bench seat, or to frame a view.

2 PLANT THE IVY
Select an ivy with long stems, and check the label to make sure that it will grow large enough to cover the arch. Enrich the soil around the arch with organic matter, and plant an ivy about 30cm (12in) away from each side. You can also plant a few 30cm (12in) from the fence or wall. Plant the ivies at the same depth they were in their original pots.

3 AFTERCARE
Use garden twine to tie the stems to the arch; they can be removed once the stems have taken hold. Water the plants frequently and trim any wayward stems in spring and summer.

Seasonal gold

The winter jasmine, *Jasminum nudiflorum*, is really a wall shrub, but its long, lax stems are easily trained over trellis or on wires to cover screens and fences. Masses of starry golden yellow flowers appear on bare stems in late winter and early spring, but unlike summer jasmine, they are unscented.

PLANTING JASMINE

Choose a spot that will be in full sun or partial shade in the winter to encourage the best blooms. Note that areas that are in sun in summer may be shaded later in the year, so check your aspect carefully (*see p.15*). In autumn, dig well-rotted organic matter, such as farmyard manure or homemade garden compost, into the soil before you start, and plant the jasmine as for wall shrubs (*see pp.234–235*).

∧ > Frosted flowers
Winter jasmine's tough little flowers continue to bloom even when dusted with frost. During dry spells, keep the plant well watered until established, and feed with a shrub fertilizer each spring.

∧ Freckled friends
The flowers of Clematis cirrhosa *var.* purpurascens *'Freckles' appear throughout the winter.*

Winter delights >
Stunningly beautiful, the flowers of Clematis armandii *emit a delicious scent, and appear for many weeks from late winter to early spring.*

Evergreen clematis

Exquisite blooms set amid evergreen foliage are the star qualities of winter-flowering clematis. Plant them in a sheltered site as they won't tolerate very low temperatures.

PLANTING TIPS

Clematis armandii has sweetly scented white or pink flowers and long, slim, dark green leaves. In some areas it may stay quite compact, but when fully established and in a suitable location, it can romp through a large tree. *Clematis cirrhosa*, with its freckled, cup-shaped flowers, can be equally vigorous in ideal conditions. Although these clematis are less likely to fall prey to clematis wilt, it is still worth planting them deeply in well-drained soil, just in case the disease strikes (*see p.217*).

AFTERCARE

Water well during dry spells for the first year until the plants are established, and clip untidy growth lightly after flowering. The lower leaves of *Clematis armandii* may turn brown and fall, which is a characteristic of this plant; use another climber or shrub to disguise the stems.

Elegant standards

Standard trees make a bold statement in the garden but can be expensive to buy, but with a little patience and the right care you can create your own, as long as the plant has a strong lead shoot.

>> **WHEN TO START**
Anytime

AT ITS BEST
All year round

TIME TO COMPLETE
Initial pruning, 30 minutes

YOU WILL NEED
A variegated holly, such as *Ilex* x *altaclerensis* 'Golden King' used here
Large container
Garden cane
Twine
Secateurs

1 ASSESS THE PLANT
Look at the plant from all angles before pruning. Decide how long you want the clean stem to be and what growth you are going to leave to make up the lollipop top.

2 REMOVE SIDE SHOOTS
Prune the lowest side shoots from the main stem, but don't remove them all in one go as they help to pull sap up the plant. Once the plant has a decent round head, you can cut them all off.

3 TIE IN AND SHAPE
Shorten the growth left at the top of the plant slightly to encourage it to bush out and form a rounded head. Push a cane into the compost to support the main stem, which will be quite weak at this early stage; tie securely in several places. Trim the head to shape each year.

Planting options

Almost any plant can be grown as a standard, and if you have the time it is worth experimenting to see which work best.

GLOBES OF FLOWERS AND FOLIAGE

Roses are traditionally trained as standards, and are particularly effective grown in this formal way with less traditional mixed cottage-style planting beneath them. The same is true of wisterias. Other commonly grown standard lollipop trees include box and bay, often used for topiary, and decorative evergreens, such as rosemary, *Euonymus fortunei,* and *Photinia*. You can also create interesting foliage and structural effects with large deciduous trees, such as acers and oaks, trimmed into standards, as long as you prune them regularly.

❶ *Rosmarinus officinalis* has silvery growth and looks good rising above a planting of cool whites and purples.
❷ *Euonymus fortunei* provides brightly coloured variegated foliage all year round, even in shady corners.
❸ *Photinia* x *fraseri* 'Red Robin' is green all year but produces a flush of bronze-red new foliage every spring.

< *Holly head*
Variegated holly, shaped into a standard tree, brings strong colour, structure and style to any mixed planting or group of containers.

Choosing conifers

Conifers comprise a wide group of mostly evergreen trees and shrubs that provide welcome colour and structure all year round. Although some have a bad name, growing into ungainly monsters, many make elegant additions to small gardens, especially when combined with other woody plants and perennials.

SIZE MATTERS

The following plants are examples of the different types of conifer you may see in garden centres and catalogues. Check their labels carefully to ensure you buy a conifer that will suit your plot. "Slow-growing" conifers are not necessarily small, they simply grow slowly, putting on 15–30cm (6–12in) of growth per year. "Dwarf" types remain compact, and grow between 2–15cm (1–6in) per year, while "Miniatures" are tiny and will only grow to about 25cm (10in) after ten years and ultimately reach no more than 90cm (3ft).

❶ The blue Colorado spruce, *Picea pungens* 'Koster', is a slow-growing conifer that reaches a height of 2m (8ft) and width of 1.2m (4ft) but may, after many years, grow even larger. ❷ This Hinoki cypress, *Chamaecyparis obtusa* 'Opaal', is a dwarf conifer reaching 1m (3ft) high and 75cm (30in) wide when mature. ❸ The dwarf mountain pine, *Pinus aristata* 'Sherwood Compact', with its decorative candle-like cones, is tiny and reaches just 60cm (24in) when mature.

Contemporary conifers >
This elegant small garden mixes well-behaved conifers, including a blue-leaved weeping Cedrus atlantica *'Glauca Pendula'* (left), Chamaecyparis obtusa *trained into a tiny lollipop* (bottom left), *and a pretty pine* (right), *together with grasses and bamboos to create a stylish modern scheme.*

Creative effects

Conifers are excellent design tools, offering a wealth of colours and shapes. You can use them en masse for a mosaic effect, choose just one striking example for a focal point in a border or lawn, or plant tiny types in pots and containers.

DESIGN OPTIONS

For year-round colour, you can't do much better than the blue spruce, *Picea pungens*, which comes in all shapes and sizes and makes a great companion for purple-leaved shrubs, such as the smoke bush, *Cotinus* 'Grace'. Alternatively, match them up with contrasting golden conifers, such as the spreading *Juniperus* x *pfitzeriana* Gold Sovereign or the rounded *Chamaecyparis lawsoniana* 'Golden Pot'. To strike a pose, look for pencil-thin plants that provide accents and can be used as focal points, or to line a path. The Italian cypress, *Cupressus sempervirens*, is a classic example, but junipers are easier plants for cooler climates. Try *J. communis* 'Compressa' or 'Sentinel', which have a similar rocket-like form.

∧ *Textured gold*
The vivid golden foliage of Abies nordmanniana 'Golden Spreader' makes a striking statement plant; the foliage is even brighter in winter.

∧ *On parade*
Use cone-shaped conifers, such as Thuja occidentalis 'Smaragd' to form a screen of sentry-like specimens.

Purple candles >
The unusual purple cones of the slow-growing Korean fir, Abies koreana, are spectacular; buy one with cones to ensure it will perform.

Options for small gardens

Conifers are quite easy-going and adapt to a range of conditions, but most thrive in a sunny site in moist soil that drains freely, although junipers will cope with drier conditions. Check labels for width as well as height, as some need space to spread.

These conifers are perfect for small areas:

Abies balsamea 'Nana'
Cephalotaxus harringtonii 'Fastigiata'
Juniperus communis 'Compressa'
Juniperus scopulorum 'Blue Arrow'
Pinus heldreichii 'Smidtii'
Tsuga canadensis 'Cole's Prostrate'

① Lawson cypress, *Chamaecyparis lawsoniana* 'Minima Aurea'; ‡45cm (18in) ↔30cm (12in) ② Juniper, *Juniperus procumbens* 'Nana'; ‡30cm (12in) ↔1.2m (4ft) ③ Japanese cedar, *Cryptomeria japonica* 'Nana'; ‡↔60cm (2ft) ④ White cedar, *Thuja occidentalis* 'Caespitosa'; ‡30cm (12in) ↔40cm (16in)

All-season colour

By planting evergreen conifers with long-lasting grasses, and then throwing in a smattering of perennials, you can have a garden that looks good all year round, with a few highlights in summer.

》 **WHEN TO START**
Autumn

AT ITS BEST
All year round

TIME TO COMPLETE
1–2 days

YOU WILL NEED
Spade and fork
Well-rotted organic matter
1. *Abies concolor* 'Wintergold'
2. *Pinus heldreichii* 'Smidtii'
3. *Erica carnea* f. *aureifolia* 'Foxhollow'
4. *Pennisetum alopecuroides* 'Little Bunny'
5. *Imperata cylindrica* 'Rubra'
6. *Pinus mugo* 'Ophir'
7. *Stipa gigantea*
8. *Kniphofia* 'Percy's Pride'

1 PREPARE THE SITE
In the autumn before planting, thoroughly remove all weeds from the border. Dig it over deeply and then incorporate plenty of organic matter, such as well-rotted manure or garden compost.

2 SET OUT THE PLANTING PATTERN
Buy the plants in spring and set them out before planting them. The dwarf conifers provide the backbone, with a ribbon of *Imperata* and *Erica* running between them. Use the *Stipa* as an accent plant, and fill gaps with the *Pennisetum*.

3 PLANT AND FEED
Plant the conifers and *Erica* first, then add the grasses and *Kniphofia*. Water the plants in well. Keep them watered throughout their first full growing season, and feed them each spring with an all-purpose granular fertilizer.

Fruit and Vegetables

Whether you have a large allotment or tiny courtyard, you can grow a range of crops for the kitchen. The step-by-step projects in this chapter are both easy and fun, and include leafy herbs in hanging baskets, raised beds filled with root vegetables, and pots of delicious strawberries and other fruits. Sow and plant regularly, and you will have home-grown crops to eat throughout the year. Keep your plants well watered and fed to fend off pests and diseases.

Grow a row of beans

Climbing French and runner beans are among the most productive vegetable plants in the garden, but you do have to treat them well to get the best crops. They are easy to care for once planted out and established, but the key to success is to nourish the soil well before planting time.

WHEN TO START
Spring

AT THEIR BEST
Summer

TIME TO COMPLETE
3 hours over a few months

YOU WILL NEED
Bean seeds
Coir pots
Seed compost
Garden canes
String
Well-rotted garden compost or
 farmyard manure

1 SOW SEED IN POTS
French and runner beans are sensitive to frost, so sow them inside, one to each pot. Set the pots on a tray in a warm, sunny spot, and water the seedlings regularly; do not let them dry out. Plant them outdoors once all risk of frost has passed.

2 PREPARE YOUR TRENCH
Dig out a trench to at least one spade's depth and fill the base with a deep layer of compost or farmyard manure. This will give your beans the energy they need. Then, use long garden canes to create a sturdy climbing frame to support them all summer.

3 TIE IN STEMS
Plant one seedling at the base of each cane and tie the stem to it, until it takes hold by itself. You can also sow bean seeds directly into the soil in late spring, after the frosts. If you do, plant two seeds per cane in case one fails to grow. If both come up, weed out the weakest.

4 WATER AND WAIT
Beans are thirsty, so water them often, especially when they start flowering. If the plants are too dry, the blooms will drop off and you will lose your crop. Harvest the pods when they are young and tender, before you can see the beans swelling inside.

TOP TIP: BLAST OFF APHIDS

Sap-sucking aphids cause a lot of damage to plants, and they love tender bean tips. A good way to tackle them that doesn't require chemicals is to blast them off with a jet of water. A hand mister is also useful during hot weather, as a fine spray on the flowers can improve pollination.

Pot up a productive patio

Awash with colourful blooms and brimming with delicious crops, this tiny patio is both pretty and productive. You can either grow vegetables and flowers from seed, or buy a range of young plug plants from the garden centre if space and time is limited.

WHEN TO START
Early spring
AT ITS BEST
Summer to early autumn

TIME TO COMPLETE
 3 hours to sow; 1 day to plant up

YOU WILL NEED
Selection of large pots and
  hanging baskets
Broken clay pot pieces
Soil-based compost
Slow-release fertilizer granules
Tomato fertilizer

1. Tomato 'Tumbling Tom'
2. Tomato 'Gardener's Delight' and
   'Costoluto Fiorentino'
3. Asparagus pea
4. Herbs
5. Pot marigolds, *Calendula*
6. Summer squash 'Sunburst' hybrid

1 SOW SEEDS
Either buy plants in late spring or sow seed earlier. If you only need one or two tomato plants, it may be easier to buy young plants. Sow chard seed directly into pots in late spring (*see p.260*). The asparagus pea is a gourmet vegetable that's easy to grow – simply sow the seed indoors in late spring and, as the weather warms up, harden off the seedlings by placing them outside during the day. To grow the squash, follow the sowing and planting methods for courgettes (*see p.276*), and sow some marigolds to brighten up the display (*see pp.108–111*).

2 PLANT AFTER FROSTS
When all danger of frost has passed, plant up the seedlings and young plants in large containers of soil-based compost (*see pp.272–273 for tomatoes in growbags*). Tumbling tomatoes are best planted in large baskets (*see pp.312*); partner them up with herbs or trailing bedding plants, such as ground ivy. Also consider buying or making small raised beds (*see pp.254–255*), which are perfect for packing lots of vegetables into tight spaces. When planting the peas, add twiggy sticks to support them (*see p.275*).

3 WATER DAILY
Crops in pots must be watered every day in summer, and the fruiting and podded vegetables benefit from a weekly feed with tomato fertilizer to encourage a bumper harvest. Pick the crops as soon as they ripen.

TOP TIP: BAGS OF FUN

Growing crops in large bags is a popular idea for small patio gardens. You can either buy proprietary products in an assortment of colours, or use strong recycling bags. Large plants, such as potatoes and courgettes, that require lots of space and soil, are ideal for bags, which are generally cheaper than containers of the same size.

∧ *Climbing crops*
Trailing courgettes, such as 'Tromboncino' are decorative plants with large leaves, sunny yellow flowers and cream fruits. Use vine eyes to fix coated wires up your wall or fence, and tie in the stems to make a screen of delicious vegetables.

Grow a crop of potatoes

Potatoes are an allotment staple and taste delicious when freshly dug up from the soil. Grow your crops in an open, sunny site in well-drained soil, and plant "earlies" one month before the last frosts are predicted, and "second earlies" and "maincrops" slightly later at the end of spring.

 WHEN TO START
Late winter

AT THEIR BEST
Summer

TIME TO COMPLETE

 3 hours over a few months

YOU WILL NEED

 Seed potatoes
Egg boxes
Well-rotted organic matter, such
   as compost or farmyard manure
String
Spade
Straw or other dry mulch

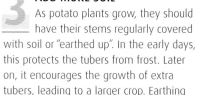

3 ADD MORE SOIL
As potato plants grow, they should have their stems regularly covered with soil or "earthed up". In the early days, this protects the tubers from frost. Later on, it encourages the growth of extra tubers, leading to a larger crop. Earthing up also prevents the tubers from being exposed to light, which makes them turn green and inedible.

1 CHIT SEED POTATOES
In late winter, buy your seed potatoes and place them in egg boxes in a cool, light, frost-free place to "chit" or sprout. They will start growing while it is still too cold to plant out.

2 PLANTING DEPTH AND DISTANCE
Dig a trench to a spade's depth, and fill the bottom with loose soil or compost. Plant "first earlies" and "second earlies" 30cm (12in) apart, in rows 50cm (20in) apart, and "maincrops" 40cm (16in) apart, in rows 75cm (30in) apart. Cover them with soil.

4 PROTECT PLANTS
When seed potatoes are first planted out, earthing up may not provide enough protection from frost. In colder regions, add a layer of straw to prevent tubers from freezing.

5 HARVESTING
When the flowers begin to open, your potatoes are ready to harvest. Use a fork to dig them up from below, accessing them from the side of the mound, to avoid damaging them.

TOP TIP: STORING POTATOES

Maincrop potatoes can be stored in paper or hessian sacks. After harvesting, brush off the soil and dry in the sun for a few hours. Pack away only the perfect tubers and check them regularly.

Bags of spuds

If you don't have an allotment or space in your garden for a vegetable patch, you can grow potatoes in containers on your patio. Large pots work well, but sacks are particularly good, as you can start with them rolled down, and unroll the sides as you earth the potatoes up. You can enjoy a surprisingly good crop by growing in this way, as long as you remember to water regularly.

》WHEN TO START
Late winter
AT THEIR BEST
Summer

TIME TO COMPLETE
🕐 1 hour
YOU WILL NEED
Seed potatoes
Several sacks or large pots
Soil-based compost, such as John Innes No.3
Watering can

1 PLANT POTATOES
Make sure your container has adequate drainage holes, then put 20cm (8in) of compost in the base. Place one or two "chitted" seed potatoes (*see Step 1, left*) per pot or sack on top of the compost. Cover them with about 10cm (4in) of compost, and water in well.

2 KEEP EARTHING UP
As the potatoes grow, unroll your sack to make the sides higher. Keep covering the new growth with compost; don't worry, the shoots will soon find their way through the soil. When you reach the top, and can earth up no more, just let the plants grow. Water regularly. New potatoes can be harvested any time after flowering.

Build a timber raised bed

If you have a heavy clay soil, you may find it easier to grow your vegetables in raised beds, which offer many advantages. Not only does the soil drain freely, making them ideal for root crops, but it also warms up more quickly in spring, allowing you to sow and plant sooner, and enjoy earlier harvests.

WHEN TO START
Winter
AT ITS BEST
Summer

TIME TO COMPLETE
1 day

YOU WILL NEED
Spade
Heavy-duty gloves
8 timbers cut to size required
 – timbers used here are 2 x 2m
 (8ft) and 2 x 1.2m (4ft)
Builder's spirit level
Tape measure
Rubber mallet
Screwdriver
Long heavy-duty coach screws
Broken pots
Top soil or soil-based compost,
 such as John Innes No.3

1 DIG OUT STRIPS OF TURF
Mark out lines on the ground where the timbers will rest, then use a sharp spade to cut out the outline of your bed, all the way around. If positioning the bed on a lawned area, ease the spade between turf and soil, and lift off the grass, which you can then use elsewhere in the garden (*see p.29*).

2 LAY TIMBERS IN POSITION
Set the first layer of timbers in position. Remove or add soil until they are level. Check the levels along and diagonally across the timbers with a builder's spirit level. Ensure the base is square by checking that the diagonals are equal in length. For a perfect square or rectangle, have the timbers pre-cut at a timber yard.

3 SECURE BASE TIMBERS
Use a rubber mallet to adjust the position of the timbers so they butt up and align neatly at the corners. Drill two holes on one side of each corner, and secure the joint using long, heavy-duty coach screws. Check that all timbers are firmly joined together.

4 ARRANGE SECOND LAYER
The next layer of timbers simply sit on top of the first. Arrange the pieces so that the joints at the four corners are staggered, as shown, to give the structure extra strength and stability. Check all levels before screwing the timbers in place, as shown in Step 3.

5 SOW SEEDS OR PLANT PLUGS
For added drainage, put a layer of broken pots or builder's rubble in the base, then fill with garden topsoil or soil-based compost, such as John Innes No.3. Water it well and leave to settle for a few days, after which you can sow seeds or plant directly.

< *Convenience food*
Position a raised bed near your patio and you can have fresh salad leaves and herbs close to the kitchen and barbecue area.

Roots for raised beds

Root vegetables, such as carrots and beetroot, commonly produce misshapen roots if they are grown in stony garden soil. Since these, and most other root crops, also prefer a free-draining soil, they are ideal for growing in raised beds, where their tasty, succulent roots can develop straight and true.

 WHEN TO START
Spring
AT THEIR BEST
Summer, autumn, and winter

 TIME TO COMPLETE
🕐 1½ hours

YOU WILL NEED
ℹ️ Seed for root vegetables, such as carrot, radish, beetroot, and celeriac

Beetroot

Reliable and easy to grow, beetroot comes in yellow, white, and striped varieties, as well as the traditional blood-red. Sow a new batch every few weeks and harvest the plump, sweet, earthy roots as you need them.

1 SOWING
Sow seeds 1.5cm (¾in) deep in rows, directly in the soil, every two weeks from late spring. Thin the seedlings shortly after germination so plants are 15cm (6in) apart.

2 HARVESTING
Beetroot is sweetest and most succulent when young, and can be harvested when roots reach the size of a golf ball. Leave some in the ground to grow larger, where they will last into winter. Pull them as required, although they will eventually become tougher and less tasty. When you harvest the beetroot, cut leaves bleed and stain; instead, simply twist off the leafy tops.

Celeriac

The edible part of celeriac is actually the swollen base of the stem, not the root. Since this develops below soil level, it is commonly regarded as a root vegetable.

Carrots

Carrots are the mainstay of the allotment and kitchen, but they are slightly fussy, and need really free-draining soil to do well. They are also prone to a troublesome pest, carrot fly larvae, which you need to guard against.

1 SOWING IN DRILLS
Sow seeds 1.5cm (¾in) deep directly into the soil from mid-spring. As they grow you can thin them out and eat as baby carrots, leaving the others in the ground to mature. Try not to bruise their leaves when pulling them out, as the smell attracts carrot fly (*see Top Tip, below*).

2 HARVESTING
Carrots are ready to harvest from midsummer. On sandy soils, you can simply pull them out of the ground, but on heavier soils use a fork, taking care not to damage the roots. Harvest young carrots to use immediately. Older ones can be stored in a cool place over winter.

1 SOWING AND PLANTING
In early spring, sow seed in modules in a greenhouse or cold frame. Germination can be slow, and the plants need a long season to mature fully. Pot them on as they grow. When they are about 7cm (3in) tall, harden them off outside (*see p.109*). Then plant them out into well-drained soil, at a distance of about 15cm (6in) apart.

2 HARVESTING
Celeriac can be harvested from late summer and throughout winter. As they do not store well once dug up, leave them in the soil until you need them. Cold weather improves the flavour of celeriac but can damage the plants. A mulch of straw applied before the first frosts will prevent this and keep your crop in a good condition until you harvest it.

TOP TIP: PROTECTIVE COVERING

The carrot fly locates carrots by scent, and then lays eggs nearby. As these hatch, the larvae burrow into the necks of the roots, at the base of the foliage, often making the carrots inedible. To prevent this, simply cover the crop with a light, transparent mesh, such as garden fleece, dug into the soil at the bottom. Alternatively, surround your crop with a solid barrier 75cm (30in) high, as the adults can only fly close to the ground.

Raised bed options

Elevating your crops in raised beds solves many problems. You can fill them with good-quality top soil, free from weeds and stones, or use them for crops such as blueberries that like specific conditions, in this case, acid soil. They are also easier to tend, and can save your back from damage. Make your own or buy a kit, and choose beds made from natural timber or woven willow, or lightweight man-made materials that last for many years.

❶ Use treated wooden planks, pushed halfway into the soil, for quick and effective temporary beds.
❷ Low beds are easy to make and ideal for leafy crops (*see pp.254–255*).   ❸ For permanent raised beds, build them from bricks, leaving small gaps in the bottom two courses to provide good drainage.
❹ Proprietary raised bed kits are easy to assemble, and some have integral mesh-covered canopies to deter pests.   ❺ Raised beds made from woven willow hurdles look great in cottage gardens. They are not very durable and will need replacing every few years.   ❻ If you buy a timber raised bed kit ensure it has the FSC logo, which means the timber is from a renewable source.   ❼ When making tall raised beds, screw each layer together, rather than just resting them on top of one another (*see pp.254–255*).
❽ Dual-purpose beds-cum-seats allow you to tend your crops without bending or kneeling. Use thick timbers for the bed, and attach the wider seating edge along the top with long coach bolts.

Plant up productive pots

Although many vegetables need space to produce a worthwhile crop in a pot, there are plenty that can be grown successfully in more cramped conditions. Grow a container planted with vegetables outside your back door, and you can nip out and grab a handful whenever you need them.

Rainbow chard

Harvest these as colourful baby leaves, little and often, and use them in summer salads or stir-fries.

 WHEN TO PLANT
Spring to early summer
AT ITS BEST
Summer to autumn

TIME TO COMPLETE
🕐 30 minutes

YOU WILL NEED
 Small chard plants
Large, wide container
Broken clay pot pieces
Soil-based compost, such as
 John Innes No.3
Watering can

1 PREPARE CONTAINER
Make sure the container has adequate drainage holes and then cover the base with clay pot pieces. Top up the container with compost.

2 TEASE OUT ROOTS
Water small plants of rainbow or ruby chard. Tip them from their pots, and carefully tease out the roots. This helps them establish quickly.

3 PLANT AND FIRM IN
Plant the chard fairly close together for a good display. Firm in and water well. Keep well watered and cut back flowering stems to prolong the crop.

Radishes

Radishes are great crops for containers. They are the fastest germinating and maturing vegetable of all, grow almost anywhere, and their peppery taste gives salads a real kick.

 WHEN TO PLANT
Spring to summer
AT ITS BEST
Late spring to early autumn

TIME TO COMPLETE
 30 minutes

YOU WILL NEED
Radish seed
Low, wide pot
Broken clay pot pieces
Soil-based compost, such as
 John Innes No.3
Watering can with fine rose

1 PREPARE AND SOW
Cover the base of the pot with broken pot pieces. Fill the container with compost and firm the top lightly. Sow seed on the surface and cover with 1cm (½in) of compost. Water with a fine rose.

2 THIN OUT
As seedlings germinate and grow, thin them out, leaving the others to mature fully. You can eat the removed seedlings as an extra early salad crop.

3 HARVEST
Water your pot regularly. Radishes are usually ready about five weeks after sowing. Do not allow them to grow for longer than this, as their taste becomes hotter and unpleasant, and they lose their crunch. To harvest, simply pull them up when ready. They store well in the fridge for a few days.

TOP TIP: BABY BEANS FOR CONTAINERS

'Hestia' is one of the smallest runner beans. Being compact, with beautiful flowers, it is well suited to growing in pots. Dwarf runner beans do not climb and need minimal support – just a few short canes to hold them up in windy weather. Prepare the pot as for radishes. Grow one plant per pot, and water them frequently. Pick regularly once the beans start appearing to prolong the harvest.

Enjoy some easy greens

There are fresh greens to be enjoyed from the garden all year round, providing a wonderful source of vitamins when there is not much else available. These are useful crops for filling gaps in the vegetable year, as they mature when others are either just starting to grow, or have finished for the season.

Spring cabbage

Spring cabbage is ready in late spring (earlier if grown as spring greens), when other crops are just getting going. Give it a sheltered position to help it survive the winter.

WHEN TO START
Late summer
AT ITS BEST
Spring

TIME TO COMPLETE
30 minutes sowing; 1 hour planting

YOU WILL NEED
Spring cabbage seed
Seed compost
Pot
Modular seed trays
Dibber or garden trowel

TOP TIP: REPEAT CROPPING

To harvest a succession of spring greens, start cutting in early spring, before the plants form hearts, cutting away the entire leafy part but leaving the stalk. Cut a cross in the top of the leftover stalks. This encourages the plant to sprout again, and produce a second flush of leaves, which you can then harvest. Do this to alternate plants in the row, leaving the others to form cabbages with rounded hearts.

1 SOW IN MODULAR TRAY
You can either sow seed directly in the soil and thin the plants later, or sow in pots and transplant into modules, planting the seedlings out once they have five leaves each. Water the soil well first.

2 PLANT OUT
Position plants 30cm (12in) apart for smaller spring greens; 45cm (18in) apart if you want fully-hearted cabbages. Do not add fertilizer – it encourages soft leafy growth, and your cabbages need to be tough to withstand the winter. In late autumn, mound up the soil around the stems to protect the plants during the worst weather. Spring greens can be harvested as soon as they are big enough to eat, while fully-hearted cabbages will be ready during the last month of spring.

Spinach

If you sow spinach every few weeks in spring and early autumn, and protect it over winter, you can harvest the tender leaves throughout the year.

WHEN TO START
Spring or early autumn
AT ITS BEST
Summer

TIME TO COMPLETE
 1 hour
YOU WILL NEED
Spinach seed
A line of string
Trowel
Watering can

SOW IN DRILLS
Stretch out your string and use a trowel to make a shallow drill. Sow the seeds into it at 2.5cm (1in) intervals. Thin the seedlings to about 7cm (3in) apart for baby salad leaves, or 15cm (6in) apart for larger leaves to use for cooking. Protect seedlings in winter with a cloche (*see p.409*).

HARVESTING
You can cut the leaves when they are large enough to eat. Whether you remove individual leaves or cut off the entire plant, new leaves will emerge and give you a second crop. Regular watering can help prevent plants running to seed in warm weather.

Oriental greens

These are some of the most useful autumn vegetables, providing a hint of the exotic, just as the weather is cooling. They provide a great range of colours, textures and flavours, and can bring real variety to your salads and cooking.

WHEN TO START
Midsummer to early autumn
AT ITS BEST
Autumn

TIME TO COMPLETE
 1 hour
YOU WILL NEED
Seed
A line of string
Trowel
Watering can

SOW SEEDS
Komatsuna, pak choi, bok choi, mizuna, mibuna and other Oriental greens are best sown in late summer, or they will quickly run to seed. They need a rich, fertile, moist soil. Sow *in situ* or in modules, thinning or planting to eventual spacings of around 15cm (6in).

PICKING THE CROP
Pick the leaves when young as a cut-and-come-again crop for salads and stir-fries, or leave them to mature fully and harvest the entire plant. If you cut the plant 2.5cm (1in) above the ground, it will produce a second crop of leaves.

Winter pickings

Winter can be a surprisingly bountiful time on the vegetable plot, but you need to plan ahead carefully for a good crop of vegetables. Start sowing the previous spring, giving your plants all summer and autumn to bulk up, and you should have plenty of fresh produce for winter dishes.

Leeks

Grow leeks as part of a crop rotation, as they will quickly succumb to diseases if replanted in the same spot year after year. Planting them deep produces white and tender stems.

WHEN TO START
Spring
AT THEIR BEST
Winter

TIME TO COMPLETE
30 minutes for sowing
1½ hours for planting out

YOU WILL NEED
Leek seed
Seed tray
Seed compost
Dibber or slim trowel

1 SOW IN TRAYS
In spring, sow seed thinly across a seed tray and keep in a cold frame or cool, sheltered spot while they germinate. When the seedlings are about 20cm (8in) tall, they are ready for planting out.

2 PLANT OUT
In a well-prepared bed, mark out a line and use your dibber to make holes 20cm (8in) deep and 15cm (6in) apart. Drop a leek into each hole, making sure the roots reach the bottom, and then water them in. There is no need to backfill with soil; this will happen slowly, of its own accord, allowing some light to reach the small leek plants.

3 CROP CARE AND HARVEST
Leeks require very little attention after planting. You only need to water during prolonged dry spells. The crop will sit happily in the ground until you want to harvest, but the stems are prone to snapping when extracted from frozen soil. If freezing conditions are forecast, lift the leeks beforehand, trim the leaves, wrap them in newspaper and store in a cool place

Parsnips

For the best winter parsnips, sow as soon as the soil has warmed up in spring. They will grow all summer, forming sweet and starchy winter roots.

>> **WHEN TO START**
Early spring

AT THEIR BEST
Winter

TIME TO COMPLETE
🕐 30 minutes for sowing
3 hours for planting out

YOU WILL NEED
 Parsnip seed
String
Straw
Wire
Plant markers

1 SOW IN DRILLS
Always sow fresh seed. On well-drained soil, mark out a line with string and make a shallow drill, then sow seed thinly along it. Once germinated, thin to 7cm (3in) apart for small, sweet roots, or slightly further apart for larger ones.

2 FROST PROTECTION
In cold weather you may need to apply a straw mulch (pinned down with hoops of wire) to prevent the soil and the parsnips from freezing.

3 HARVEST CROPS
Parsnips taste sweetest after a light frost, so don't harvest too early. The leaves die down in winter, so you will need to mark the rows well so that roots are easily found. Dig up and eat as required; their taste will improve as the winter wears on.

Brussels sprouts

Love them or hate them, no winter vegetable patch is complete without Brussels sprouts. They are big plants that need lots of attention, but they will reward you well.

>> **WHEN TO START**
Spring

AT THEIR BEST
Winter

TIME TO COMPLETE
🕐 30 minutes – sowing
3 hours – planting out

YOU WILL NEED
🌱 Brussels sprout seed
Seed trays
Compost
Cage
Fine woven mesh

1 COVER PLANTS
Sow in seed trays and add manure to your beds at the same time. Plant out the seedlings about four weeks later, at least 1m (3ft) apart. Cover plants with a fine mesh to keep out cabbage white butterflies, which lay their eggs on the foliage, as well as pigeons.

2 CROP CARE AND HARVEST
Keep plants well watered until established, and remove withered leaves as they may carry diseases. As they grow, draw up soil around the stems to give them extra stability. Flavour is at its best after a good, hard frost. Harvest sprouts as you need them, picking from the base of the stalk and moving up. After picking all of the sprouts, chop off the top leaves and cook as you would greens.

Grow year-round salads

Growing cress and sprouting seeds indoors provides a constant supply of fresh ingredients for salads and sandwiches all year round. Sow cress every couple of weeks, and prepare jars of sprouts on a daily basis. These easy projects are ideal for children, who love to watch the plants develop.

WATER THE POTS
2 Repeat for several pots – you will need a few if growing for salads. Set the pots on a plant tray or saucers, and water them to dampen the towels.

Easy cress

One packet of seed will be sufficient for a few sowings. Reseal the packet after use and store in a container in the fridge.

TIME TO COMPLETE

🕐 30 minutes

YOU WILL NEED

ℹ️ Cress seed
Small pots
Kitchen paper towels
Non-toxic felt-tip pen
All-purpose compost
Plastic bags

FOLD KITCHEN TOWEL
1 Fold a sheet of kitchen towel in four. Invert a pot over it and draw around the rim with a pen. Cut out the circles of paper. Fill the pot with compost to just below the rim and place the four paper circles on top.

SOW THE SEEDS
3 Sprinkle some seeds onto the paper. Place each pot in a plastic bag, seal loosely and store in a cool dark place. When the seedlings are 1cm (½in), remove the bag. Set pots on a windowsill out of direct sun, and keep moist until the cress is ready.

Crunchy sprouts

Delicious and packed with nutrients, sprouting beans add crunchy texture to salads, and you can choose from many different varieties. From spicy onion to mild broccoli, you will find a taste to suit, or try a few and mix them together.

TIME TO COMPLETE

🕐 5 minutes each day

YOU WILL NEED

💧 Packets of beans or seeds
   Sprouting jars with lids or tiered sprouters
   Storage containers

VARIETIES TO TRY

🌱 Adzuki
   Alfalfa
   Beet
   Broccoli
   Chickpea
   Fenugreek
   Lentil
   Mung
   Onion
   Red cabbage
   Rocket
   Snow peas
   Wheatgrass

1 CLEAN THE CONTAINER
Proprietary sprouting jars with meshed lids and tiered sprouters are widely available from garden centres and DIY stores. Make sure you clean them thoroughly before each use. Then pour seeds into your jar (or sprouter), fill it with water, and leave the seeds to soak for 8–10 hours.

2 RINSE AND DRAIN
After soaking, invert the jar over the sink and allow the water to drain out. Rinse the seeds again in fresh cold water and drain again. Make sure there is no water left in the bottom of the jar, and place it in a light area out of direct sun.

3 KEEP RINSING
Rinse and drain the seeds with cold water twice a day to keep them clean and moist. Many seeds sprout and are ready to eat in four or five days. When they are ready, give the sprouts a final rinse, drain, and leave for eight hours to allow excess water to evaporate.

4 STORE AND USE
When the sprouts are dry, use them immediately, or you can store them in the fridge for up to five days. If any go mouldy, discard the whole batch. You can also store the beans in a dark cupboard which will produce white sprouts that have a slightly different flavour to the green ones grown in light.

Edible flowers

Some flowers can be eaten as well as admired: lavender and roses have a light, perfumed flavour; French marigolds taste spicy; nasturtium peppery; mallow is sweet; and tangy pot marigold petals add a golden hue to food. Most flavours are delicate, and while they may add a subtle taste, edible flowers are most often used as adornments – sweet ones to decorate cakes and puddings, and savoury types sprinkled over salads.

❋❋❋ fully hardy   ❋❋ hardy in mild regions/sheltered sites   ❋ protect from frost over winter
☼ full sun   ☼ partial sun   ☀ full shade   ◊ well-drained soil   ◔ moist soil   ● wet soil

1 Wild pansy, *Viola tricolor*; ↕12cm (5in) ↔15cm (6in) ☼ ☼ ◔ ❋❋❋   **2** Pot marigold, *Calendula officinalis*; ↕50cm (20in) ↔ 40cm (16in) ☼ ☼ ◊ ❋❋❋   **3** Bergamot, *Monarda didyma*; ↕90cm (36in) ↔45cm (18in) ☼ ☼ ◔ ❋❋❋   **4** Rose (scented species), eg *Rosa* 'Summer Wine'; ↕3m (10ft) ↔2.2m (7ft) ☼ ◔ ❋❋❋ **5** Lavender, *Lavandula angustifolia*; ↕1m (3ft) ↔1.2m (4ft) ☼ ◊ ❋❋❋
6 Courgette; ↕45cm (18in) ↔90cm (36in) ☼ ◊ ◔ ❋   **7** Nasturtium, *Tropaeolum majus* Alaska Series; ↕30cm (12in) ↔45cm (18in) ☼ ◔ ❋   **8** *Anchusa azurea* 'Loddon Royalist'; ↕90cm (36in) ↔ 60cm (24in) ☼ ◔ ❋❋❋   **9** Annual mallow, *Malope trifida*; ↕90cm (36in) ↔24cm (10in) ☼ ◔ ❋❋❋
10 French marigold, *Tagetes* Gem Series 'Tangerine Gem'; ↕23cm (9in) ↔30cm (12in) ☼ ◊ ❋
Warning: the pollen of some flowers may cause a reaction in those who suffer from asthma or hayfever.

Grow tasty bulbs

Onions, shallots, and garlic are among the most essential of all vegetables, adding strong, savoury flavours to a vast number of traditional and exotic dishes. Try out a range of cultivars for different tastes. Dry them well, and you can store the bulbs for use throughout winter.

Onions

Onions can be grown from seed or sets (small bulbs). Sets are more costly, and there is a smaller range of cultivars available, but they are quick, reliable, and a good choice for beginners.

 WHEN TO START
Early spring
AT THEIR BEST
Midsummer

 TIME TO COMPLETE
 1 hour
YOU WILL NEED
Onion sets
Spade
Horticultural grit for heavy soils
Rake
String line

1 PLANT SETS
Onions need good drainage, so add horticultural grit to heavier soils. Stretch a line of string between two pegs to make a straight row. Use a rake to form a shallow furrow, and plant the sets 15cm (6in) apart, with the tips protruding. Weed regularly, and water during dry spells.

2 LIFT AND DRY
Onions are ready for harvesting in midsummer, when the leaves turn yellow and fold over. Lift them and leave them in a cool, airy place to dry out for a couple of weeks. Use any with thick necks straightaway, and store the others for later.

Shallots

Many people prefer the sweet, milder flavour of shallots, as an alternative to onions. They can also be harvested earlier, and store longer than onions.

 WHEN TO START
Early spring
AT THEIR BEST
Mid-autumn

TIME TO COMPLETE
 1 hour

YOU WILL NEED
 Shallot sets
Horticultural grit for heavy soil
String line
Rake

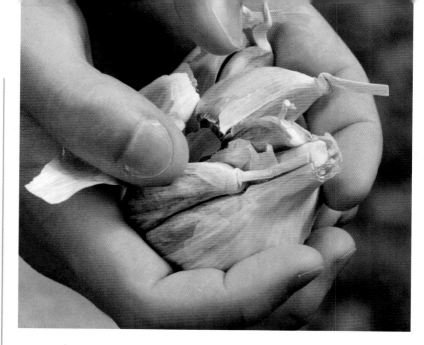

1 WHEN TO PLANT
In late winter or early spring, prepare the bed as for onions (*see left*). Plant shallots into well-drained soil, spacing them 15–20cm (6–8in) apart. Make a small hole, then push the shallot into the ground so that the top is just showing.

2 LIFT BULBS
Shallots form small clumps of bulbs, which you should lift intact. Dry and store them whole, somewhere dry and well ventilated, and break off individual bulbs as you need them. They will store well for up to 12 months.

Garlic

Despite its reputation as an ingredient used in warmer countries, garlic is surprisingly easy to grow in cooler climes, although it needs a long growing season. Always use bulbs from a reputable supplier.

 WHEN TO START
Autumn
AT THEIR BEST
Summer

TIME TO COMPLETE
 1 hour

YOU WILL NEED
 Garlic bulbs
Dibber
String line
Rake
Horticultural grit for
heavy soils

1 HOW TO PLANT
Plant into well-drained soil; add horticultural grit to heavy soils, or make and plant into a low ridge of soil. Split the bulb into individual cloves, plant with the point facing up, 10cm (4in) deep, 20cm (8in) apart, and cover with soil.

2 HARVEST AND DRY
Garlic is ripe when the leaves turn yellow in summer. Lift the bulbs and hang them to dry. Store individually or plait them together while the stems are dry but flexible. Starting with three bulbs, plait the stems until there is room to add more, then join the new stems to the other strings of the plait. Store in a cool, dry, well-ventilated place.

Bag up some tomatoes

Tomatoes grow very successfully in grow bags in a greenhouse or outdoors. Crops can be improved by inserting bottomless pots full of compost into the grow bag to increase the volume for better root growth. Buy young plants in late spring, or sow seed indoors earlier in the season.

 WHEN TO START
Mid-spring
AT THEIR BEST
Early autumn

 TIME TO COMPLETE
 2 hours over a few months

YOU WILL NEED
Two tomato plants
Grow bag
Two plastic pots
Stanley knife
Some extra compost
Stake (bamboo cane or
  chestnut stake)
Garden twine

 VARIETIES TO TRY
'Black Russian'
'Gardener's Delight'
'Marmande'
'Shirley'
'Summer Sweet' F1
'Sungold' F1

1 CUT OUT HOLES
Cut the bottom off of the pots, then place them onto the grow bag and cut around them. Push the pots into the bag and fill them up with the spare compost.

2 PLANT INTO THE POTS

Plant one tomato per pot at the same level as it was growing in its container. Plant straggly plants a little deeper. This encourages new roots to form along the buried stem, helping to stabilize the plants.

3 PINCH OUT SIDESHOOTS

As the plants grow, small sideshoots appear off the main stem. These should be removed as soon as possible, as they will take energy away from the ripening fruits. When they are small, simply pinch them out with your fingers.

4 TIE IN MAIN STEMS

Tomato plants need to be regularly tied in to a sturdy support. Make a figure of eight using twine, tying tightly around the support, and loosely around the plant stem, to allow room for growth.

5 NIP OUT THE TOP

You can help the plant to put all its energy into ripening the fruits by preventing it from putting on too much growth. After outdoor plants have set four trusses of fruits, and greenhouse plants six, nip out the top shoot with your fingers.

6 FRUITING AND HARVESTING

Tomatoes are best when picked fully ripe, but you are likely to have some green tomatoes at the end of the season. Cutting back on watering can help to shock the plant into ripening the fruits. If it is turning cold and your tomatoes must be harvested, pull up the whole plant and hang it by its roots somewhere cool and dark to finish ripening.

TOP TIP: CAREFUL WATERING

Cracks can appear in the skin just as fruits are ripening. The problem is due to changes in growth rate, caused by fluctuating temperatures and erratic watering; as growth slows during a cool, dry period, skins harden and do not have the elasticity to cope if growth later picks up and fruits swell. It is a particular problem in

soft-grown plants: those that have been fed too much nitrogen. While you cannot control temperatures, you can make sure watering is regular, and that you provide the correct feeding regime. Make provisions for watering if you go away, even for a few days, and feed weekly with a specially formulated tomato feed, one rich in flower- and fruit-promoting potassium.

Sow peas and pods

Sweet and crunchy, peas of every kind are delicious vegetables, and especially loved by children who can pop them in their mouths the moment they are picked. Sugarsnaps and mangetout are expensive to buy in the shops, too, but are both surprisingly easy to grow and very productive.

Peas

Peas are at their finest the moment they are picked. Grow your own and you will never eat shop-bought ones again.

WHEN TO START
Winter

AT THEIR BEST
Summer

TIME TO COMPLETE
 1½ hours

YOU WILL NEED
 Pea seed
Fork
Spade
String line
Pea sticks or pea netting

1 SOW SEED
Dig the area in winter and leave it until early spring. Remove any weeds, and create a trench 3cm (1¼in) deep along a string line. Plant the seeds 5cm (2in) apart, in two rows 20cm (8in) apart, and cover with soil. Water well. Keep soil moist for bumper crops and to prevent powdery mildew.

Mangetout

Mangetout means "eat all" in French, and that is exactly what you do with these tender, crunchy pods. The young pods of any peas can be eaten whole, but these have soft inner walls, are flat, and the peas inside do not swell. Add them to stir fries, lightly steam, or eat them raw in salads.

2 SUPPORT YOUR PEAS
Peas are short, climbing plants and need support as they grow. Insert short twiggy pea sticks (*see p.307*) next to each plant, or stretch closely woven pea netting along the row between two upright supports.

3 WHEN TO HARVEST
Peas are ready about three weeks after flowering. The pods at the base of the plant mature first. Pick them when they are young for the sweetest taste. Keep picking, and the plant will keep producing. After harvesting, cut the plant off and leave the roots in the ground to release nitrogen – a natural fertilizer.

≫ **WHEN TO START**
Spring
AT THEIR BEST
Summer

TIME TO COMPLETE
🕐 1 hour

YOU WILL NEED
Mangetout seed
Spade
Rake
Pea sticks or pea netting

1 BEFORE YOU PLANT
Choose a sunny, open spot, and dig the soil over about a month before sowing time. Use a rake to make a trench 3cm (1¼in) deep, and sow the seed 5cm (2in) apart. Cover the seed with soil and water in well.

2 SUPPORT AND CARE
Push pea sticks into the ground close to the seed. Keep the plants well watered, especially when they are flowering, and during warm weather. Harvest frequently, as soon as the pods reach 5–6cm (2–2½in) long.

Sugarsnap peas

This is another pea relative that is eaten whole, pod and all. The difference between these and mangetout is that sugarsnaps have a firm inner pod that gives them more of a crunch. They also swell up like normal pea pods.

PLANTING AND CARE
Sugarsnap peas grow well in cool conditions, and can be sown directly in the soil from early spring for a summer crop; sow in midsummer for an autumn crop. Sow a small amount of seed every couple of weeks, using the same method as peas, to give a succession of crops. Since some sugarsnap peas grow tall, provide a sturdy frame 2m (6ft) high with long pea sticks, or pea netting stretched between upright poles. Keep the peas well watered. Harvest the pods while young and tender, which will encourage the plants to produce more.

Grow sweet squash

Summer and winter squashes, which include courgettes and pumpkins, as well as butternut varieties, are satisfying and fun plants to grow. They are tender and need protection at the beginning of the year, but once the danger of frost has passed, they will grow quickly, forming strong, bountiful plants.

1 PLANT SEEDS
Fill small pots with seed compost. As courgette seedlings are large, plant just one seed into each pot. Water them in and cover the pots with clear polythene bags to encourage germination.

Bags of courgettes

Courgettes are so easy to grow that you don't even need a pot, let alone space in the border. A large, well-made plastic bag can contain enough compost to keep a single courgette plant happy and productive.

2 CHOOSE A SUNNY SITE
Once the seedlings have germinated, remove the bags and place the pots in a warm, sunny spot. Keep them indoors, or in a warm greenhouse, until all danger of frost has passed in late spring or early summer.

⟩⟩ **WHEN TO START**
Spring

AT THEIR BEST
Summer

TIME TO COMPLETE
 30 minutes to sow; 30 minutes
to plant

YOU WILL NEED
 Courgette seeds
Seed compost
Multi-purpose compost
Large, sturdy plastic bags
Scissors
Small pots
Mulch, such as bark chips

3 PLANT INTO A LARGE BAG
Once the weather has warmed, harden off your plants by standing them outside by day, and bringing them inside at night, for a couple of weeks. Set your plastic bag in a sheltered sunny spot outside. Make drainage holes with scissors in the bottom of the bag, fill it with compost, and plant the courgettes.

4 ADD LAYER OF MULCH
Firm the plants in and water them well. To help retain moisture, cover the compost with a thick mulch of chipped bark or organic matter. Water every day during summer, and feed weekly with a tomato fertilizer. The plants grow rapidly, and will soon form large golden flowers that develop into tasty courgettes.

Plump pumpkins

Pumpkins and winter squash are left to mature all summer, and can then be stored, ready for use in the kitchen throughout autumn and winter.

 WHEN TO START
Spring
AT THEIR BEST
Autumn and winter

TIME TO COMPLETE
🕐 30 minutes to sow; 1 hour to plant

YOU WILL NEED
🛈 Pumpkin and squash seeds
Seed compost and small pots
Well-rotted organic matter
Straw

1 SOW AND PLANT OUT
Sow the seeds indoors in spring and keep frost-free until the weather warms (*see Steps 1 and 2 opposite*). Choose a sunny spot, and enrich the soil with plenty of organic matter before planting. Mulch with straw to seal in moisture, and to prevent the fruits lying on wet soil and rotting.

2 HARVEST AND STORE
Cool weather can lead to the formation of male, non-fruiting flowers at first, but later female flowers (*right*) will come. Pumpkins need a long summer to grow and ripen. They are ready to harvest when the stalk starts to crack. Cut with stalk intact, keep the large orange fruits dry for at least 10 days, then store in a cool, dry place.

TOP TIP: MAKE A RESERVOIR FOR WATERING

Pumpkins, squash, and courgettes are thirsty plants that hate dry soil. Plant into a depression in the soil or make a ridge of soil up around them to create a well. Water will then pool around the plant roots and seep into the soil, rather than flowing away.

SELECTIONS»

Squash and pumpkins

Winter squash and pumpkins are as beautiful as they are tasty. They come in a variety of vibrant and bizarre colours and shapes, and many, such as 'Turk's Turban' (*below*) are prized as much for their ornamental value, as for their flesh. They love plenty of sun and moisture and, once fully grown and mature, the fruit can be stored well into winter. Delicious roasted, they are the quintessential autumn vegetable: comfort food at its best.

❋❋❋ fully hardy   ❋❋ hardy in mild regions/sheltered sites   ❋ protect from frost over winter
☀ full sun   ☀ partial sun   ☀ full shade   ◊ well-drained soil   ◖ moist soil   ● wet soil

Individual fruits vary in size and weight according to variety, from tennis- to beach ball-sized, so check the packet first. Grow varieties with large fruit, such as pumpkins and butternut squash, as groundcover, where they will spread 4m (15ft). Smaller-fruited varieties can be grown up sturdy supports. Reaching 1–2m (3–6ft) high, and taking up little ground space, they are ideal for smaller gardens.

1 Squash 'Turk's Turban'   **2** Squash 'Hasta La Pasta'   **3** Squash 'Red Kuri'   **4** Squash 'Sweet Dumpling'   **5** Pumpkin, *Cucurbita maxima* cultivars   **6** Squash 'Little Gem Rollet'   **7** Bush marrow 'Badger Cross' F1   **8** Squash 'Hooligan' F1 hybrid   **9** Butternut squash 'Pilgrim'   **10** Squash 'Tromboncino'. Conditions required by all cultivars: ☀ ◊ ◖ ❋.

Heat up your windowsill

Chillies are easy to grow if you have a warm windowsill or hot, sunny patio. Sow seeds in spring and you can look forward to fresh chillies from summer to the autumn, or all year round if you dry them. Experiment with different coloured varieties and levels of heat.

 WHEN TO START
Mid-spring

AT THEIR BEST
Summer to autumn

TIME TO COMPLETE
 1 hour

YOU WILL NEED
 Chilli seeds
8cm (3½in) pots
Seed compost
Clear plastic bag
Larger pots
Multi-purpose compost
Small canes
Tomato fertilizer

1 SOW SEED
Select seed to suit your taste – some are much hotter than others. You can also sow seed from dried chillies grown the previous year, but they may revert to a common type if you planted a named hybrid. In spring, fill small pots with moist seed compost. Place about two or three seeds on the surface and cover lightly with more compost. Water, label, and place pots in a plastic bag. As soon as the seedlings appear, remove the bag.

2 SEEDLING CARE
When 2cm (1in) tall, separate seedlings into their own small pots and set on a sunny windowsill. Keep well watered. When they are about 20cm (8in) tall, pot them on into larger containers.

3 GROW THEM ON
Pinch the growing tips out when the plants reach 30cm (12in) to encourage more shoots, and stake as necessary. Harden plants off if you plan to keep them outside (*see p.109*). Feed weekly with tomato fertilizer when buds appear, and pick the fruit when green for a milder taste, or leave till they are red hot.

Grow fabulous fungi

Mushroom picking in the wild is only for the experts, but you can grow your own at home with a specialist kit. Some come in the form of dowels impregnated with mycelium that you plant into logs; others, like the one used here, are simple kits in boxes, ideal for beginners.

WHEN TO START
Early spring

AT THEIR BEST
Summer

TIME TO COMPLETE
1 hour

YOU WILL NEED
Mushroom kit
Measuring jug

1 FILL BOX WITH COMPOST
Box kits come with mushroom compost that has been injected with mycelium, and a "casing layer", which holds water and protects the developing mushrooms. First, line the box with a plastic bag (most kits come with this too) and add the mushroom compost.

2 ADD WATER TO THE CASING
Open the bag of casing and slowly add 0.5 litres (1 pint) of water. Leave for about an hour to allow the moisture to soak in. Take a small handful of the mushroom compost and mix it into the casing layer in the bag.

3 RUFFLE THE SURFACE
Empty the contents of the bag onto the compost in the box. Spread the casing evenly over the compost and ruffle the surface with a small fork. This creates a microclimate where the young mushrooms can form. Rest the lid at an angle on the box so air can circulate.

4 CHECK DAILY
Place the box in a warm spot at 20–24°C (68–75°F) but not in an airing cupboard or by a radiator. After a few days, white mycelium will form on the surface. Remove the lid and place in a dark location at 16–20°C (61–68°F). Mist to keep the compost moist. Mushrooms should appear after six days.

Unwrap tender treats

Among the greatest delights of the vegetable patch are those crops that hide their bounty beneath tactile wrappers. Sweetcorn, with its squeaky skin that peels back to reveal the cob, and broad beans, with soft, fur-lined pods, are particularly pleasing for children, who love discovering the treats within.

Sweetcorn

Sweetcorn is a tender plant that is easily damaged by cold weather. Sow it indoors in mid-spring, and only plant out once the danger of frost has passed – late spring at the earliest, depending on where you live.

 WHEN TO START
Mid- to late spring
AT THEIR BEST
Late summer

 TIME TO COMPLETE
A few hours over several weeks

 YOU WILL NEED
Sweetcorn seeds
Compost
Small pots for sowing
Seed labels
String
Ruler

1 HOW TO SOW
Sweet corn will be ready for planting out about six weeks after sowing indoors in pots. Clear all weeds from the soil and dig it over thoroughly. Plant out in square blocks, which aids pollination, spacing plants 35cm (14in) apart. You can also sow direct from late spring onwards, but sow two seeds per station in case one of them fails to grow.

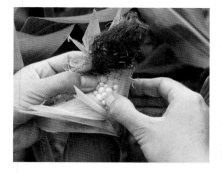

TEST FOR RIPENESS

Once the tassels turn brown, test regularly for ripeness. Press a nail into a kernel – if a milky liquid comes out, it is ready; if watery, it is under-ripe; but if doughy, the corn has passed its best.

HARVESTING THE COBS

Pick the cobs by twisting them off, only when you are ready to eat them; their natural sugars quickly turn starchy once picked. Sweetcorn is delicious wrapped in foil and grilled on a barbecue.

TOP TIP: INTERCROPPING

Try growing other crops among your sweetcorn, as its foliage lets lots of light through to the ground. Use quick-maturing crops such as lettuces, or sweetcorn's traditional intercropping partners, winter squash and pumpkin.

Broad beans

This is a gourmet crop that matures in early summer when most other vegetables are still getting started. The beans are easy to grow and very hardy. In well-drained soils, sow them in autumn for an early crop; in heavier soils, you may have to wait until spring. Plant them in a sunny, sheltered site.

» **WHEN TO START**
Early autumn or spring
AT THEIR BEST
Early summer

TIME TO COMPLETE
30 minutes for sowing

YOU WILL NEED
Bean seeds
Dibber
Wooden pegs
String
Garden canes

SOW SEED

Peg out a length of string and make holes along its length, 6cm (3in) deep, 25cm (10in) apart, and drop a single seed into the base of each one. Mark out and sow successive rows at 20cm (8in) intervals. Refill the holes with soil, and water the seeds in well.

PINCH OUT GROWING TIPS

To reduce the risk of aphid damage, snap off the soft tips of the bean plants once they have started to produce pods.

SUPPORT PLANTS

Broad beans can grow up to 1.2m (4ft) tall and become heavily laden with pods, which can cause the plants to collapse. To stop this, support the plants by using garden canes and string to make an open frame around them, particularly in windy areas.

HARVEST

Broad beans are usually ready to harvest four to five months after planting. Check the pods regularly, and pick them once they are clearly swollen with beans but still look glossy. Once the pods turn leathery, although the beans inside are still edible, they will be tough.

Make a box of herbs and leaves

Growing herbs and salads in a windowbox provides a fresh supply close to the kitchen, and by making a box to your own specifications, you can ensure it fits your space perfectly. All you need are some simple tools and a few basic DIY skills to create this timber design.

WHEN TO START
Any time
AT ITS BEST
Spring and summer

TIME TO COMPLETE
🕐 4 hours

YOU WILL NEED
 Herbs and small lettuce plants
Drill, saw and tape measure
5cm (2in) self-tapping screws
Treated timber
Battens (about 12mm thick)
Copper anti-slug tape
12mm roofing tacks
Multi-purpose compost

1 MEASURE TIMBER
Decide on the length of your windowbox and buy pieces of wood long enough to make two sides, two ends, and a base, and mark them out.

2 CUT INTO LENGTHS
Double-check the measurements and cut out the pieces. To create straight cuts and a neater finish, support both ends of the timber as you saw.

3 SCREW SIDES TOGETHER

Use self-tapping screws to attach one side piece to an end piece; two screws should be enough. If the wood is hard, drill small pilot holes first. Repeat with the other side and end pieces. Screw the two sections together.

4 ATTACH BATTENS TO BASE

Attach the base by screwing it to both side and end pieces. Cut two battens to size, to fit the underside of the box. These will lift the base off the windowsill, allowing space for drainage. Turn the box upside down and attach the battens with short screws.

5 DRILL DRAINAGE HOLES

Good drainage is essential for healthy plants. With the box still upside down, use a drill to make a 1cm (½in) hole every 10cm (4in) along the base of the trough. Take care not to damage the surface below.

6 FIX COPPER TAPE

Attach a band of copper tape around the trough to deter snails, and to provide a decorative finish. Check you have sufficient tape to wrap all the way around without leaving any gaps.

8 PLANT WITH HERBS AND SALAD LEAVES

Fill the trough with compost and plant up with a range of herbs, and a few young lettuce plants. Make sure none of them forms a bridge over the copper tape as they grow, which would enable snails to bypass it and climb in.

7 NAIL TAPE SECURELY

To keep the tape in place, hammer small tacks along it, at 10–15cm (4–6in) intervals. Add more to make a feature of them, if desired. Make sure the tape seam is secure.

Sow a bowl of salad

Salads are "must-grow" vegetables, and taste so much better when picked fresh rather than bought. They are among the easiest of vegetables to grow, require little space, and mature in a few weeks.

Sowing in pots

Grow salad leaves in containers, and you can just step outside and cut them when you need them. Cut-and-come-again leaf crops make the most of limited space and give a ready supply.

 WHEN TO START
Spring and throughout summer
AT ITS BEST
Summer into autumn

TIME TO COMPLETE
 30 minutes

YOU WILL NEED
 Mixed salad leaf seed
Containers
Multi-purpose compost
Scissors

∧ > *Cut and come again*
While it is possible to grow traditional "headed" lettuce in containers, you will get more salad from the space, and a more attractive effect, if you choose leaves that grow back after cutting.

1 CHOOSE A VARIETY
For an attractive and colourful display, and an interesting bowl of salad, look for seed mixes containing a variety of different colours and textures. Lettuce mixes are a good choice early in the season, as they germinate well and grow abundantly in cooler conditions. The cooler night-time temperatures in spring, and lengthening days, can make baby Oriental leaf mixtures flower and go to seed all too quickly; sow these after midsummer. Ensure your containers have drainage holes in the bottom, and cover them with broken clay pieces. Then fill with compost and firm it down.

2 SOW ON SOIL SURFACE
Sow thinly across the surface, cover lightly with compost, and water well. Cut-and-come-again crops can be sown thickly, but you should thin the seedlings to a spacing of about 5cm (2in), once they are large enough to handle.

3 HARVEST THE LEAVES
When the leaves reach about 15cm (6in) high, cut them with a pair of scissors. Keep them fresh until needed in a sealed, moistened, plastic bag. The plants will re-grow several times before they are exhausted and need replacing.

Growing in beds

Beds provide more space than pots, so use them for larger, traditional, headed lettuces, although cut-and-come-again crops will flourish here too.

1 SOW IN DRILLS
Both types of lettuce should be sown in shallow drills. The only difference is that headed lettuce should be sown much more thinly. Once seeds have germinated, thin them out to 15–30cm (6–12in) apart, depending on their final size.

2 TAKE CARE
Protect your plants from slugs using mini cloches made from clear plastic bottles (*see p.426*). You may also need to net them to prevent birds eating your crops. Water them regularly during summer. They are prone to bolting in hot weather, so plant them close to taller crops, such as beans, that will provide shade.

Leafy options

Rocket has a strong, piquant taste that gives a kick to milder lettuce-based salads. Lamb's lettuce (corn salad) is a winter crop with a nuttier flavour.

PLANTING AND AFTERCARE
Rocket is best sown in spring and early autumn, when the cooler temperatures make it less likely to bolt. Sow thinly and protect the plants from flea beetles, which nibble the leaves, by covering them with a fine mesh or garden fleece.

Lamb's lettuce can be sown at any time in spring and summer. It is a useful crop to sow late in the season to provide a tasty winter substitute for lettuce. For the best quality leaves, grow lamb's lettuce under cloches, or in a glasshouse or polytunnel.

∧ *Tasty leaves*
Lamb's lettuce (top) and rocket will make a tasty addition to your lunchtime sandwiches.

Spring onions

Spring onions fit in almost anywhere, and will germinate quickly and mature between other crops. These shallow-rooted plants will even grow and produce a crop in a seed tray or container.

GROWING AND HARVESTING
Spring onions are an ideal crop for pots and containers. Sprinkle a small amount of seed on the surface of the compost once every two weeks throughout spring and summer, to ensure a constant supply. Spring onions sown in late summer can be left in the soil during winter, to harvest the following spring.

∨ *Pack a punch*
Simply lift the tangy bulbs from the soil as you need them and use in salads or stir-fries.

Salad leaves

With such a wide variety of salads on offer, you can grow leaves for your salad bowl all year round, if you can provide some frost protection in winter. From mild, buttery lettuce to spicy mizuna, oriental mustard and salad rocket, and bitter chicory and endive, salads will never be boring again. You can even snip in a few chives for a hint of onion. Grow a range with different tastes and colours, and provide shelter from hot sun for the best leaves.

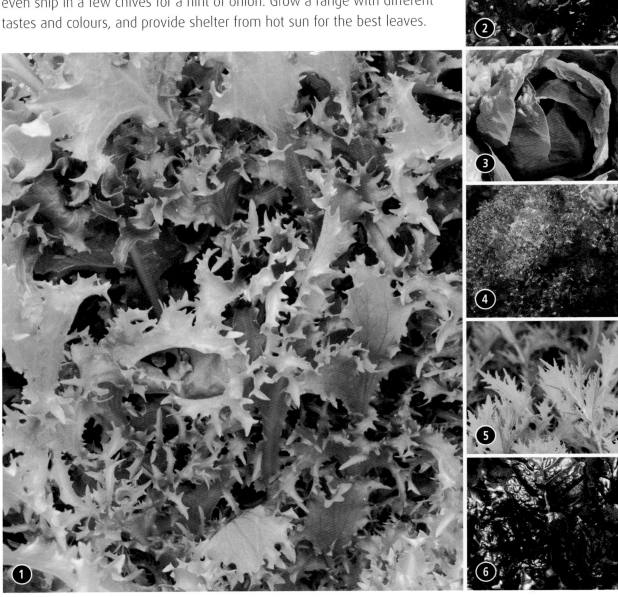

❀❀❀ fully hardy   ❀❀ hardy in mild regions/sheltered sites   ❀ protect from frost over winter
☼ full sun   ☼ partial sun   ☀ full shade   ◊ well-drained soil   ◐ moist soil   ● wet soil

① Endive 'Pancalieri'; ‡10cm (4in) ↔30cm (12in) ☼ ◐ ❀❀❀   **②** Lettuce 'Red Oakleaf'; ‡20cm (8in)
↔30cm (12in) ☼ ◐ ❀❀   **③** Lettuce 'Tin Tin'; ‡30cm (12in) ↔20cm (8in) ☼ ◐ ❀❀   **④** Lettuce 'Lollo
Rosso'; ‡20cm (8in) ↔20cm (8in) ☼ ◐ ❀❀   **⑤** Mizuna; ‡30cm (12in) ↔30cm (12in) ☼ ◐ ❀❀❀
⑥ Lettuce 'Rosemoor'; ‡30cm (12in) ↔30cm (12in) ☼ ◐ ❀❀   **⑦** Radicchio; ‡30cm (12in) ↔30cm
(12in) ☼ ◐ ❀❀❀   **⑧** Rocket; ‡30cm (12in) ↔10cm (4in) ☼ ◐ ❀❀❀   **⑨** Oriental mustard; ‡30cm
(12in) ↔30cm (12in) ☼ ◐ ❀❀❀   **⑩** Chives; ‡30cm (12in) ↔30cm (12in) ☼ ◐ ❀❀❀
⑪ Red-veined sorrel; ‡20cm (8in) ↔30cm (12in) ☼ ◐ ❀❀❀

Pot up delicious strawberries

Growing strawberries in containers suits them perfectly because it lifts the fruits off the ground, keeping them away from slugs, mice, and other pests, as well as wet soil that can cause the berries to rot. Replace your strawberries with fresh, young plants every few years.

 WHEN TO PLANT
Early spring

AT THEIR BEST
Summer

TIME TO COMPLETE

 1½ hours

YOU WILL NEED

 Three strawberry plants
Large pot
Broken clay pot pieces
Multi-purpose compost
Slow-release granular fertilizer
Bark chips
Straw

1 PREPARE TO PLANT
Take three young, healthy plants and water them thoroughly, an hour before planting. Cover the holes in the base of the large pot with broken clay pieces to prevent compost from blocking them, and then add compost until the pot is two-thirds full. Firm down lightly.

2 EASE PLANTS FROM SMALL CONTAINERS

Take the plants out of their pots and check the roots. If they are root bound, and running in tight circles inside the pot, tease them out carefully to help the plants establish quicker.

3 PLANT AROUND EDGE OF POT

Place the three plants around the edges of the pot so that the fruits will dangle over. Fill all around them with compost, add some fertilizer granules and then firm down. Water well, and daily thereafter.

4 REMOVE FLOWERS

You will have healthier plants in the long run if you sacrifice the first year's fruits, allowing them to concentrate on root growth. Nip out the flowers as they appear. The following year, apply a tomato fertilizer every week after the flower buds form.

TOP TIP: PROTECTING THE FRUITS

Strawberry fruits can rot if they come into contact with wet soil. While most grown in a pot will hang over the sides, avoid any problems by placing a straw mulch around the top of the pot to lift fruits away from the compost.

Tip-top berries

Strawberries can also be grown in hanging baskets or windowboxes. Dainty, tasty alpines are the best choice for this type of container.

WHEN TO PLANT
Early spring

AT THEIR BEST
Summer

TIME TO COMPLETE
1½ hours

YOU WILL NEED
Alpine strawberry plants
Hanging basket or windowbox
Multi-purpose compost
Slow-release granular fertilizer

1 PLANT THE WINDOWBOX

Plant small plants fairly close together to give an impressive show, and a good harvest. Add some slow-release fertilizer granules to the compost as you plant, and keep the plants well watered throughout the year.

2 HARVESTING AND CARE

Harvest and eat the berries as they ripen throughout summer. Check the plants frequently and pick regularly to encourage later fruits to ripen. The plants will need lifting out of the pot and dividing every three or four years.

Make space for autumn berries

The sweet, refreshing taste of raspberries and the mellow, hedgerow flavour of blackberries make them great additions to the productive garden. They can be eaten fresh, cooked and made into delicious puddings, or preserved as tasty jams or jellies to eat throughout the year.

Raspberries

Vigorous and easy to grow, autumn-fruiting raspberries look after themselves once established, and just need regular pruning to stop them from spreading.

 WHEN TO PLANT
Autumn
AT THEIR BEST
Early to mid-autumn

TIME TO COMPLETE

 2 hours

YOU WILL NEED

 Raspberry canes
Well-rotted organic matter, such as farmyard manure
Spade
Mulch
Stakes and thick wire

1 SELECT SITE AND PLANT
Raspberries prefer a moist soil and grow in sun or partial shade. Dig in plenty of organic matter and plant canes in a row. Water well and apply a mulch.

2 SUPPORT AND TRAIN
Cut the canes to the ground after planting. They can grow quite unwieldy in summer and it is important to provide a strong support. Hammer two sturdy wooden stakes into the ground and string thick wires between them at 60cm (24in) intervals. Tie in the stems.

3 ROUTINE CARE
During the first year after planting, pinch off any fruits that form, to allow the plant to concentrate its energies on root growth. Then, each year after fruiting, cut the fruited canes to the ground. Tie new canes to the support – these will produce fruit the following year.

Blackberry pot

Blackberries are usually big plants and unsuitable for pots, but the thornless varieties are less vigorous and can be successfully grown in a large container. They are amenable plants and can grow well in sun or in partial shade.

WHEN TO PLANT
Autumn
AT ITS BEST
Late summer to early autumn

TIME TO COMPLETE
1 hour

YOU WILL NEED

Blackberry plant, 'Loch Maree' used here
Large pot
Soil-based compost, such as John Innes No.3
Broken clay pot pieces
Canes or trellis for support

1 PLANT UP AND FEED
Place the clay pieces in the bottom of the container to aid drainage and to prevent the holes from blocking up. Fill with compost and plant. Most compost contains enough nutrients for the first few months, but in summer in subsequent years apply a tomato feed every week to promote flowering and fruiting.

2 TIE IN STEMS
Blackberries produce long growths that need tying in. Insert a few strong canes into the compost, or place the container up against a sturdy trellis. When tying, create a "figure of eight" so that the stem does not make direct contact with the support, which could lead to rubbing and the creation of wounds.

3 PRUNING AND CARE
Blackberries always fruit on the previous year's stems. Therefore, just after you have harvested your crop, remove any stems that have fruited by cutting them at their base. Tie any new stems into the supports; these should fruit the following year. Replace the top layer of compost with fresh every spring.

Grow super fruit

Every few years another food is labelled a "super food" because of its high levels of antioxidants, vitamins, and nutrients. Many of these berries are easy to grow in your own garden, and on a patio in a large container, giving you instant access to some of the healthiest foods available.

Aronia berries

Commonly known as chokeberry, *Aronia* has the highest level of cancer- and age-fighting antioxidant, anthocyanin, of any fruit. The berries are tart when eaten raw, and are best combined with other ingredients or sweetened.

GROWING TIPS

Aronia grows well in a range of conditions, but is best in a moist, acidic soil, in partial shade or full sun. Incorporate plenty of organic matter before planting. It is a large, shubby plant, reaching 2m (6ft) tall, with a 3m (10ft) spread. As attractive as it is productive, *Aronia* flowers in late spring, and has superb autumn colour that complements the dark berries, so plant where it will be seen.

AFTERCARE

This plant should be kept moist at all times, especially during the first year. Apply a thick mulch of chipped bark after planting to help retain moisture and suppress weeds. *Aronia* takes a few years to establish and reach full productivity, so be patient. You may need to protect plants from birds when the berries are ripe; they develop their best flavour after hard frosts.

∧ *Nutritious berries*
Dark purple Aronia *berries have even higher levels of health-promoting antioxidants than the celebrated blueberry.*

∨ *Autumn blaze*
The foliage turns pretty shades of red and orange in autumn, just as the berries are ripening.

Goji berries

These berries contain large amounts of vitamin C and iron. In China they are most often used in savoury dishes, such as soups – a handful is thrown in towards the end of cooking – or they are stewed to make tea.

GROWING TIPS
Goji plants are fully hardy shrubs, and prefer fertile, well-drained soil in a sunny spot. When planting, incorporate lots of well-rotted organic matter, such as farmyard manure, and keep them well watered for the first year. They flower in late spring and summer, but are unlikely to produce a worthwhile crop until the third year after planting.

DRYING BERRIES
Use the berries when fresh, or dry them for storing. Place them in the oven on its lowest temperature, with the door open, for a few hours, then store the berries in clean, dry, airtight jars.

Honeyberries

Honeyberries have a blueberry-like appearance and taste, although they are not generally thought to be as sweet and flavoursome. However, they will grow in any soil, unlike the blueberry, which requires acidic conditions.

GROWING TIPS
You need two plants of different cultivars for one to pollinate the other, otherwise they will not fruit. It can be tricky finding cultivars that flower at the same time, so ask suppliers when purchasing. This is a hardy shrub that prefers semi-shade, and moist, well-drained soil. Plants can have a wayward habit, so prune after fruiting. Pick when the fruit is soft but leave them for two days before using to allow the flavours to develop. Honeyberry fruits the second year after planting.

Jostaberries

This is a cross between a blackcurrant and a gooseberry and is extremely vigorous, so only plant it where you have plenty of space. The fruit makes particularly good jam.

GROWING TIPS
Jostaberries are unfussy about soil, but will benefit from plenty of organic matter. Choose a sheltered spot in full sun. They are self-fertile and resistant to many of the pests and diseases that affect gooseberries and blackcurrants. Their vigour means they are useful as informal hedging. Birds love the fruit, so net the plant well at ripening time, or plant in a fruit cage.

Plant fruit in a small space

Even if you have no garden soil in which to plant, you can still grow a fruit tree if you make your choice carefully. Almost all fruit trees can be bought grown on dwarfing rootstocks, and are happy in large containers, as long as they're well watered and fed. Such small trees can be surprisingly bountiful.

 WHEN TO START
Late winter

AT ITS BEST
Autumn

TIME TO COMPLETE

 1 hour

YOU WILL NEED

 A large pot
Broken clay pot pieces
John Innes No.3 compost
Slow-release granular fertilizer
A dwarf fruit tree
Pebbles or chips for mulch

1 BEFORE PLANTNG
Fruit trees grown in containers are almost totally dependent on the fertilizer and water you give them. So, to give your tree the best start and to help it establish, soak the root ball before planting, as it is hard to wet dry roots thoroughly afterwards. The best way to do this is to immerse the pot in a large bucket of water and leave it to soak for about an hour, or until the soil surface is damp. Then, lift the tree from the bucket and allow it to drain.

2 PREPARE TO PLANT
Choose a large pot with a wide base so that the tree is not easily blown over, and stand it in a sunny, sheltered spot. Make sure it has plenty of drainage holes, or drill your own, and cover them with a layer of broken clay pot pieces to prevent compost blocking them up. Fill the base with compost, and add a sprinkling of slow-release fertilizer.

3 TEASE OUT ROOTS
Place the tree in the pot, adding or removing compost, until the top of the root ball is about 5cm (2in) below the rim. Then lift the plant, remove its original pot, and tease out the roots from the root ball. This encourages the roots to grow out into the compost, stabilizing the tree, and helping it to establish quickly. Place the tree in the container.

4 BACKFILL, STAKE AND MULCH
Fill the gaps around the root ball with more compost and water well. Unless the tree already has a stake or cane, insert one now to hold the tree upright and to help anchor it in the pot. If it has a cane, carefully push it down into the new compost below. To conserve moisture and suppress weeds, apply a mulch of small pebbles or chipped bark.

Fruit trees are commonly grown on dwarf rootstocks, which limit the size of the tree. To grow fruit in containers, choose apples grown on M26, M9 or, for really small containers, M27. Look for pears grown on Quince C, cherries on Gisela 5, and for plums and damsons, choose those grown on Pixy.

5 WATERING AND FEEDING

It is essential to keep the fruit tree well watered, filling the pot to the brim each time. To encourage the best crop, don't allow it to dry out when in flower or fruit, and feed using a tomato fertilizer every two weeks during spring and summer. Although dormant, also water the tree during mild dry spells in late autumn and winter.

Fruit for large containers

You can grow a mini-orchard of fruit in patio containers if you're happy to water and feed regularly. Choose from soft fruits, such as currants and gooseberries, or tree fruits like apples, pears, and cherries, grown on dwarfing rootstocks. Renew the top layer of compost every year for the best crop.

RED, WHITE, AND BLACKCURRANTS

These delicious fruits need moisture-retentive soil, and those in pots must be watered regularly during the growing season. Plant them in large containers filled with soil-based compost, such as John Innes No.3, mixed with well-rotted organic matter — garden compost or manure is ideal. You can either grow them as bushes or train them on a trellis like a climber (*see pp.118–119*). Apply a general fertilizer for fruit crops in spring, and top up with tomato fertilizer every week from late spring until the fruits ripen. Cover the blooms with fleece if frosts are forecast. Site in a cool, partly shaded spot. For pruning, see gooseberries (*below*).

GOOSEBERRIES

The sharp sweetness of gooseberries is perfect for summer puddings and pies. Planting and feeding requirements are the same as for currants (*see above*), and if the crop is heavy, thin the fruits in late spring. Every winter, cut back the main stems by one half to an outward-facing bud, and prune the sideshoots to one bud from the main stems (beware of the spines). Keep the plants well watered and harvest ripe fruit in summer.

PEACHES AND CHERRIES

The best fruit trees for pots are those grown on dwarfing rootstocks that produce full-sized fruit. Cherries are grafted on to Colt or Gisela 5 rootstocks, and peaches on Pixy or St Julien A. Good cherries include 'Compact Stella' and 'Maynard Mini Stem'; for peaches try, 'Bonanza' and 'Garden Lady'. Plant in large pots of soil-based compost, such as John Innes No.3, keep in a sheltered, sunny spot, and protect the blossom with fleece. Feed in spring with all-purpose fertilizer, and apply tomato food every fortnight after flowering. No pruning is needed.

APPLES AND PEARS

Popular for pots, apples grown on the dwarf rootstocks M27, M9, or M26, which should be stated on the label, are widely available. The choice of pears is smaller, but look for those grown on Quince C or Quince A. All these compact trees produce full-sized fruit. If you have space, grow several and enjoy a variety of different flavours from late summer and throughout the autumn. Popular apple varieties include 'Egremont Russet', 'Cox's Orange Pippin', 'Discovery', golden yellow 'Elstar', and 'Blenheim Orange', with its crisp, nutty flavour. The pear varieties 'Williams' Bon Chrétien', 'Doyenné du Comice' and 'Dwarf Lilliput' are ideal for containers. If space is really limited, you can buy two different fruits grafted on to one rootstock, offering two flavours for the price of one. Planting and care is the same for apples and pears (*see pp.296-297*). Keep pots well watered throughout the spring and summer.

❶ 'Fiesta' apples are widely available on dwarf rootstocks, and are sometimes sold as 'Red Pippin'. The red fruit has a flavour very similar to English 'Cox's Orange Pippin', and is ready to pick in mid-autumn.

❷ Disease- and frost-resistant, 'Red Falstaff' has a sweet, mellow flavour. It is ready to harvest in mid-autumn and stores well.

❸ 'Pixie' is a small, sweet apple that is produced in abundance even on small trees. To avoid too many tiny fruits, thin them in early summer. Pick your crop in mid-autumn.

❹ Commonly referred to as the Williams pear, 'Williams' Bon Chrétien', is the most widely grown, and should be harvested while the fruit is still hard.

❺ Harvest the nutty-flavoured 'Egremont Russet' in early autumn and the fruit will store till spring. Heavy cropping and resistant to disease, it is a great apple for those who enjoy something a bit different.

Plant tasty tart fruit

Some fruits lend themselves to cooking. With the addition of a little sugar or honey, cooked rhubarb is transformed from super-sharp to pure nectar. Blueberries can be delicious raw, depending on how ripe they are, but their flavour really comes to life when they are baked in muffins or cakes.

1 CHOOSE AN OPEN SUNNY SITE
Dig in organic matter, plant and water in well. Protect your plant from slugs, either using a copper slug ring or with a few slug pellets (*see p.426*).

TOP TIP: FORCING RHUBARB

Forcing rhubarb, by excluding all light when it first sprouts, results in sweeter, more tender stalks. As soon as you notice new shoots starting to appear in spring, cover the plant with a light-excluding barrier, such as a metal bucket, a box, or a rhubarb forcer, which will draw up the sweet stalks. The tender stems will be ready to pick about four weeks later – a month or so earlier than other rhubarb. Pick this crop, then leave the plant to recover for the rest of the year, and the following year.

Rhubarb

Once established, rhubarb looks after itself year after year. All you need do is pull as many stalks as you can eat.

> **WHEN TO PLANT**
> Late autumn
>
> **AT ITS BEST**
> Early summer

TIME TO COMPLETE

🕐 1 hour

YOU WILL NEED

🛈 Rhubarb plant
Well-rotted organic matter, such as farmyard manure
Spade
Slug pellets or a slug ring

2 HARVEST STALKS
Water during dry spells. Feed every spring with an organic liquid fertilizer, and mulch with well-rotted manure. Do not pull any stalks the first year and only one or two in the second year. After that you can harvest more. To harvest, pull and slightly twist the stems.

Blueberry pots

These small, delicious berries are regarded as "super foods" because they are particularly high in vitamins and antioxidants. They need an acidic soil, and to guarantee fruit you should grow two different cultivars together.

WHEN TO PLANT
Mid-autumn

AT THEIR BEST
Summer

TIME TO COMPLETE

 1½ hours

YOU WILL NEED

Two blueberry plants
Two large pots
Broken clay pot pieces
Ericaceous compost and fertilizer
Mulch, such as bark chippings
Rainwater

1 PLANT IN LARGE POTS
Place broken clay pieces in the base of each large pot and part-fill with ericaceous compost. Plant the blueberry plants at the same depth as they were in their original pots, and fill in around the root balls with more compost, to within 5cm (2in) of the rim.

2 ADD FERTILIZER
To ensure a good crop, add a slow-release ericaceous fertilizer to the compost, following the instructions on the packet. Most slow-release fertilizers last for a limited period, so re-apply as specified. Don't use non-ericaceous fertilizers, as these could harm your plants.

3 WATER AND MULCH
As tap water often tends to be alkaline, use rainwater to water the plant thoroughly. Then place a mulch of bark chippings over the compost to help retain moisture. Water daily with rainwater. The berries will ripen over a few weeks; pick as required.

Grow Thai herbs and spices

Deliciously spicy, Thai and other Asian cooking relies on three key ingredients: the seeds and leaves of coriander, lemon grass, with its citrus-flavoured stalks, and hot ginger roots. Instead of buying them at the supermarket, grow these easy, tender plants at home on a windowsill, or in the garden in summer.

Coriander

Grow this annual herb in a sunny spot for its lemony seeds and spicy leaves, which add a fresh taste to dishes.

 WHEN TO PLANT
Spring

AT ITS BEST
Spring to autumn

TIME TO COMPLETE
 30 minutes

YOU WILL NEED
 Coriander seeds or plug plants
Modular seed tray
Seed compost
Deep container
Broken clay pot pieces
Soil-based compost, such as
 John Innes No.2
Watering can with fine rose

1 SOW AND PLANT UP
Fill a modular seed tray with seed compost. Scatter seed on the surface, cover with a little compost, and water. Keep in a sunny spot and water frequently. Thin congested seedlings once they have a few leaves. Coriander plants have long roots, so when the seedlings are growing well, line the base of a deep container with clay pieces, and fill it with soil-based compost.

2 CARE FOR YOUR PLANTS
Plant up the coriander, and keep it well watered; drought stress will cause plants to run to seed. Remove any flower stems immediately. Cut the stems and leaves when mature; a new set may then grow, giving a second crop. Alternatively, allow plants to run to seed, put the cut seedheads in a paper bag, and hang them upside down until the seeds drop.

Lemon grass

The stems of this tender aromatic herb have a tangy lemon taste. Fresh stems, bought from specialist Asian groceries and supermarkets, root easily to create new plants. Select firm stems that have a woody, light brown base.

 WHEN TO PLANT
Spring
AT ITS BEST
All year round

 TIME TO COMPLETE
30 minutes

YOU WILL NEED
 Fresh lemon grass stems
Glass or jar of water
Sharp knife
8cm (3½in) plastic pots
Soil-based compost
Liquid houseplant fertilizer
Decorative indoor planter

∧ *Leafy house plant*
As well as spicing up Asian dishes, lemon grass makes a beautiful house plant. The stems bulk up quickly, ready for harvest.

1 ROOT THE STEMS
Buy fresh lemon grass stems and put the bulbous ends in a jar of water. Stand them on a bright windowsill for a few weeks until a good root system has developed. Change the water weekly.

2 TRIM AND PLANT
Fill small pots with soil-based compost, such as John Innes No.2. Trim off the top of each stem and pot the young plants up. Water well, and keep on a warm, sunny windowsill, or in a greenhouse.

3 AFTERCARE
Water well during summer, and apply a liquid fertilizer every two weeks. Pot them on into larger pots as they grow. In winter, keep the compost just moist. To harvest, cut the stems close to the roots.

Ginger

Ginger plants grow up to 1m (3ft) tall and make stunning house plants, as well as providing tasty edible roots that you can use fresh or freeze. It is not hardy, so grow it indoors, except in summer.

YOU WILL NEED
 Ginger roots
8cm (3½in) plastic pots
Soil-based compost, such as
 John Innes No.2
Large pot
Liquid fertilizer

1 PREPARE THE POT
Choose a ginger root with some pale knobbly eyes, which will grow into shoots. Fill a pot with compost and plant the ginger, just covering the eyes. Water well, and keep in a light spot.

2 PLANT ON
When shoots appear, move it out of direct sunlight, and repot the plant as it grows. In summer, stand it outside and feed fortnightly with liquid fertilizer. In autumn, allow it to dry out and the foliage to die back. Harvest the roots but keep a piece to grow again next spring.

Grow citrus fruit

Citrus prefer to grow outdoors in the summer, and only need frost-free conditions to see them through the winter. With a little care, they flower and fruit well, and make beautiful patio plants.

Lemon tree from a pip

Growing lemon trees from pips is good fun, especially for children, and although they flower as quite young plants, it takes a number of years before they fruit. In the meantime, they make attractive, highly fragrant, house and patio plants.

>> **WHEN TO START**
Spring

AT ITS BEST
All year round

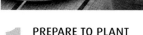

TIME TO COMPLETE
 30 minutes

YOU WILL NEED
 Lemon pips
Pots
Seed compost
Soil-based compost

1 PREPARE TO PLANT
Cut open a lemon, remove the pips, and dry them. Plant several pips per pot, 1cm (½in) deep, in seed compost. Water them in and put the pots in a warm area. Keep them well watered.

2 POT ON
Once the young seedlings are growing well, remove them from their pots and carefully tease their roots apart. Pot them on individually into their own small pots of soil-based compost. Water them in.

3 AFTERCARE
Place the pots in a sunny spot, and keep well watered. Grow in a cool room indoors, or in a greenhouse over winter; place outside in the summer and early autumn, until the first frosts are forecast. Water with rainwater, if possible, and watch out for aphids, scale insects and mealy bugs.

Citrus options

Citrus have a fabulous variety of fruit colour and texture, and many of these beautiful plants can be grown fairly easily. Some may survive the winter outdoors in milder areas, but they grow best with a little protection.

GROWING AND CARE

Citrus plants need plenty of water during spring and summer, less during winter. Use rainwater where possible, particularly in hard water areas. Feed with a specially formulated citrus fertilizer throughout the growing season. Indoors, mist daily with rainwater to keep humidity high and to help ward off red spider mite. A little warmth in late winter and spring will encourage the citrus to flower, and then, hopefully, fruit.

❶ Calamondin orange, x *Citrofortunella microcarpa*, is a kumquat–orange hybrid, and one of the easiest citrus to grow indoors. It produces scented flowers all year round and has sour fruit. ❷ Kaffir lime, *Citrus hystrix*, is most often grown for its fragrant leaves, an essential ingredient in Thai cooking, but it also bears knobbly, very sour fruit. ❸ Key lime, *Citrus aurantifolia*, with its thin skin and delicious flavour, is the lime commonly used to make daiquiris and margaritas. ❹ Kumquat, *Fortunella japonica*, is one of the most attractive, and easiest of all citrus to grow. It is hardy and flowers in summer.

< *Perfect for patios*
This pretty lemon tree, like other citrus fruits, is happiest outside in summer, and makes a great patio feature. Just bring it indoors for the winter.

Grow nuts

Nuts are attractive trees, and produce tasty autumn treats that are expensive to buy in the shops. They grow well in cool climates, and require just a little attention once planted. Almonds and hazels are the smallest of the nut trees, and both are very easy to grow in the garden.

Almonds

As well as producing nuts in autumn, almonds produce a beautiful display of pale pink blossom in spring.

WHEN TO PLANT
Late autumn
AT THEIR BEST
Spring and late summer

TIME TO COMPLETE
 3 hours
YOU WILL NEED
Almond tree
Spade
Stake
Tree tie
Secateurs
Pruning saw

1 SITE AND PLANTING
Choose an open, sunny spot with deep, fertile, well-drained soil. Avoid planting in frost pockets, as almonds flower in spring and their blooms are easily damaged. Plant and stake the tree (*see pp.178–179 for planting instructions*). If your tree is not self-pollinating, you will need to plant two.

2 PRUNE AND HARVEST
Prune your almond trees to keep a good, open shape, but only in summer, as they are susceptible to silver leaf disease (*see p.432*). Once the almond hulls have cracked open, harvest the nuts by knocking them from the tree. Slit the hulls, remove the nuts, and dry them.

Hazel and cobnuts

Hazels are round, hard, chewy nuts that commonly grow in hedgerows. Cobnuts are a slightly elongated, cultivated form of hazel, and are particularly good for eating. Both grow well in a range of conditions, and produce nuts from a young age.

 WHEN TO PLANT
Late autumn or spring
AT THEIR BEST
Late summer

 TIME TO COMPLETE
🕐 2 hours

YOU WILL NEED
Hazelnut plant
Spade
Stake
Tree tie
Organic matter for mulch

1 SITE AND PLANTING
Hazels prefer well-drained soil and a position in full sun or partial shade. Plant two hazel trees in your garden to guarantee cross pollination and a good crop of nuts. Plant bare-root plants in late autumn; pot-grown ones in spring. Plant and stake the tree (*see pp.178–179 for planting instructions*). After planting, water well, and apply a layer of mulch.

2 PRUNE AND HARVEST
Water the tree regularly for the first year. Once the plant is established, and has been growing for at least two years, prune the strongest, upright stems to the ground to encourage flowering side shoots. Hazelnuts can be harvested young and eaten fresh and green, or left to turn brown on the plant, and then harvested and stored.

Home-grown hazel pea sticks

As well as nuts, hazel produces woody stems that are particularly useful in the garden. Pea sticks (as they are known) make great supports for peas, which is how they got their name, as well as annual climbing flowers and a range of other tall vegetables. Longer hazel poles can be made into rustic obelisks and sturdy frames for runner beans.

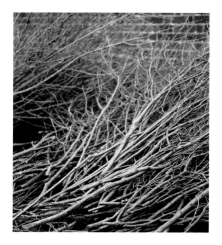

 WHEN TO START
Winter
AT THEIR BEST
Summer

 TIME TO COMPLETE
🕐 2 hours

YOU WILL NEED
A mature hazel plant
Pruning tool, such as loppers or
 a pruning saw

1 GROW PEA STICKS
Allow your hazel tree to grow unpruned for three or four years. The most useful pea sticks are those stems with shrubby, branching growth, which will be well developed on a mature plant. Then, in winter, simply thin out your hazel plant, take the stems you need, and leave the rest to grow and produce nuts. Store the stems in a cool, airy place until you need them in late spring or summer.

2 GROW HAZEL POLES
For long, straight poles cut all the stems of an established hazel plant to the ground in winter (*see also p.230*). New growth forms poles, which will be ready to harvest in five years. Grow several plants to get a regular harvest.

Create a parterre

A parterre is a pattern of box or other evergreen hedging, with the areas in between filled with other plants. Traditionally, the hedging would be the permanent structure, and the infill made up of temporary plants, such as bedding or vegetables. However, they also make beautiful herb beds, as shown here.

» WHEN TO START
Spring
AT ITS BEST
Summer

TIME TO COMPLETE

 4 hours for the small parterre, measuring 1m (3ft) x 1.2m (4ft), above.

YOU WILL NEED

Small box plants,
Buxus sempervirens 'Suffruticosa'
1 bay tree, *Laurus nobilis*

Shrubby herbs, such
as rosemary, lavender, curry plant, cotton lavender, and thyme – 3 plants per segment
Spade
Grit
Organic matter
Rake
Landscape fabric
Measuring tape
Chalk
Short canes or pegs
Sharp knife
Slate chippings

1 PREPARE THE SOIL
First, decide on the design you want and sketch it on paper – this parterre is a simple cross pattern. Then clear the area of grass and weeds, and add organic matter, such as well-rotted farmyard manure or garden compost, to improve the soil's structure. Silver-leaved herbs like well-drained soil, so if yours is heavy, add plenty of grit to help water drain away. Level the area carefully with a rake.

2 LAY AND SECURE LANDSCAPE FABRIC

The entire area should be covered in a good quality landscape fabric to suppress weeds and keep moisture in. Pin down the edges securely or slide them under the existing turf.

3 MARK OUT A HEDGING PLAN

Use a measuring tape and chalk to mark out your pattern. Space the hedging plants at 20cm (8in) intervals; insert short canes to mark their positions. The plants will quickly spread to form a dense hedge.

4 PLANT UP

With a sharp knife, cut a cross in the landscape fabric at each planting point. Make small planting holes. Insert the box plants and firm them in. Then fold the landscape fabric back around the stem of the plants.

5 ARRANGE HERBS FOR THE FINAL DESIGN

Place your selected herbs, while still in their pots, in the gaps between the hedging plants, and arrange them until they look right. Put the bay tree in its terracotta pot at the centre of your parterre to create a focal point.

6 APPLY A LAYER OF SLATE CHIPPINGS

Plant the herbs, water them in and then cover the whole parterre in a layer of slate chippings. This will hide the landscape fabric and further help to seal in moisture. Other mulching materials can be used, such as gravel or shingle.

TOP TIP: ENCOURAGE BUSHY GROWTH

Allow the box plants to grow a little taller than their required height, but nip off the tips of the side shoots to encourage bushy growth. When the plants are tall enough, set a line of string at the right height and clip along the hedge with shears.

Essential kitchen herbs

Herbs are easy to grow, look good, taste and smell amazing, and many of them are magnets for bees and butterflies. Most take up little space – a trough or a sink will fit a selection of the most useful – and planted up in this way, you can keep them within arms' reach of the kitchen door. You can freeze or dry them, and even grow them on a windowsill indoors during winter. Just keep picking the leaves to keep your plants compact and bushy.

✿✿✿ fully hardy   ✿✿ hardy in mild regions/sheltered sites   ✿ protect from frost over winter
☼ full sun   ☀ partial sun   ☀ full shade   ◊ well-drained soil   ◑ moist soil   ● wet soil

1 Basil; ↕45cm (18in) ↔45cm (18in) ☼ ◑ ✿   **2** Apple mint; ↕70cm (28in) ↔70cm (28in)
☼ ◑ ✿✿✿   **3** Thyme; ↕12cm (5in) ↔75cm (30in) ☼ ◊ ✿✿✿   **4** Flat-leaved parsley; ↕30cm (12in)
↔30cm (12in) ☀ ◑ ✿✿✿   **5** Golden oregano; ↕30cm (12in) ↔30cm (12in) ☼ ◊ ✿✿✿
6 Variegated lemon balm; ↕60cm (24in) ↔40cm (16in) ☀ ◑ ✿✿✿   **7** Chives; ↕30cm (12in) ↔30cm
(12in) ☼ ◑ ✿✿✿   **8** Coriander; ↕40cm (16in) ↔30cm (12in) ☼ ◊ ✿   **9** Rosemary; ↕1.2m (4ft)
↔1.2m (4ft) ☼ ◊ ✿✿✿   **10** Variegated sage; ↕1m (3ft) ↔1m (3ft) ☼ ◊ ✿✿✿   **11** Fennel; ↕2m (6ft)
↔45cm (18in) ☼ ◑ ✿✿✿

Grow a basket of crops

Hang a basket brimming with leafy herbs and succulent tomatoes close to your kitchen door for easy access to fresh ingredients. With a sprinkling of annual flowers, this pretty mix is a match for any bedding scheme, and the herbs emit a wonderful scent at just the right height for you to enjoy.

>> **WHEN TO START**
Mid- to late spring

AT ITS BEST
Summer

TIME TO COMPLETE
 2 hours

YOU WILL NEED
 Large hanging basket with liner
Soil-based compost mixed 50:50
with multi-purpose compost

Slow-release granular fertilizer
Plastic bags
Gravel mulch
Liquid tomato fertilizer
Tomato plants
Violas and nasturtiums
Herbs; those used here are:
 Basil 'Magic Mountain'
 Chives
 Flat-leaved parsley
 Thyme

1 PREPARE THE BASKET
Buy the largest basket you can find, ideally with an integrated liner — because tomatoes are greedy feeders and need lots of water, they may not be as successful in a small basket that holds a limited amount of compost, water, and food. Line the base of the basket with a sheet of plastic to create a reservoir at the bottom. Stand the plants in a tray of water for 30 minutes until the top of the compost is moist. Remove, and leave them to drain.

2 PLANT THE SIDES
Half-fill the basket with compost. Cut two or three crosses in the liner above the compost. Tip a thyme plant from its pot and wrap the leaves in a plastic bag. Carefully push the bag from the inside out through a slit, so the root ball is resting on the soil. Repeat with the other thymes.

Basket care >
Never allow your basket of tomatoes to dry out or the fruits may split (see p.273). Remove spent flowers to encourage more to form.

3 MIX IN FERTILIZER
Fill in around the thyme root balls with compost mixed with slow-release fertilizer. Top up the basket with more compost to 10cm (4in) from the rim.

4 ADD THE PLANTS
Set out your plants in their pots to check that they fit. Then plant them up at the same level they were at in their pots, with the tomato plants at the edge and the basil in the middle of the basket.

5 WATER DAILY
Add a gravel mulch. Hang the basket on a strong bracket (*see p.130*) in a sunny spot. Water daily and feed every week with a tomato fertilizer. Harvest leaves from the herbs as you need them, and pick the tomatoes when ripe.

Herb circle

Herbs make an inspiring feature when grown together, and tend to like similar conditions. Soften an area of hard landscaping by allowing space for a circle of these colourful, low-growing, culinary plants.

WHEN TO PLANT
Spring
AT ITS BEST
Summer

TIME TO COMPLETE
🕐 4 hours

YOU WILL NEED
Horticultural grit
Spade
Trowel
3 small terracotta pots
A selection of herbs, for example:

1. Chives and fennel (here planted in a central pot)
2. Oregano
3. Parsley
4. Violas (as a decorative filler)
5. Lemon balm
6. Mint
7. Thyme (also in pot)

1 LIGHTEN THE SOIL
Most herbs prefer to grow in well-drained soil, so in all but the lightest soils it is important to dig in plenty of horticultural grit before planting. Do not add to individual planting holes, but dig it in thoroughly over the whole area.

2 ADD PLANTS
Lay out the herbs before planting. Place three of each plant in a triangle so that they will form the "wedges" of the circle once they have grown together. Plant the mint in individual terracotta or plastic pots to contain the roots, and sink these into the soil.

3 AFTERCARE
Water the herbs in well after planting and keep them watered while they settle in. All plants are hardy and can be left in the bed, but the parsley and violas will need refreshing with new plants every year or two.

TOP TIP: PROMOTE NEW GROWTH

Harvesting and pruning are the same job when you are growing herbs. Nip out the tips of the plants regularly to use in the kitchen, and to help keep the plants bushy and compact.

Enjoy fruit from the Med

Juicy peaches and fresh figs in cream are irresistible, and you can grow these delicious fruits at home. Just plant them against a sheltered, south-facing wall, and they should produce plenty of fruit.

Figs for a wall

Figs are handsome plants but their roots must be restricted if they are to fruit well. Plant them in a sheltered spot, protect the young figs over winter, and feed in spring with a granular fertilizer and a dose of high-potash fertilizer in late summer.

 WHEN TO PLANT
Winter
AT THEIR BEST
Summer

TIME TO COMPLETE
 2 hours to plant; 1 hour to prune

 YOU WILL NEED
Two-year-old pot grown fig tree
Paving stones
Rubble, eg, broken bricks
Wires, vine eyes and twine
Well-rotted organic matter, such
 as farmyard manure
Granular tree and high-potash
 fertilizers
Secateurs

1 DIG A PIT
To restrict the fig's roots, dig a pit 60cm (2ft) square and deep, next to the wall. Line the sides with paving stones, but not the base. Add a 25cm (10in) layer of rubble to the base for drainage, and top up with garden soil.

2 PLANT THE FIG
Fix horizontal wires to the wall (see p.212). Water the tree, then plant it in the centre of the pit at the same depth it was in its pot. Firm in, and water well. Apply a mulch of organic matter, keeping it clear of the stem. Tie the side stems to the wires, and remove any growing towards or away from the wall. Water regularly for the first year, and in dry periods thereafter.

3 AFTERCARE AND HARVEST
In late spring the tree will produce some figs; then, in late summer, you will see a second crop of embryo fruits. In late autumn remove fruits larger than a pea, as they tend to rot over winter, and protect the embryos against frost with fleece; these will then ripen the following summer. Trim the tree in summer to encourage more fruit (see Top Tip, right).

TOP TIP: PRUNING FIGS

In the spring after planting, cut back the main stem to encourage side shoots. The following spring, cut back these new stems by half, and remove weak growth. Cut over-long branches to 5cm (2in) to promote fresh growth.

< ∨ *Cutting back*
Prune out stems that block light from fruits (left). *In summer pinch out new shoots so five leaves remain on each stem* (below).

Peach fan

For a good crop of peaches, grow a fan-shaped tree against a warm wall, and protect the flowers from spring frosts. Mulch around the base of the tree in early spring with well-rotted organic matter, and feed with granular fertilizer. Enrich sandy soil with plenty of organic matter to help retain moisture and nutrients.

 WHEN TO PLANT
Late autumn

AT ITS BEST
Summer

TIME TO COMPLETE
 2 hours to plant; 1 hour to prune

YOU WILL NEED
Fan-trained peach tree
Wires and vine eyes
Well-rotted organic matter, such as farmyard manure
Bamboo canes
Granular shrub and tree fertilizer
Garden twine
Secateurs

1 BUY AND PLANT

Buy a partially trained two- or three-year-old fan, and check that it has eight branches. Fix wires to the wall (*see p.212*) and tie canes in a fan shape to the wires. Plant the peach 45cm (18in) from the wall and lean it towards the cane fan. Tie the stems, with four on each side, to the canes with twine.

TOP TIP: THIN OUT FRUIT

Peaches form in clusters and should be thinned to allow large fruit to form. When hazelnut-sized, remove fruit growing towards the wall, and thin to one per cluster. A few weeks later, thin to one fruit every 15cm (6in).

2 PROTECT FROM FROST

Water the tree regularly for the first year, and during dry spells thereafter. The blossoms appear in early spring and must be protected from frost. Fix a roll of fleece to the top of the wall. Secure a few long canes just in front of the tree, and roll the fleece down over the canes to cover the blossoms. Lift the screen after each frost to allow insects in to pollinate the flowers.

3 PRUNE FOR FRUIT

In early spring, remove stems growing towards or away from the wall. Then look for flowering stems, and select one strong side shoot at the base and another further up the same stem. Tie in these two new shoots to a cane or wire, and cut back all other side shoots along the stem to one leaf.

4 PRUNE AFTER FRUITING

After the flowering stem has produced fruit in summer, cut it back to the new shoot at its base, or if this failed, to the shoot further up. Also shorten overlapping stems and remove congested or dead wood. Ripe fruit is soft and gives slightly when pressed gently near the stalk. Eat as soon as possible.

Train fruit trees

If you think your garden is too small for a fruit tree, you may be wrong. Fruit trees are some of the most amenable plants; they can be trained along walls and fences, taking up very little space, and look beautiful and even fruit better when grown in this way.

 WHEN TO START
Winter
AT ITS BEST
Spring and autumn

TIME TO COMPLETE
 5 hours

YOU WILL NEED
Several bare-root cordon apple or
  pear trees
Bamboo canes
Well-rotted organic matter, such
  as farmyard manure
Spade
Wires, vine eyes, and twine
Mulch

1 MEASURE PLANTING DISTANCES
Fix horizontal wires to the fence or wall at 60cm (24in) intervals (see *pp.212–213*). Cordons can be planted as close together as 30cm (12in), depending on the effect you wish to create. Decide on your spacing, and measure along the wall or fence, marking each planting spot with a cane. Dig holes large enough to accommodate the root balls easily.

2 PLANT AND TRIM ROOTS
Plant the cordon at an angle of about 45° degrees. Examine the roots of each plant and cut off any that are large or woody, to encourage new feeding roots. Also, thin those that are above the soil. Ensure the graft union (scar on the stem) is above the surface.

3 ATTACH TREES TO CANES
Firm in the soil around the roots with your foot. Push the canes into the soil at the same angle as the trees. Tie the cordons to the canes, and tie the canes to the horizontal wires. Make sure all of your plants are securely fastened and aligned.

4 APPLY MULCH

Water the trees well after planting and apply a mulch of chipped bark, keeping clear of the stems, to retain moisture and suppress weeds. Water the trees regularly during their first year. Apply a tree and shrub granular fertilizer around the trees every spring, and replenish the mulch afterwards.

TOP TIP: ROUTINE PRUNING

Remove the flowers the first year after planting to encourage strong roots. Prune cordons each year in late summer. Shorten all woody sideshoots to within a few leaves of the stem to help promote fruiting spurs.

Plant a tiny orchard

Fruit trees work hard for their keep, providing a strong winter outline, a spring show of beautiful blossom, and a bountiful harvest in summer and autumn. They need little care once established and are well suited to small- and medium-sized gardens, particularly when they are grown on dwarfing rootstocks.

 WHEN TO START
Late autumn
AT THEIR BEST
Summer to autumn

TIME TO COMPLETE
 2 hours

YOU WILL NEED
Fruit tree or trees
Spade
Well-rotted organic
 matter, such as
 farmyard manure
Mulch
Stake
Tree tie

Apples and pears

These fruit-bowl regulars make characterful garden trees and their crop is unlikely to go to waste in most households. As they age, the trees take on a wonderfully gnarled appearance which sets off their spring blossom perfectly.

CHOOSING VARIETIES
Depending on the variety you choose, apples and pears ripen from late July to late autumn. You can choose pears with a soft, buttery flesh or a more solid texture. The taste of apples varies enormously between varieties so read descriptions before buying. If you want a tiny apple tree go for one on M27 rootstock. For a tree about 3m (10ft) high, choose MM106. Pears grown on Quince A rootstock will reach 3–6m (10–20ft) in height.

Keep within bounds >
Choose a pear tree that has been grafted on to a dwarfing rootstock.

Beauty in age >
Apple trees become twisted and more distinctive over the years.

PLANTING AND CARE
Autumn and winter are the best times to plant apples and pears. Bare-root trees become available at this time of the year, and they are less expensive and establish just as quickly as pot-grown trees. Plant bare-root types as soon as you can after receiving them. Dig over the area around the planting hole and add some organic matter. Plant at the same level as the trees were in the field (look for the dark stain on the stem). Firm in well. Water in, then insert a stake (*see p.179*) and tie the tree to it. Mulch with bark chippings or compost, and keep well watered for the first two years.

Cherries and plums

Luscious and juicy, cherries and plums taste of summer. Both are grown as standard trees, but cherries can also be trained along a warm, sheltered wall.

CHOOSING VARIETIES

You can grow sweet or sour cherries. Sweet are the best for eating from the tree and sour are ideal for cooking and jam-making. Cherries can grow into large trees, so select one grown on dwarfing rootstocks – Colt or Giselle 5 – and a self-fertile cultivar if you only want one tree. Some varieties of plum are particularly good for eating, some are better for cooking, and others are dual purpose.

Simply the best >
Plums can be enjoyed straight from the tree or cooked in delicious pies, jams, and puddings.

PLANTING AND CARE

Plums and cherries should be planted in autumn or winter, much like apples and pears. Once they are established and fruiting, it is important to protect cherries from birds, or they will quickly finish off the crop. A net thrown over the tree will provide some protection, but for best results, grow them in a specially constructed fruit cage. Plums and cherries should always be pruned in summer, and never in winter, as they are susceptible to silver leaf disease (*see p.432*), which is more prevalent in winter.

< Cherry ripe
Grow cherries for their eye-catching, sweet and juicy summer fruit, as well as their attractive spring blossom.

Pruning tips

All fruit trees fare better if they are regularly pruned. Pruning encourages the tree to produce the best fruiting wood, and removes any growth that may lead to problems.

WHEN TO PRUNE

Prune apple and pear trees in winter, and cherry and plum trees in summer. Start by removing any growth that is dead or diseased, or that is crossing the centre of the tree: you want an open centre to increase air flow and to allow sunlight in. It is important to create a main framework in the first few years, and to prune back to that. You can then shorten new stems by about one third to an outward-facing bud, and shorten the side-growths that grow from them to about five buds.

∧ Remove branches
Cut back branches that are growing in towards the centre of the tree as these will reduce airflow and light, and may lead to disease problems.

∧ Spur pruning
Shortening the side shoots creates "spurs", which are lengths of thickened wood that are more likely to produce flower buds and fruit.

Wildlife Gardening

Birds, small creatures, and insects not only bring your garden to life, many are beneficial to plants too. Insects help to pollinate flowers, while frogs and toads eat slugs, and thrushes love to feast on snails. To lure these allies into your garden, provide food – berries and fruit for birds and nectar-rich flowers for insects – and plenty of fresh water to drink. As well as wildlife-friendly planting ideas for ponds and gardens, this chapter also includes lots of advice on composting.

Make a wildlife pond

Providing the perfect home for some of the most decorative foliage and flowering plants, a pond also mirrors the sky, reflecting light into the garden. A wildlife pond is especially beautiful, and will also attract a whole host of beneficial animals, birds, and insects. Make one with sloping sides, to allow easy access for creatures to come and go, and leafy edges that offer habitats and cover for hibernation. Site your pond in an open area, not too near overhanging trees, as decaying autumn leaves sully the water.

WHEN TO START
Late winter or early spring
AT ITS BEST
Spring to early autumn

TIME TO COMPLETE
 2–3 days

YOU WILL NEED
Hosepipe
Spade
Long length of wood
Spirit level
Old carpet or pond underlay
Butyl pond liner (see Step 1 for quantities)
Sharp knife
Large stones
Mortar
Trowel
Pond plants
Aquatic compost
Pond baskets
Gravel

1 MARK OUT THE POND
Using a hosepipe, mark out the pond with sweeping curves for a natural effect. Calculate the area of liner you will need by adding twice the total depth (D), plus 45cm (18in) extra, to the length (L). Then add twice the depth (D), plus 45cm (18in) extra, to the width (W), and multiply the two answers (see also Step 2): (2xD+45cm+L) x (2xD+45cm+W).

2 DIG DOWN
Dig out the whole area of the pond to a depth of 45cm (18in), and angle the sides so that they slope slightly. Leave a 30–45cm (12–18in) wide shelf around the sides at this depth. Then dig out a central area 1m (3ft) deep, and an adjacent area, about 75cm (30in) deep, creating two deeper areas to keep plants and wildlife frost-free in winter.

3 LEVEL UP
It is essential that the top edges of the pond are level all the way round, or water will drain out unevenly. Place a spirit level on a straight plank of wood and test the level in six or seven different places, building up or removing soil as necessary.

4 LINE THE BASE
Smooth the edges, and remove large or sharp stones from the sides and base. Line the pond with old carpet or a proprietary pond underlay. Do not use sand because it falls away from the sides and will fill up the hole.

continued...

5 LINE WITH BUTYL

Centre the liner over the hole and push it down in the middle, allowing pleats to form against the sides and base. Fill the deepest part with water; the weight will pull the liner into place.

6 FILL WITH WATER

Fold the liner in neat pleats over the shelf and top edges, and check that it is bedded into the bottom of the pond. Top up with more water, which will force the liner against the shelf and sides.

7 TRIM TO FIT

As you fill the pond, move around so that the liner is pulled evenly into the hole. When the pond is full, trim the liner with a sharp knife, leaving up to 45cm (18in) excess around the edges.

8 EDGE WITH TURF OR STONES

To turf up to the edges, leave 25cm (10in) of excess liner; butt the turves up to it and allow the grass to encroach. Or add stones by mortaring them onto the liner, ensuring that no cement falls in the water.

9 PLACE THE STONES

When positioning the stones, make sure that they do not overhang the edge by more than 5cm (2in). This will prevent them from tipping up and both you and the stones falling into the water when you walk on the edge.

TOP TIP: CHOOSING POND PLANTS

There are four main types of pond plant; deep-water aquatics, oxygenators, marginals, and bog plants. Water lilies are deep-water aquatics and sit on the bottom of the pond, although some will grow in shallow water. Check the depth required on the label (measured from the pot surface) and raise them up on bricks as required.

Oxygenators are essential plants that help to keep the water clear (see Top Tip, opposite).

Marginals, such as the marsh marigold, *Caltha palustris* (right), prefer the shallows around the edge of the pond, and will be happiest on the shelf (see Step 2, p.324).

Site bog plants in the damp area around the pond – not in the water (see pp.330–331).

10 FINISH OFF

Place rocks in the water but protect the liner from damage by placing them on cushions of folded plastic sacks or spare rolled-up liner. Ensure the rocks are stable, but do not mortar them in. The pond is now ready to plant. Use the shelves around the sides for marginal plants, and the deeper areas for submerged aquatics, such as water lilies (see Top Tip, right).

Plant up your water feature

Choose a variety of different plants for your pond to establish a natural balance that will help to keep the water clear, and provide the best habitat for plants and wildlife. All submerged pond plants can be planted up in the same way, and should be divided and repotted every two or three years.

WHEN TO PLANT
Mid- to late spring

AT THEIR BEST
Summer

TIME TO COMPLETE
30 minutes per plant

YOU WILL NEED
Aquatic plant basket or fine-netted pond bag
Aquatic compost
Trowel
Water lily or pond plant
Pea gravel

TOP TIP: PLANTING OXYGENATORS

These vital plants release oxygen, absorb nutrients, and obscure light, helping to keep the water clean and clear of green algae. Establish them in baskets on the pond shelves, before sinking them to the bottom. Avoid invasive types, like parrot's feather, *Myriophyllum aquaticum*, and curly waterweed, *Lagarosiphon major*. Good oxygenators to choose include:

Water moss, *Fontinalis antipyretica*
Hornwort, *Ceratophyllum demersum*
Curled pondweed, *Potamogeton crispus*
Hart's pennyroyal, *Mentha cervina*

1 FILL A BASKET
Choose an aquatic pond basket that has small holes in the sides to stop the soil leaking out into the water. Place a layer of aquatic compost in the bottom. Do not use garden soil because it may contain nutrients that encourage algae.

2 ADD THE PLANT
Carefully remove the water lily or pond plant from its original pot and place it in the centre of the basket at the same level. Fill in around the plant with more aquatic compost, firming it down with your fingertips as you go.

3 MULCH WITH GRAVEL
Check the plant carefully, and clean off any duckweed (small round leaves) or algae from the stems and leaves. To stabilize the soil surface, add a layer of pea gravel; rinse it first several times to remove any impurities or dirt.

Design a fishpond

Fish bring a pond to life (*right*), complementing the planting with colour and movement, but before buying, check that your feature is wide and deep enough to create a happy home for them. A small waterfall increases oxygen levels, but site it away from water lilies.

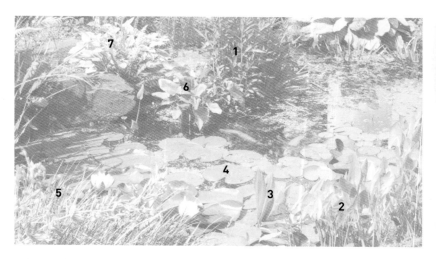

>> **WHEN TO PLANT**
Mid- to late spring

AT ITS BEST
Early summer to early autumn

TIME TO COMPLETE

🕐 1 day

YOU WILL NEED

ℹ Aquatic compost
Aquatic planting baskets

1. *Lobelia* 'Hadspen Purple'
2. Pickerel weed, *Pontederia cordata*
3. Golden club, *Orontium aquaticum*
4. Water lily, *Nymphaea* 'Albida'
5. Reed sweet-grass, *Glyceria maxima* var. *variegata*
6. Arum lily, *Zantedeschia aethiopica*
7. Variegated hosta

1 SIZE MATTERS
Make sure that your pond has a water surface area of one square metre (3ft) for each small fish you plan to keep, and a depth of at least 75cm (30in), which will provide an ice-free place for them in winter.

2 CHOOSE PLANTS
Include mixed plantings in your pond to create a beautiful and healthy environment for both fish and plants. Choose water lilies to partially cover the surface, and leafy marginals that sit just below the water at the pond edges. Also add some oxygenators (*see p.327*), which help to keep the water clear. Together, these regulate the water temperature on hot days and their roots take up fish waste matter, helping to maintain the biological balance. As well as those featured in this pond, try the tough plants opposite in your pool.

3 PLANT YOUR POND
Fish root around plants for food, and dig them up if they are not planted carefully. Plant in aquatic baskets (*see p.327*) and cover the soil surface with small pebbles to keep the fish at bay. Water lilies and other floating foliage plants are essential, providing the fish with shade and hiding them from predators, such as herons.

Fish-friendly planting

The best fish for small ponds are common goldfish and shubunkins, while koi carp require larger pools and special filters. All fish feed on pond plants, so choose tough types that will regenerate easily when munched.

❶ Spring-flowering marsh marigold, *Caltha palustris*; plant at water level, ↕60cm (24 in) ↔45cm (18in)

❷ Sweet flag, *Acorus calamus* 'Argenteostriatus' forms a grassy foliage effect; plant 20cm (8in) below water level, ↕75cm (30in) ↔60cm (24in)

❸ Flowering rush, *Butomus umbellatus*, has delicate summer flowers on long stems; plant 5–15cm (2–6in) below water level, ↕1m (3ft) ↔unlimited

❹ Japanese iris, *Iris laevigata*, flowers in late spring; plant at 10–15cm (4–6in) below water level, ↕75cm (30in) ↔1m (3ft)

INTRODUCE FISH

Fish are sensitive to changes in temperature, so acclimatize them to their new pond. Float the bag in which you bought them on the water and open the top to allow more air inside. After about 20 minutes, gently release the fish into the pond. Don't worry if fish hide for a few days, they will soon appear when they have adjusted to their new home.

Create a beautiful bog garden

Some of the most fabulous plants will only grow in soil that is permanently moist, and even if you don't have a boggy area in your garden, it is quite easy to create one. This type of planting looks particularly natural next to ponds or among trees, but can be equally effective in any part of the garden.

>> **WHEN TO START**
Anytime

AT ITS BEST
Summer

TIME TO COMPLETE
2 days

YOU WILL NEED
Hosepipe
Pond liner
Bricks
Gravel
Well-rotted organic matter, such as farmyard manure
Topsoil
Perforated hose
Scissors
Rake
Fork
Spade
Bog plants

1 DIG OUT BORDER
Next to your pond or other suitable area, use a garden hose to make a curved and natural outline for your bog garden. Dig it out to a depth of about 60cm (24in) and keep the soil.

2 PLACE LINER AND STABILIZE

Lay the liner in the hole and push it into the corners. To hold it in place, overlap the edges of the hole with at least 30cm (12in) of liner, and weigh it down with bricks. Make sure the liner is not pulled tight or it could rip when filled.

3 PERFORATE LINER WITH FORK

Although you want the soil in your bog garden to be moist, it should not be completely saturated or it will lack oxygen, which is vital for healthy plant roots. To provide some drainage, pierce the liner with a garden fork at 1m (3ft) intervals.

4 COVER BASE WITH GRAVEL

To ensure that the drainage holes do not become blocked over time, causing the soil in your bog garden to stagnate, cover the liner with a layer of gravel or coarse grit. A depth of about 8cm (3in) thick should be sufficient.

5 TRIM EDGE OF LINER

Fill the bog garden with the soil you excavated when digging the hole, together with some well-rotted organic matter, and press it down. This will settle the liner into its final position. Use sharp scissors to cut any visible excess liner from around the edges.

6 PLACE PERFORATED HOSE ROUND PERIMETER

A perforated hose, which allows water to seep out slowly, will make it easier to keep your bog garden topped up during dry periods. Sink it into the soil all the way around the inside edge of the bog garden, just leaving the hose attachment above ground. You can then simply attach a garden hose to it when necessary. As the hose attachment will eventually be hidden by plants, remember to mark its position in the garden.

7 PLANT UP

Lay your bog plants out in their pots, and when you are happy with the design, plant them so that they are at the same level as in their pots, or slightly deeper. Mulch with organic matter. Keep well watered until the plants are fully established.

Striking bog plants

The plants that thrive in boggy conditions are as varied and colourful as any other group, and there are many attractive effects you can create by choosing carefully. Several have impressive and boldly-shaped foliage for maximum drama, including giant rhubarb-like *Gunnera*, hand-shaped *Rodgersia* and golden-leaved *Carex*. Others, such as *Iris sibirica* and *Primula japonica*, bring a more refined and delicate beauty to your bog garden.

❀❀❀ fully hardy ❀❀ hardy in mild regions/sheltered sites ❀ protect from frost over winter
☼ full sun ☼ partial sun ☀ full shade ◊ well-drained soil ◔ moist soil ● wet soil

1 Arum lily, *Zantedeschia aethiopica*; ‡90cm (36in) ↔90cm (36in) ☼ ◔ ❀ **2** *Darmera peltata*; ‡1.9m (6ft) ↔1m (3ft) ☼ ☼ ◔ ❀❀❀ **3** *Carex elata* 'Aurea'; ‡70cm (28in) ↔45cm (18in)☼ ☼ ◔ ❀❀❀ **4** *Iris sibirica* 'Shirley Pope'; ‡80cm (32in) ↔45cm (18in) ☼ ☼ ◔ ❀❀❀ **5** *Rodgersia sambucifolia*; ‡90cm (36in) ↔90cm (36in) ☼ ☼ ◔ ❀❀❀ **6** *Primula japonica* 'Miller's Crimson'; ‡45cm (18in) ↔45cm (18in)☼ ☼ ◔ ❀❀❀ **7** Globeflower, *Trollius europaeus*; ‡80cm (32in) ↔45cm (18in) ☼ ☼ ◔ ❀❀❀ **8** *Filipendula purpurea*; ‡1.2m (4ft) ↔60cm (24in)☼ ☼ ◔ ❀❀❀ **9** *Gunnera manicata*; ‡2.5m (8ft) ↔3m (10ft)☼ ☼ ◔ ❀❀❀ **10** *Eupatorium purpureum*; ‡2m (6ft) ↔1m (3ft) ☼ ☼ ◔ ❀❀❀ **11** *Ligularia stenocephala* 'The Rocket'; ‡1.5m (5ft) ↔1m (3ft) ☼ ☼ ◔ ❀❀❀

Plant up boggy pots

If you have no space for a bog garden but would like to grow some of the plants that prefer damp soil, create a container display. Simply plant up a large, non-porous pot — made from glazed earthenware, synthetics, or galvanized steel — with your favourite plants to perk up a shady patio or pool-side.

WHEN TO PLANT
Late spring

AT ITS BEST
Early to late summer

TIME TO COMPLETE
2 hours

YOU WILL NEED
Large, non-porous container
Plastic sack
Gravel
Soil-based compost
Well-rotted organic matter

Bog plants; those used here are:
Astilbe 'Fanal'
Carex 'Silver Sceptre'
Persicaria microcephala
  'Red Dragon'

1 LINE THE CONTAINER
Select a large non-porous container, and make sure it has a drainage hole; drill one if it doesn't. Line the container with a thick plastic sack, such as an old compost bag. With a kitchen fork, pierce a few small holes around the sides of the sack, about 5cm (2in) from the bottom.

2 PREPARE TO PLANT
Fill the base with 8cm (3in) of gravel, which will prevent soil from clogging the drainage holes around the sides and create a water reservoir at the bottom of the pot. Then add a layer of soil-based compost mixed with some well-rotted organic matter.

3 ADD THE PLANTS
With the plants still in their pots, check that they will sit at least 5cm (2in) below the rim of the pot when planted. Then water the plants, and remove them from their pots. Place them on the layer of compost, and fill in around them carefully with more of the mixed compost and organic matter.

4 MULCH AND WATER
Firm in the plants, water well, and add a mulch of organic matter. Set the container in a partially shaded area, and water frequently. Reduce watering in winter to prevent the compost freezing. In spring, replace the top 7cm (3in) of compost with fresh material. Add slow-release fertilizer.

Planting ideas

Large containers are ideal for bog plants because they hold more soil and water, and provide the best conditions for good growth.

PLANT CHOICES
Any plants that like boggy soil can be added to a container display, as long as you match the size of the pot to your plants. Check plant labels carefully for heights and spreads. For example, the gigantic leaves and stems of an imposing *Gunnera manicata* will need a large pot to support them, while a group of primulas will be happy in a smaller container. Most bog plants are fully hardy, and can spend the winter outside, but choose a pot made from thick material to insulate the roots.

∧ *Chic mix*
These galvanized metal containers, filled with white arum lilies, Zantedeschia aethiopica 'Crowborough', and variegated hostas, H. 'Great Expectations', make a smart duo on a contemporary terrace. Line the pots with bubble plastic to insulate the roots in winter.

Create a lush stream-side

Take advantage of permanently moist soil, or areas near streams, to grow some of the many beautiful plants that associate well with water. Primulas, sedges, and horsetails all look at home in this environment, and thrive in the damp, humid conditions found there.

< Final touches
To make your stream look realistic, disguise the pond liner and pump tubing with flat stones or pebbles. These will also create small eddies and cascades, providing a mellifluous tune to accompany the colourful planting.

》 **WHEN TO START**
Spring
AT ITS BEST
Spring to summer

TIME TO COMPLETE
3 hours

YOU WILL NEED
Well-rotted organic matter, such as farmyard manure
Spade and pond liner

1. *Canna indica*
2. Sedge, *Carex comans*
3. *Primula pulverulenta* Bartley hybrids
4. Horsetail, *Equisetum hyemale*
5. *Persicaria microcephala* 'Red Dragon'
6. *Dryopteris filix-mas*

1 CREATE A STREAM
To make a stream, dig a shallow, sloping trench with a large hole at the lower end. Then add a pump (*see Top Tip, below*) to move the water.

2 PREPARE TO PLANT
If the soil is dry, consider creating a bog garden (*see pp.330–331*). Even if your soil is damp, add some well-rotted organic matter to further increase its moisture-holding capacity.

3 PLANTING AND AFTERCARE
Arrange the plants in naturalistic drifts along the banks in groups of threes and fives, where possible. Plant at the same depth as they were in their original pots. Water in the plants and mulch with chipped bark to help retain moisture and suppress weeds. Water the plants frequently during their first year.

TOP TIP: MAKING THE WATER FLOW

Buy a pump powerful enough to push the water along the length of your trench. You will also need a power source (*see p.345*). Place a bucket in the hole at the lower end (*top right*). Cover the trench and bucket with pond liner, and cut a hole where it covers the bucket. Place the pump in the bucket, and raise it up on bricks so the nozzle is above the liner (*bottom right*). Cover with galvanized wire mesh, and cut a hole for the water outlet (*far right*). Attach a long tube to the outlet and run it along the trench — water will then trickle from the top to the bottom of the trench when you turn on the pump.

Make a home for frogs

Add a new dimension to a small garden or patio with a tiny pool made from a wooden barrel. Fill it with compact pond plants and soon you will find frogs, toads, water skaters, and other wildlife making their homes there too. The pool is best placed in a sunny spot that is in shade for part of the day.

WHEN TO START
Early spring

AT ITS BEST
Spring to late summer

TIME TO COMPLETE
3 hours

YOU WILL NEED
Wooden half barrel
Strong plastic or butyl pond liner
Sharp knife or scissors
Galvanized nails and hammer
Aquatic pond baskets
Aquatic compost
Gravel and bricks

Marginal plants, those used
  here are:
Iris laevigata
Water forget-me-not, *Myosotis
  scorpioides* 'Alba'
Ragged robin, *Lychnis flos-cuculi*
Marsh marigold, *Caltha palustris*

1 LINE THE CONTAINER
Set the barrel where you intend to keep it because it will be very difficult to move once full of water. Place the pond liner over the top of the barrel, and push it down in the centre. Smooth it over the bottom and around the edges, pleating it neatly so that it lines the barrel evenly. Make sure that the liner reaches about 10cm (4in) above the rim at this stage.

2 ATTACH THE LINER
Fill the barrel with about 20cm (8in) of water and trim off excess liner just above the rim. With galvanized nails, shorter than the width of the wood, tack the liner to the barrel, then trim it above the nails.

3 FILL THE POOL
Fill the pool to about 10cm (4in) below the galvanized nails. Then plant up your pond plants (*see p.327*). Add gravel to the top of each basket to prevent the soil from floating out.

4 ADD THE PLANTS
Check the label of each plant to see what depth it prefers. Most marginals like to grow with the tops of their baskets between 2–30cm (1–12in) below the water surface. To provide the correct depth, stand the plants on bricks in the barrel. The raised baskets also act like stepping stones, providing small creatures, such as frogs and toads, with easy access to and from the pool. To keep the water clear, include one or two oxygenating plants (*see p.327*).

5 CREATE A WILDLIFE SANCTUARY
In spring, ask friends or neighbours with a pond for some frog or toad spawn, or tadpoles, to add to your barrel. Position other potted plants around the pool, so that the amphibians have landing places to hop in and out of the water. Snails and water insects will soon find their way to your pool too. From time to time, remove excess duckweed (small round leaves that float on the surface) with a net or old kitchen sieve, and take out algae using a stick.

Miniature Monet

If Monet's lilies have inspired you, but your garden is too tiny for a large, naturalistic feature, make a small formal pool like this one. Place a seating area close by from which to enjoy the flowers and the cloud patterns reflected in the water.

≫ **WHEN TO PLANT**
Early spring
AT ITS BEST
Summer

TIME TO COMPLETE
3 days to dig out and plant

YOU WILL NEED
Aquatic plant baskets
Aquatic compost
Gravel
Well-rotted organic matter
Oxygenating plants

1. Arum lily, *Zantedeschia aethiopica*
2. *Bergenia*
3. *Nymphaea* 'Pygmaea Rubra'
4. *Nymphaea alba*
5. *Iris laevigata* 'Variegata'
6. *Iris laevigata* var. *alba*
7. *Lysimachia nummularia* 'Aurea'

1 DIG THE POND
Follow the steps for a wildlife pond (*see pp. 324–326*) but use strings and pegs to mark out straight edges, rather than curved sides. Like the wildlife pond, this one needs a shelf for the marginals and a deeper area for the lilies.

2 CALL IN THE EXPERTS
The raised brick edging and patio around the pond are best built by a professional landscaper, unless your DIY skills are up to the job. Make a bog garden around the pond (*see p. 330–331*), enrich the soil with organic matter, and plant up.

3 PLANT THE POOL
Plant the lilies and set them on the bottom of the pool, and place the irises and arum lily on the shelf (*see p. 327*). Include a few oxygenating plants (*see p. 327*) to keep the water clear.

< *Small yet stylish*
Perfect for a small plot, this pretty pool packs in all the elements of a large feature, with a mix of water lilies, irises, and elegant arum lilies.

Lilies for a small pond

You don't need a large pond to enjoy the stately beauty of water lilies; many smaller species and cultivars are perfectly suited to small pools or well-sealed containers. Choose from shades of red, pink, white, and yellow, and look out for those with unusual foliage markings too. The flowers only open fully when in sun, so plant them in a brightly lit position. They also need still water, and will not thrive in a pond with a fountain or waterfall.

SELECTIONS»

※※※ fully hardy　※※ hardy in mild regions/sheltered sites　※ protect from frost over winter
☼ full sun　◐ partial sun　● full shade　⊥ planting depth

1 *Nymphaea tetragona*; ↔40cm (16in) ⊥ 30cm (12in) ☼ ※※※　**2** *N.* 'René Gérard'; ↔1m (3ft) ⊥ 30–75cm (12–30in) ☼ ※※※　**3** *N.* 'Gonnère'; ↔1.2m (4ft) ⊥ 1m (3ft) ☼ ※※※　**4** *N.* 'Escarboucle'; ↔1m (3ft) ⊥ 75cm (30in) ☼ ※※※　**5** *N.* 'Lemon Chiffon'; ↔75cm (30in) ⊥ 30–60cm (12–24in) ☼ ※※※　**6** *N.* 'Rose Arey'; ↔1m (3ft) ⊥ 50cm (20in) ☼ ※※※　**7** *N.* 'Froebelii'; ↔1m (3ft) ⊥ 75cm (30in) ☼ ※※※　**8** *N.* 'Marliacea Chromatella'; ↔1.2m (4ft) ⊥ 75cm (30in) ☼ ※※※　**9** *N.* 'Virginalis'; ↔1.2m (4ft) ⊥ 1m (3ft) ☼ ※※※　**10** *N.* 'Odorata Sulphurea'; ↔1.2m (4ft) ⊥ 75cm (30in) ☼ ※※※

Make a bubble fountain

Easy to install, this beautiful bubble fountain makes a wonderful feature in a small gravel garden, or use it as a focal point in a formal setting. You can buy kits that come complete with a water reservoir and lid, which means you then just need a small water pump and a decorative pot to stand on the top.

WHEN TO START
Spring
AT ITS BEST
Spring to autumn

TIME TO COMPLETE
6 hours

YOU WILL NEED
Spade
Sand
Bubble fountain kit and piping
Small pump with flow adjuster
Electrical tubing
Frost-proof pot with drainage hole
Pebbles and gravel

1 PREPARE THE SITE
First ask a qualified electrician to install an electricity supply and an outdoor socket to an easily concealed location close to the fountain. Then dig a hole larger than the reservoir.

2 LAY A SANDY FOUNDATION
Remove any sharp stones from the hole and pack damp sand around the edges, sides, and base. Place the reservoir in the hole, and use a spirit level to check that it is level in all directions.

3 CHECK LEVELS
Pack more sand around the reservoir, as necessary, and check that it is level again. It is essential that your fountain is horizontal to prevent water draining out, and to ensure that the pot on top will be stable.

4 PLACE THE PUMP
When level, place the pump in the reservoir. You may need to fit an extension pipe onto the pump to reach through the hole in the base of the decorative pot. Put the lid on the reservoir, and over the pipe from the pump.

5 ADD THE POT
Place the decorative pot on the reservoir lid, making sure that the pump pipe passes through the drainage hole in the bottom. Seal the pump pipe in place with silicone sealant, and leave to dry and harden for 24 hours.

6 ATTACH THE FLOW ADJUSTER
Attach a long section of pipe to the water flow adjuster. Then attach this to the pump pipe in the base of the pot. Trim the water delivery pipe so it reaches just below the rim of the decorative pot.

7 FILL WITH WATER
Use a hose pipe or watering can to fill the reservoir through the holes in the lid, and top up the decorative pot to just below the delivery pipe.

8 PROTECT THE FLEX
The electrical flex must be protected by special piping, which a qualified electrician can advise you about. For safety, make sure that all electrical connections in the garden are fitted with an RCD circuit breaker.

9 DISGUISE THE RESERVOIR
Plug in the pump and check that it pushes the water over the top of the pot, and adjust the flow as necessary. Disguise the reservoir with pebbles and gravel, leaving a gap to allow you to top it up – you need to do this once a week in summer.

TOP TIP: SOFTEN WITH PLANTING

Plant up around your pool, leaving a margin between your planting and the reservoir, to avoid dislodging it. Plants from the Mediterranean, such as euphorbias (*right*), lavender, and rock roses (*Cistus*) make great companions for an urn. If you prefer a more traditional look, try roses, honeysuckle, and daisies.

Plant trees for wildlife

Trees are among the best features for wildlife. In urban areas, in particular, they act as beacons in a sea of streets and housing, signalling to birds that rest and shelter are on offer. They provide nesting and roosting sites, a home for insects and other wildlife, and many are a great source of food. Every garden should have one; no matter how small the site, there are trees to suit.

INSECT FEASTS

Fruit trees, such as apples and pears, provide a sweet feast late in the year, but they are also rich sources of nectar when they blossom in spring. As soon as their first flowers open, these trees are alive with hungry bees, pollinating the flowers as they feed and ensuring a bountiful harvest later in the year. Native trees, such as hawthorn (*Crataegus*) and elder (*Sambucus*), are particularly good for wildlife, producing an abundance of nectar.

< ∧ *Spoilt for choice*
Even cultivars of native trees, such as 'Paul's Scarlet' hawthorn (left) and elder flowers (above), provide spring nectar for insects.

FOOD SOURCES FOR BIRDS

Berries are an attractive feature in a garden, glowing in the low autumn sun, and they also provide a sustained food source for birds and animals that can last well into the winter months. If you have space, plant several fruiting trees that ripen at different times to ensure an enduring supply. Good choices for an abundance of berries are whitebeam (*Sorbus aria*), rowans (*Sorbus*), mulberries (*Morus nigra*), elderberry (*Sambucus*) and cherries (*Prunus*). No berries will go to waste, with any windfalls readily eaten by birds, small mammals, and even butterflies. If you have a bumper crop of fruit and berries, consider freezing some to put out in late winter when food is scarce.

Food for all >
Mulberries are loved by people and birds alike (top left), and rowan berries (far right) are a food source that can last for many months. Windfalls benefit birds, ground-dwelling animals, and insects (right).

NESTING SITES

Trees become more valuable to wildlife as they get older; a mature tree will become home to birds that regularly return, year after year. Trees with dense crowns and bare trunks are particularly prized by birds, as they provide sheltered nesting sites, and keep predators at bay. Once mature, a holly tree (*Ilex*) has everything: berries, dense growth, and thorns that keep out all but the most determined intruders. Other excellent prickly trees are hawthorn (*Crataegus*) and blackthorn (*Prunus spinosa*). If you don't have space for mature trees, all three make great wildlife hedges that offer similar protection for nesting birds (*see pp.192–193*). Older trees require maintenance, and it is essential that you carry out any pruning and routine care outside of nesting time, otherwise you risk upsetting nesting birds or fledglings, which is against the law.

< Best for nests
Birds feel safe nesting in the thick, dense, impenetrable growth of holly (left), and can hide in the dark foliage of the purple-leaved plum (Prunus cerasifera 'Pissardii', far left).

Sow a flower meadow

Romantic, colourful, and easy to maintain, meadows are also perfect habitats for wildlife. The flowers and grasses will thrive on infertile soil in a sunny site, and they need just one cut each year after the plants have set seed. Meadows look best on a large scale and are ideal if you have lots of space to fill.

WHEN TO START
Early autumn

AT ITS BEST
Summer

TIME TO COMPLETE
8 hours

YOU WILL NEED
Wildflower seed
Horticultural sand
Spade
Wheelbarrow
Bamboo canes
Spring-tined rake
Garden rake
String and bird-scarer, such as
ribbons or old CDs

< *Mellow meadow*
This cool collection blends annual grasses with blue cornflowers, purple corn cockles, pink cosmos, white daisies, and cow parsley.

1 MIX SEED WITH SAND
To sow seed over a large area, first mix it with clean, dry horticultural sand. This helps to spread the seed more evenly, and makes it obvious which areas you have already sown. Wildflower mixes should be sown at 3 grams per square metre, so weigh out this amount of seed and mix it up with the sand in batches in a clean container.

2 REMOVE A LAYER OF TOPSOIL
Topsoil is full of nutrients that encourage strong grasses to grow at the expense of delicate wild flowers. Use a spade and wheelbarrow to remove the top few centimetres, and recycle it elsewhere in the garden. Also remove any weeds and roots you find that could regrow and compete with the flowers.

3 PREPARE THE SEEDBED
Remove stones from the area and rake over the soil to break up the surface. Leave the site for two or three weeks, and then weed it again. To prevent the seeds washing away, water the area before sowing, not afterwards. Use canes to mark out the area into square metres, and sow each square with your batches of seed and sand mixture.

4 AFTER SOWING
Use a spring-tined rake (*see right*) to lightly cover the seeds with soil after sowing. To avoid walking over sown areas, sow a small area at a time and then rake over it, before moving on to the next.

5 FIRM SOIL GENTLY
Use the back of a garden rake to gently compact the soil, ensuring good contact between seed and soil, which helps germination. It also makes the seed less visible to birds, who will happily eat their way through the lot if given the chance.

TOP TIP: KEEP BIRDS AT BAY

To prevent hungry birds from eating the wildflower seed, set up a series of strings with old CDs threaded on to them across the sown area. The CDs reflect light as they move in the wind, which frightens off the birds.

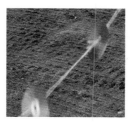

A feast for bees

Bees are suffering an alarming decline in numbers, so plant a border of nectar-rich flowers to keep these essential insects well-fed. Prolong the food supply by growing early- and late-flowering plants.

WHEN TO PLANT
Autumn and spring

AT ITS BEST
Summer

TIME TO COMPLETE
3 hours to prepare; 4 hours to plant

YOU WILL NEED
Spade
Fork
Well-rotted organic matter, such as farmyard manure

1. *Lupinus* 'The Governor'
2. *Pittosporum tenuifolium* 'Silver Queen'
3. *Anchusa azurea* 'Loddon Royalist'
4. *Achillea* 'Moonshine'
5. *Rosa* 'Rose of Picardy'
6. *Verbascum* 'Gainsborough'

1 **PREPARE TO PLANT**
In autumn, weed the border carefully. Then dig it thoroughly, incorporating plenty of organic matter. Plant the *Pittosporum* and roses in autumn (*see p.36 and p.93*) so they can become established the following spring.

2 **PLANT THE PERENNIALS**
In spring, buy the perennials (*Achillea*, *Anchusa*, lupins and *Verbascum*). Position them in swathes of colour running between the shrubs, then plant (*see pp.30–31*).

3 **AFTERCARE**
Water well after planting, and regularly for the first year. In spring, prune the roses (*see p.415*) and support taller-growing plants (*see p.67*). In late winter, cut back the old perennial stems, ready for new spring growth.

Plants to attract insects

Bugs may not all be beautiful but the beneficial kind are essential to the environment. They not only pollinate flowers, ensuring good crops, but some, such as ladybirds and hoverfly larvae, also help to keep pests at bay. Plant annuals, like sweet alyssum and viper's bugloss, or perennial Shasta daisies, asters, bee balm, and ice plants to welcome these insect allies. Shrubs, such as hebe, roses, lavender, and honeysuckle, will also help to lure them in.

❋❋❋ fully hardy   ❋❋ hardy in mild regions/sheltered sites   ❋ protect from frost over winter
☼ full sun   ☀ partial sun   ☀ full shade   ◊ well-drained soil   ◔ moist soil   ● wet soil

❶ Shasta daisy, *Leucanthemum* x *superbum*; ‡90cm (36in) ↔60cm (24in) ☼ ☀ ◊ ❋❋❋   **❷** Viper's bugloss, *Echium vulgare* 'Blue Bedder'; ‡60–90cm (24–36in) ↔30cm (12in) ☼ ◊ ❋❋❋   **❸** *Hebe* 'Great Orme'; ‡1.2m (4ft) ↔1.2m (4ft) ☼ ☀ ◊ ❋❋❋   **❹** Sweet alyssum, *Lobularia maritima* 'Snow Crystals'; ‡25cm (10in) ↔25cm (10in) ☼ ◊ ❋❋❋   **❺** Dog rose, *Rosa canina*; ‡4m (12ft) ↔3m (10ft) ☼ ☀ ◔ ❋❋❋   **❻** Lavender, *Lavandula angustifolia* 'Hidcote'; ‡60cm (24in) ↔75cm (30in) ☼ ◊ ❋❋❋   **❼** *Aster amellus* cultivars; ‡40cm (16in) ↔45cm (18in) ☼ ◊ ❋❋❋   **❽** Honeysuckle, *Lonicera periclymenum*; ‡7m (22ft) ☼ ☀ ◔ ❋❋❋   **❾** Bee balm, *Monarda* 'Mahogany'; ‡90cm (36in) ↔45cm (18in) ☼ ☀ ◔ ❋❋❋   **❿** Ice plant, *Sedum spectabile*; ‡45cm (18in) ↔45cm (18in) ☼ ◊ ❋❋❋

Wildlife wall

Many beneficial garden insects, such as ladybirds and ground beetles, struggle to find habitats in our neat gardens. Consider creating a wildlife wall to lure them in and keep them happy. It creates perfect homes for many different species, and its textures and patterns make it an attractive garden feature.

» **WHEN TO MAKE**
Spring or summer

AT ITS BEST
Winter

TIME TO COMPLETE
4 hours

YOU WILL NEED
Sedum or *Sempervivum* plants
Bricks (with holes in them)
Small blocks of wood, drilled
 with different sized holes
Roof tiles
Sheets of plywood or planks
 of wood
Straw, corrugated cardboard,
 slate chippings, bamboo canes,
 clumps of moss, twigs
Compost

1 CONSTRUCT THE WALL
In a quiet area of the garden, make a layer of bricks and tiles, leaving plenty of gaps. Place plywood or planks of wood on top and then add another layer of bricks and tiles. Top the structure off with the roof tiles, to keep excess moisture out.

2 STUFF THE GAPS
Cut the bamboo canes into short lengths and pack them into gaps to make homes for solitary bees. Roll up corrugated cardboard to create laying sites for ladybirds. Moss, slate chippings, straw and twigs pushed into the other holes will be colonized by many different garden insects. Plant the top with *Sedum* or *Sempervivum* to create a living roof.

3 AFTERCARE
Your wildlife wall, once built, should be left well alone; the more established (and decrepit) it becomes, the better it will be for wildlife, so don't be tempted to disturb it. However, you may need to occasionally top up some of the materials, particularly those such as straw that may be taken away as nest-building materials by birds.

Make a dead hedge

This is a simple way to make a wildlife-friendly corner from vines and twigs that cannot be composted. Small birds and insects will love it for shelter and food.

CONSTRUCTION TIPS
Use strong, long-lasting chestnut poles for the uprights, hammering them securely into the ground. For a neater look, use lengths of willow to weave loose sides. Then simply pile in shrub trimmings, lengths of ivy and bramble, and any other twigs the garden produces. Eventually, they will rot or compact down, and you can then add more to the top.

TOP TIP: CREATE A LOG HOME

A pile of old logs in the garden will attract beetles, frogs, toads, and other wildlife. Make a well-constructed pile, supported by a few posts hammered into the ground to prevent rolling. Leave the logs to rot down.

Install a green roof

Environmentally-friendly green roofs attract wildlife and help to insulate buildings in winter and keep them cool in summer. The easiest way to install one is with sedum matting which you can buy by the metre.

⟩⟩ **WHEN TO START**
Spring
AT ITS BEST
All year round

TIME TO COMPLETE
 2–3 hours, or longer, depending on roof size

YOU WILL NEED
Heavy-duty polythene sheet, such as butyl pond liner
Sand or gravel, or proprietary underlay
Sedum matting
Sharp knife
Slow-release granular fertilizer

1 ASSESS YOUR ROOF
If you want to cover a roof on your house, it is best to consult an expert first to ensure that the proposed area can take the weight of the planting and growing medium, and that it has sufficient drainage. Green roof specialists can be found on the internet or in local directories.

2 FIRST STEPS
For flat or gently sloping shed roofs or similar garden structures, sedum matting is the best option for DIY installation as it is easy to lay and maintain. Sedum mats come complete with mature plants already established on a special material and in growing medium. Lay them soon after delivery. The matting is heavy, especially when wet, and will require two people to lift it on to the roof.

3 INSTALL AN UNDERLAY
First, lay heavy-duty polythene, such as pond liner, over the roof to create a waterproof root barrier, then add a layer of sand or gravel, or a proprietary underlay sold by the suppliers. Ensure that the surface is even to prevent puddling when it rains since the plants do not tolerate waterlogging.

4 LAY YOUR SEDUM MATTING
Place your sedum matting on the roof and trim with a sharp knife. The matting has an extra flap of material at each side. To butt up two sections of matting, unfold this flap on the first piece, and lay the second on top of it. This creates a perfect seam, and anchors the matting. Don't use small pieces of matting at the edge of the roof, as they will dry out quickly and the plants may die.

5 MAINTENANCE
To ensure that the plants thrive, don't walk or kneel on them when installing the matting. Water plants during dry spells until they are fully established. After the first year they will only require extra irrigation during severe droughts. Apply a slow-release granular fertilizer each spring, and replant any bald patches with young plants. Some green roof suppliers offer specialist fertilizers, but one formulated for succulents and drought-tolerant plants will also do the job. Most weeds find it difficult to survive in the thin, dry soil, but remove any that do appear as soon as you see them.

Roof plants

Although sedum mats come already planted up, you can add plants of your own as bald patches appear. Choose from the following to create a sea of colour throughout the year.

❶ *Thymus* 'Doone Valley'; ↕12cm (5in) ↔35cm (14in) **❷** *Sedum acre*; ↕5cm (2in) ↔ 60cm (24in) **❸** *Scabiosa lucida*; ↕20cm (8in) ↔30cm (12in)

< *Rustic roof*
This sedum-covered roof has been installed in a wildlife garden on a small wood store made from logs – an idea that could be adapted to make a bike shelter. Smothered with flowers, the roof attracts a wealth of butterflies and beneficial insects into the garden.

Composting essentials

Composting conveniently disposes of your garden cuttings and trimmings, while at the same time creating a free, and wonderful, soil improver. It can be as simple as throwing all your waste into a pile and forgetting about it, but you will get better results if you follow a few simple guidelines.

CHOOSING A BIN

Bog standard plastic compost bins are functional, rather than attractive, but do hold lots of garden and kitchen waste. They are also the most inexpensive, and can often be bought at a discounted price through your local council. If you are concerned about how your compost bin fits in with the rest of the garden, there are more attractive options, including wooden bins designed to look like bee hives that can be stained to suit your garden design. These are a good choice for smaller gardens where the bin would be on view. Impatient gardeners may prefer "tumbler" bins. These allow you to make small batches of compost in weeks, not months, by turning the bin to increase airflow, which naturally speeds up the composting process.

^ *Types of compost bin (clockwise from top left)*
A standard plastic compost bin, the sort available from local councils; an attractive, wooden bin, designed to look like a beehive; a vertical "tumbler" type, suitable for smaller amounts of compost; a horizontal "tumbler" bin, designed for easy turning.

FILLING YOUR BIN

To produce good compost it is important to have the right mix of ingredients. If you add too much soft, green material, such as grass clippings, the heap may turn into a slimy, smelly sludge. Put in too much dry, woody material, and it will rot down slowly, if at all. Ideally aim for a ratio of about 50:50. During most of the year, it is likely that you will be producing more green than dry material, so you will need to search around for dry waste to add. Woody prunings are best, but brown cardboard, crumpled newspaper, and even the insides of used toilet rolls all make suitable alternatives.

Make a bin

A home-made bin is just as good as a bought one, and you can make it whatever size and shape that best suits your garden, and the quantity of material you want to compost.

TIME TO COMPLETE

🕐 1 day

YOU WILL NEED

4 posts about 1.5m (5ft) long
Mallet
Chicken wire
Fencing staples
Cardboard boxes
Old carpet

QUICKENING THE PACE

Air is essential to the composting process, so the contents must be turned regularly to ensure good airflow throughout your bin or heap. Turning also allows you to check how things are going, to wet the mix if it is too dry, or to add dry material if it is too wet. This task is easier if you have two bins, but if you only have one, simply empty it out onto a tarpaulin, mix the contents well, then refill the bin.

1 ATTACH WIRE TO POSTS

Set the posts 75cm (30in) apart in a square and drive them 30cm (12in) into the ground, using a mallet. Wrap the chicken wire around the posts and attach it with fencing staples. Snip off excess wire, and make sure that no sharp strands are left sticking out.

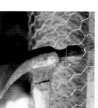

TOP TIP: BOKASHI COMPOSTING

Cooked foods, meat, and fish should never be composted in an ordinary bin as they attract rats and harmful bacteria. Instead, compost this type of waste using the Japanese bokashi system. This involves using a special sealed bin that you fill in layers, each one sprinkled with bran dust, inoculated with micro-organisms. The content of the bin then effectively pickles, and after about two weeks, it can be emptied out and buried in the garden or added to the compost heap. This method also produces a liquor that can be diluted and used as a liquid feed.

The bokashi bin >
Food scraps pickle in the sealed bin for two weeks and give off very little smell. The bin can be kept indoors or outside.

2 ADD CARDBOARD SIDES

Flatten the cardboard boxes and put several layers on each side, slotting them between the posts and the netting. Put a layer on the base then start filling your bin. Place a piece of old carpet on top of the waste; replace it each time you add more. This helps keep out the rain and insulates the bin, speeding up the composting process.

Rake up a leafy conditioner

Leafmould is one of the finest soil conditioners, and makes excellent use of a resource that is free and abundant in autumn – fallen leaves. All you need to make rich, crumbly leafmould is a plastic bin liner, some leaves from deciduous trees and a good dollop of patience.

WHEN TO START
Autumn

AT ITS BEST
The following autumn

TIME TO COMPLETE
 1 hour

YOU WILL NEED
A rake
Leaves
Plastic bag
Hand fork
Watering can

1 RAKE UP FALLEN LEAVES
When leaves start to fall in autumn, rake them up. For larger supplies, collect leaves from local parks or woods, but do not use those close to main roads.

2 PLACE IN A PLASTIC LINER
You can make a leafmould bin, but a plastic bin liner works just as well and has an added advantage, which is that it can be kept in a small space, such as behind a shed. Put leaves into the liner, pushing them down as you go.

3 SPRINKLE WITH WATER
As you pack the leaves in, occasionally stop and sprinkle them with water. Wet leaves will rot down much quicker than dry ones. Keep filling and wetting until the bag is full. One bag of leafmould won't go very far, so try to collect enough leaves to fill a few.

Nature's helpers

Inside a wormery, worms break down kitchen waste and turn it into rich compost. They can even cope with scraps, such as cooked food. Wormeries are available from specialist suppliers.

4 **TIE BAG SECURELY**
Your bag is going to be left for a long time, so make sure you tie it up well. This will prevent small creatures making a home in the leaves.

5 **PUNCH A FEW AIR HOLES**
Leaves also need air to rot down efficiently, so punch some holes in the sides with a fork. Put the bag away and forget about it for at least a year.

TOP TIP: USING LEAFMOULD

After a year or two, your leafmould will be ready to use. It works particularly well as a mulch, and is especially loved by woodland plants. Alternatively, it can be sieved and used as an ingredient in potting compost.

TIME TO COMPLETE
🕐 1½ hours

YOU WILL NEED
A wormery, with tigerworms included
Food waste
Soft "bedding" such as coir or shredded newspaper

1 **ADD THE WORMS**
Place the tigerworms on the bedding, then start by adding a small amount of food waste (referring to the pack instructions). Worms take a week to settle in and get up to full speed. Do not add any more food during this time.

2 **FEED YOUR WORMS**
After the settling in period, you should be able to use most of your food scraps, making sure you add some every day. It is best to use a variety of food and other ingredients, such as leaves and moist newspaper, to ensure the texture does not become too dense. Worms can cope with most foods, but they struggle with citrus fruits and meat.

3 **FINAL COMPOST**
Wormeries can become acidic, so occasionally add lime, such as calcified seaweed. When the compost is ready it will be dark, fairly soggy and slightly spongy. The worms are just below the surface, so can be easily removed. You can then use it on garden borders or mix it in with your other compost.

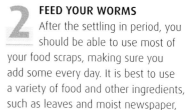

Homes for birds and bees

Birds and beneficial insects not only make a garden a more interesting place, they also help to control pests and improve flower pollination. Gardening organically helps make them feel welcome, but providing a specially made home really rolls out the red carpet and encourages them to stay.

Bee hotel

Solitary bees are excellent pollinators, but they can struggle to find nesting sites. A home-made nest looks attractive and provides them with shelter, as well as ensuring you have bumper harvests.

>> **WHEN TO START**
Summer
AT ITS BEST
Autumn to winter

TIME TO COMPLETE
30 minutes

YOU WILL NEED
Secateurs
Bamboo canes
Modelling clay
Raffia or string
Small terracotta or plastic pot

1 CUT LENGTHS OF BAMBOO
Use sharp secateurs to cut short lengths of bamboo cane that will fit into your pot. The natural variation in diameter will attract different bee species.

2 PUSH THEM INTO A POT
Fill the base of a terracotta pot with modelling clay and push the cut bamboo canes firmly into it. Continue doing this until the pot is packed tightly.

3 HANG YOUR HOTEL
Tie raffia or string firmly around the pot and suspend it from a hook or attach it to a wall. Choose a sheltered, sunny site, and angle the open end of the pot downwards so that the bamboo canes do not fill up with water when it rains.

TOP TIP: FLOWER FOOD

To make life even better for your resident bees, position the nest close to a border planted with nectar-rich flowers. They will then have only a short distance to travel for food, which will be a great help to them in spring.

Choosing and siting a nest

Encourage birds to visit your garden and you will have a ready army of pest-eaters on your side. If you can persuade them to make their nests and rear their young there too, they will make a fascinating animated addition to the flowers and foliage. Put up one or two nest boxes, and see who moves in.

CHOOSING THE RIGHT BOX

Birds are picky about where they live, so it is important to choose the right type of box. Select one that is made from an insulating material, such as wood or woodcrete to prevent them from becoming too hot or cold, and avoid any made from ceramic or those with metal roofs. Correct hole size is also important: too small, and the birds you want to attract may not fit; too large, and wind, rain, and even predators may get in. The box should be robust, waterproof, safe, and comfortable. Different bird species have different needs, so if you want to make a home for a particular type of bird, do some research first and find out what suits it.

SITING YOUR BOX

Nest boxes should be sited in a sheltered place, away from strong sunlight, wind and rain. Position them in the quietest area of the garden, away from feeding areas, and at least 1.5m (5ft) above the ground. This mimics the nesting places birds naturally prefer, and keeps them safe from predators. Choose a position away from large branches where cats can lurk, but where there are flimsy twigs nearby to give fledglings somewhere to perch when they first leave the nest. The best time to put up nest boxes is outside the breeding season, between midsummer and late winter.

❶ Birds use roosting pockets to hide from predators during the day. Smaller species, such as wrens, may even nest in them.
❷ Boxes with a smaller 25mm hole, are attractive to a wide range of garden birds, including blue tits, coal tits, and marsh tits.
❸ Open-fronted nest boxes appeal to robins, wrens, and pied wagtails, who prefer to see out of their home.

TOP TIP: HOME-MADE BOX

If you want to make your own bird box, wood is probably the easiest and best material to use. There are plenty of plans and designs available to follow that only require simple tools and basic carpentry skills. Wood needs to be treated to stop it decaying, and you may also decide to stain or paint it. In all cases, choose products that are non-toxic and wildlife-friendly to help keep your birds healthy.

Plants for your Home

Bring the essence of your garden inside with some beautiful house plants. Grow bold sculptural foliage types to make a statement in a modern home, or brighten up a windowsill with flowering plants, such as exotic orchids and the delicate blooms of Cape primroses, *Streptocarpus* (*left*). You will also find great ideas in this chapter for displaying and grouping plants to create elegant arrangements, and learn how to bring your beauties back into flower year after year.

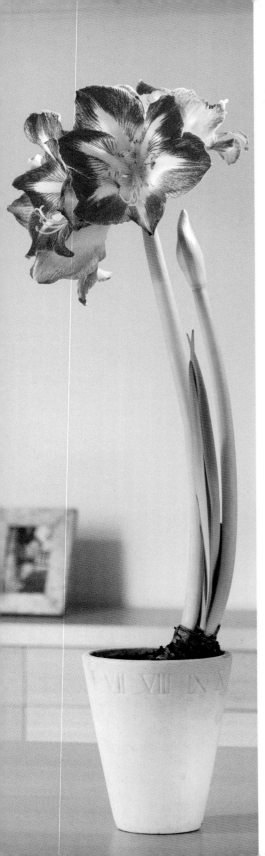

Dramatic amaryllis

Hippeastrum (commonly known as amaryllis) provide the biggest, boldest flowers of winter, and can even be bought pre-forced, so that they bloom in time for the Christmas holidays. For such exotic-looking blooms, their needs are simple: a nice tight pot, water, light, and a short rest in late summer is all they require.

WHEN TO PLANT
Autumn
AT ITS BEST
Winter

TIME TO COMPLETE
A few hours during the year

YOU WILL NEED
1 *Hippeastrum* bulb
Basin
Multi-purpose compost
Container
Balanced liquid fertilizer

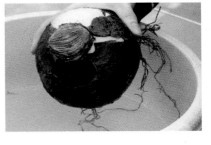

1 SOAK BULB
Soak the bulb roots in a basin of lukewarm water for a few hours. This will soften them, and encourage the bulb to come into growth again.

2 PLANT IN CONTAINER
Choose a pot, just larger than the bulb itself, that has a drainage hole. Fill the base with compost, place the bulb on top, and add more compost. Leave the top third of the bulb protruding.

3 LEAVE TO SHOOT
Water the bulb well to help settle the compost, then place the pot in a bright, warm spot at about 21°C (70°F). Water sparingly until new leaves appear; then water regularly, keeping it moist.

Hippeastrum go into dormancy at the end of summer. If yours doesn't, stop watering and feeding it, and cut back the leaves to encourage it to do so. Repot into a slightly larger pot. After several weeks, when new growth appears, resume watering.

∧ A firm hand
Ensure the bulb is firmly planted so that it does not topple over when in flower.

4 AFTERCARE
Turn the pot frequently to prevent the flower stalk growing to one side. Move the plant to a cool spot when it starts flowering, to prolong the display. Feed weekly after flowering.

Flower choices

Hippeastrum are excellent festive plants, and offer an equally vibrant alternative to the traditional poinsettias. They usually flower in shades of red and white, but some have orange, salmon, and even green-tinted blooms. Their large trumpet-shaped flowers are often heavily patterned, and vary greatly in shape; some are broad and round, while others are slender and elegant.

❶ 'Lucky Strike' is an early-flowering cultivar with deep red, rounded flowers that make a particularly festive choice for a Christmas windowsill. ❷ 'Apple Blossom' is scented, with pink-blushed, white flowers. Each bulb produces several spikes, with around four flowers apiece. ❸ 'Giraffe' has slender cream petals, decorated with vivid red stripes and splashes. It usually flowers about ten weeks after planting. ❹ 'Prelude' is possibly the most spectacular of all the *Hippeastrum*, producing an abundance of huge red and white flowers on tall, upright stems. It usually flowers in as little as five weeks after planting.

Mix and match a display

Solitary small and medium-sized house plants can look lost on a shelf or windowsill, but when grouped together on a tray, they form a lively display of contrasting colours, shapes, and textures. A layer of pretty pebbles sets off the flowers and foliage, and when the tray is filled with water, they help to provide the humid atmosphere that these plants enjoy.

TIME TO COMPLETE

🕐 2 hours

YOU WILL NEED

📍 Tray
Plastic sheet
Pebbles
House plant containers

1. *Fatsia japonica*
2. Creeping fig, *Ficus pumila*
3. *Peperomia caperata* 'Luna Red'
4. Mind-your-own-business, *Soleirolia soleirolii*
5. *Streptocarpus* 'Bethan'

1 POT UP THE PLANTS
Experiment with different-sized containers that fit into the tray, mixing tall and short ones, or even cups and saucers. For a stylish display select pots of the same colour. When you have the right grouping, buy plants that fit the pots, rather than vice versa.

2 LINE THE TRAY
Line your tray with a plastic sheet (cut from an old compost bag, for example), covering the sides to create a 1–2cm (½-1in) deep reservoir. Arrange the pots on the tray, and fill in around them with small pebbles. Fill the tray with water to just below the top of the plastic liner.

Alternative effects

As well as grouping containers, create displays by using different plants in one large pot, or repeating a single house plant species throughout your home.

MATCHING HOUSEPLANTS
When using one large pot for a variety of plants, make sure that you marry up those that enjoy the same conditions. Groups of ferns were very fashionable in Victorian times and are now *de rigueur* once more; these leafy shade-lovers look great in a large glass bowl or contrasting smooth white pots. You could also try large foliage plants, such as angel wings, *Caladium*, edged with delicate maidenhair ferns like *Adiantum*. For a hot, sunny windowsill or table, create succulent and cactus displays where natural desert conditions are easy to emulate.

∧ *Flowering desert*
Mix a group of cacti of contrasting shapes and sizes in one container, and pack them together to create a desert display for a warm, sunny room.

∧ *Contemporary trick*
Plant up identical containers with the same plant, such as this textural fern, Nephrolepis exaltata, *to create a chic, contemporary look.*

Hang a basket indoors

House plants are usually grown individually in pots, but trailing types can look great mixed together in a hanging basket. Ideal if you have limited windowsill space, colourful baskets also create an attractive "living" feature for your home. Plants will need removing and potting on every few years.

 WHEN TO START
Spring
AT ITS BEST
All year round

 TIME TO COMPLETE

 2 hours

YOU WILL NEED
Hanging basket
Plastic bowl and plastic sheet
Electric drill
Multi-purpose compost
Horticultural grit
Slow-release granular fertilizer

Plants used here:
Lipstick vine, *Aeschynanthus*
Begonia rex
Small-leaved ivy, *Hedera helix*

1 TRIM LINER
Use a piece of thick plastic to line the inside of the basket. Trim the edges to ensure that the base and sides are fully covered, but the liner is not visible over the edge.

2 DRILL DRAINAGE HOLES
Take a low, wide plastic bowl and drill lots of small drainage holes in the base. This will act as your pot, while the lined hanging basket acts as a saucer to catch any excess water.

3 ADD A LAYER OF GRIT
Cover the small drainage holes with a layer of horticultural grit to stop them blocking up. Then add a layer of compost mixed with slow-release fertilizer, leaving space for the plants.

4 PLACE PLANTS

Remove the plants from their pots and arrange them around the basket. Plants such as begonias and spider plants (*see right*) make good focal points, and they are best planted towards the centre of the basket.

5 FIRM IN WITH COMPOST

Use small amounts of compost to fill in around the plants. Firm it down with your fingers and add more until the surface of the compost is level, leaving a 2cm (1in) gap below the rim. Hang it in a bright spot out of direct sunlight.

TOP TIP: WATERING

Water every two weeks in spring and summer. Make sure the whole surface of the compost is wetted. The liner will act as a saucer and catch excess moisture. After an hour, take down the basket and tip out any excess so that the compost doesn't become waterlogged, which could harm your plants. Reduce watering in winter.

Hanging basket options

For indoor hanging baskets choose trailing plants that will cascade over the sides in curtains of texture and colour. Flowering plants, such as lipstick vine (*Aeschynanthus*), give seasonal colour in summer, while those with brightly coloured foliage provide interest all year. Although these plants are familiar and widely sold, brought together, they create a spectacular and long-lasting display.

❶ *Begonia* 'Bettina Rothschild'; ↕↔40cm (16in)   ❷ Spider plant, *Chlorophytum comosum* 'Variegatum'; ↕20cm (8in) ↔30cm (12in)   ❸ Polka dot plant, *Hypoestes phyllostachya* cultivar; ↕30cm (12in) ↔25cm (10in)   ❹ Thousand mothers, *Tolmiea menziesii*; ↕↔30cm (12in)   ❺ Wandering Jew, *Tradescantia fluminensis* 'Variegata'; ↕15cm (6in) ↔20cm (8in)   ❻ Purple velvet plant, *Gynura aurantiaca*; ↕↔30cm (12in)

Spectacular orchids

Orchids are arguably the most exquisite flowering plants you can grow indoors, their variety of colour and shape unmatched by any other plant group. Once you have succeeded with one, and got the bug, you will be hooked. Many flower throughout the winter months, offering an extra treat for colour–starved gardeners, and are well worth the effort involved in growing them. For detailed growing conditions, refer to plant labels.

☼ bright, indirect light   ☀ partial shade   ◊ allow to dry out between waterings   ◑ keep moist in summer, water sparingly in winter

❶ *Cymbidium lowianum*; ↕90cm (36in) ↔90cm (24in) ☼ ◑   ❷ *Miltoniopsis* hybrid; ↕25cm (10in) ↔25cm (10in) ☀ ◑   ❸ Moth orchid, *Phalaenopsis* pink hybrid; ↕40cm (16in) ↔35cm (14in) ☀ ◊   ❹ *Coelogyne nitida*; ↕25cm (10in) ↔30cm (12in) ☼ ◑   ❺ x *Doritaenopsis* 'Taida Pearl'; ↕70cm (28in) ↔30cm (12in) ☼ ◑   ❻ *Dendrobium* 'Sweet Dawn'; ↕60cm (24in) ↔15cm (6in) ☼ ◑   ❼ *Cymbidium* 'Minuet'; ↕30cm (12in) ↔45cm (18in) ☼ ◑   ❽ *Paphiopedilum callosum* hybrid; ↕30cm (12in) ↔15cm (6in) ☀ ◑   ❾ *Oncidium* 'Jungle Monarch'; ↕30cm (12in) ↔30cm (12in) ☼ ◑   ❿ *Epidendrum prismatocarpum*; ↕45cm (18in) ↔ 45cm (18in) ☼ ◊

Grow exotic orchids

Sophisticated, stylish, and highly fashionable, it's little wonder we all fall for elegant orchids. The problem is, many die off after flowering because they don't receive the right care, or aren't suited to life in a typical modern home. But choose your orchids carefully, and they can live long and happy lives.

CHOOSING PLANTS AND POTS

When choosing an orchid, unless you are an expert, select one that enjoys conditions that you can provide at home, such as a moth orchid, *Phalaenopsis*, or a *Cymbidium*. If you can keep your plants in a heated greenhouse, your choice is wider. Hybrids of the following orchids are generally reliable, given the right conditions (*see opposite*): *Cattleya, Dendrobium, Epidendrum, Oncidium,* and the slipper orchid, *Paphiopedilum*.

Before buying an orchid, look over the plant for any signs of pests and diseases, and make sure it has plenty of flowers and firm buds. Check that the aerial roots are firm and pale with green tips, and that any roots visible through a clear plastic pot (which orchids are often grown in) are equally healthy, and not black.

Most tropical orchids have aerial roots that absorb water and photosynthesize like leaves, taking energy from the sun and converting it into food. This means they can survive in very little compost, and require only small containers. Some should be grown in transparent pots to enable the roots to absorb sunlight.

Shop around >
Buy your orchids from a reputable source, such as a specialist nursery. Avoid those that have been sitting around in a draughty shop for weeks, as they may not survive for very long.

WATERING AND FEEDING

The most common cause of an orchid's early demise is over-watering. Although different orchids have different needs, most require watering once or twice a week in spring and summer, and once a fortnight in winter. In the case of *Cattleya*, water just enough to prevent the pseudobulb (the swelling at the base of the stems) from shrivelling. Keep *Dendrobium* almost dry in winter. Use a can filled with tepid rain- or filtered water, and pour it into the pot until it runs from the base. For plants with congested roots, submerge the pot to just below the rim in a bowl of water, and leave until the compost surface is damp, then remove and leave to drain. Also provide some humidity by misting the leaves with

∧ *Wipe away excess moisture*
After watering your plants, leave them to drain and wipe off any excess moisture on or between the leaves with a soft cloth to prevent rotting.

rain- or filtered water, avoiding the flowers; or sit the pots on a tray of damp pebbles or gravel (*see pp.368–367*).

Orchid compost contains no nutrients, so start feeding your plants with a

∧ *Warm mist*
Do not mist orchids with cold water; leave rain- or filtered water to warm up to room temperature, and spray in the morning.

proprietary orchid fertilizer as soon as you get them home, following the instructions on the packet. Some orchids, such as *Phalaenopsis*, should be fed weekly, while others need less frequent applications.

POSITIONING YOUR ORCHIDS

As with watering, the light requirements of orchids differ depending on the type. *Epidendrum* grow on tropical tree branches in the wild and like bright indirect light. *Cymbidium* hybrids also prefer bright light, and should be set outside in a sheltered spot during the summer, then given a bright, cool position indoors out of direct sun, such as a conservatory or a frost-free porch, in

∧ *Fuss-free orchid*
The large exotic blooms of the moth orchid belie its easy-going nature. It requires soft light and is quite happy in a warm room.

autumn and winter. *Cattleya* and *Oncidium* prefer a bright position that offers some shade at midday, such as an east- or west-facing windowsill, but move them to a bright spot that receives sun all day in winter when light levels are significantly lower.

If you do not have a light area in which to keep an orchid, choose a *Phalaenopsis* or *Paphiopedilum* hybrid. These dislike strong sunlight, preferring a shady site from late spring to autumn.

< *Dainty Dendrobium*
Position a Dendrobium *where it will receive bright filtered light and keep humidity levels high in the growing season. It will then reward you with these exquisite flowers.*

Orchid types

Before buying, check you can give your chosen orchid the temperature it needs. Remember that most require a 5°C (10°F) drop between day and night.

WARM-GROWING

Tender orchids, such as *Dendrobium* hybrids and *Phalaenopsis*, require warmth all year, with a minimum winter temperature of 16–18°C (61–64°F). They will tolerate occasional dips, and are fine in centrally-heated houses, if moved away from cold windowsills at night.

INTERMEDIATE

Cattleya, *Epidendrum*, and *Paphiopedilum* require more warmth than cool-growing orchids in winter, but will tolerate slightly higher temperatures in summer (*see below*). Most grow well indoors, but should be moved away from cold windowsills at night during winter.

COOL-GROWING

This group includes *Cymbidium* and *Oncidium*, which prefer low temperatures all year. Stand them outside in summer in a sheltered spot, then bring them in to an unheated room, such as a cool conservatory or greenhouse, for winter, keeping them at around 8–10°C (46–50°F).

∧ *Cool customer*
With its spidery green and maroon flowers, Cymbidium kanran *is a fantastic orchid for those with a cool room to keep it in throughout winter.*

Display stunning orchids

Stems of rich ruby-red flowers, set off by a basket-weave container, create a spectacular display for an east- or west-facing windowsill, or a bright spot out of direct sun. The orchid shown here, *Colmanara* 'Massai Red', will flower for many weeks and is very easy to look after.

WHEN TO PLANT
Late spring

AT ITS BEST
Late spring to summer

TIME TO COMPLETE
 30 minutes

YOU WILL NEED
 Large plastic-lined basket
Expanded clay pebbles, such as Hortag (available from garden centres and orchid nurseries)
Sphagnum moss or moss-like substitute
Thin wooden stakes
Colmanara 'Massai Red'

1 LINE THE CONTAINER
If your container does not have an integrated lining, use a sheet of plastic to line it. Then add a layer of expanded clay pebbles, which absorb water and slowly release it to increase humidity.

2 ADD THE ORCHIDS
Keeping the orchids in their pots, arrange them in the basket. Make sure that their flowering stems are well spaced out for maximum impact. Stake any wayward stems to create a fan-like shape.

3 FILL THE GAPS
Hold the orchid pots upright and fill around them using more expanded clay pebbles. Firm them down gently to ensure they hold the plants in place, which can be top-heavy when in flower.

4 TOP WITH MOSS
Finally, add a layer of garden moss, or a moss substitute, over the clay pebbles and the top of the orchid pots. Water the pots and add some water to the pebbles as well.

5 AFTERCARE
Place the orchids in a bright room, away from full sun; keep them at 15–23°C (59–73°F) during the day, and 10–15°C (50–59°F) at night. Throughout the year, water the plants when the compost is almost dry and apply an orchid fertilizer with every other watering. Spray every few days with rainwater or filtered tap water to maintain humidity.

Staying power >
Each flower spike of Colmanara *'Massai Red' lasts up to seven weeks. Keep the plant at room temperature for most of the year, but slightly cooler when in flower to prolong the blooming period.*

Force bulbs for winter

The winter garden may be asleep, but you can bring spring colour and scent indoors by growing bulbs as house plants. Most effective are those that have been "pre-forced", which simply means they have been chilled and fooled into thinking that winter has already passed, so that they bloom for Christmas and New Year.

≫ **WHEN TO START**
Early autumn

AT THEIR BEST
Winter to early spring

TIME TO COMPLETE
🕐 1 hour

YOU WILL NEED
🔻 Pre-forced bulbs,
    at least three per bowl
Containers (with drainage holes);
    use deep pots for narcissi
Free-draining compost
Bulb fibre
Moss for decoration

Hyacinths

With colourful flowers and a delicious scent, hyacinths are ideal for growing indoors. Plant them in early autumn, and they will flower in the coldest depths of winter.

2 STORE IN DARK
Put the bowl in a cool, dark place for eight weeks. Check regularly and keep the compost slightly moist. Pale yellow leaves will eventually appear, and you should also be able to see the flower buds poking through in the middle.

1 PLANT IN BOWLS
Put a shallow layer of compost in a bowl. Place the hyacinths on top, not touching each other, with pointed ends up. Add more compost, leaving the top third of the bulbs uncovered. Water well.

3 AFTERCARE
Bring the plants out into the light to flower. Place them in a cool, light spot, but not in bright sun. Water them enough to keep the compost just moist, and turn the bowl daily.

Narcissi

Treated miniature daffodils, such as 'Tête-à-Tête', and 'Soleil d'Or' are easy to force, but need lots of light.

PLANT AND STAKE

Plant bulbs in a pot, with the pointed tips just below the compost. Water to settle the compost. Place the pot in a sunny spot to encourage strong growth. Then wait for shoots to appear. Keep the compost moist, and support taller stems with canes.

TOP TIP: GROWING IN WATER

Forced bulbs can be grown simply in water alone. Special hyacinth vases hold the bulbs just above the surface, or you can use pebbles in a vase of water to create the same effect. Change the water regularly, and keep it topped up, so that it always sits just below the base of the bulb.

< *Maximize flowering*
Both hyacinths and narcissi will flower for longer in cool conditions. If you use them to decorate a warm room, store in a cooler spot at night.

Plants for focal points

Tiny containers can look cute, but to create a statement, go for big, bold, sculptural plants in dramatic pots. Flowers also add punch but they are seasonal, so for year-round glamour focus on the leaves first when making your choices. Set more delicate plants in tall urns or on tables to raise their profile.

CHOOSING A STATEMENT PLANT

Before buying a plant, think about where you would like to position it, and how much space you can afford. Plants with large dark leaves tend to prefer shade, while those with variegated foliage and palms enjoy more light. Cacti are happy in hot spots near south-facing windows, and the large types make striking features. Beware of their spines and hairs, though, as these will irritate your skin.

Also consider how quickly your plant will grow. Some, such as the bamboo palm, *Dypsis lutescens*, stay the same size for many years, while vigorous plants, like the sentry palm, *Howea belmoreana*, and Swiss cheese plant, *Monstera deliciosa*, can double their size in a couple of years, given the right conditions.

PLACING YOUR PLANT

Use your plant as a focal point to draw attention to an area of the room, or to provide a leafy contrast to the hard lines of cupboards and other furniture. Also, ensure the plant won't be an obstacle, and choose a pot that matches your decor.

TOP TIP: CLEAN LEAVES

Dust-covered foliage ruins the look of a plant, and restricts the light reaching the leaves, inhibiting its growth. Use a damp soft cloth to wipe away grime and dirt, or place your plant in the shower and wash off the dust. Add a shine to large-leaved plants by wiping a little milk over the surfaces.

< *Peaceful home*
The large glossy leaves and elegant white flowers of the peace lily, Spathiphyllum wallisii, *are matched by this simple metal container. Choose a large variety for a big statement.*

Architectural plant options

When choosing a house plant to make a bold statement in your home, either opt for one single dramatic specimen, or select a few smaller ones that combine well to create more impact. Unusual shapes and textures draw the eye, too, and can make up for size in smaller homes. If you love bright colours, select plants with blowsy blooms, such as amaryllis, or fiery bracts, like the *Vriesea* species.

❶ The shade-loving *Calathea rufibarba* 'Blue Grass', and dumb cane, *Dieffenbachia seguine* 'Saturn', make perfect partners in a large ceramic pot.   ❷ *Vriesea* species have colourful bracts that last for many weeks.   ❸ Japanese sago palm, *Cycas revoluta,* is an excellent house plant that strikes a pose but grows very slowly, so buy one to fit your space, and position it in bright light — a conservatory is ideal.   ❹ These two tiny plants create a talking point when combined in a bowl on a stand. However, they need different conditions and are planted in separate pots: the grassy *Isolepis cernua* requires lots of water to thrive, while the string of beads, *Senecio rowleyanus*, prefers dryer compost.

Shade-loving house plants

All houses have a shady corner that may need brightening up, and there are lots of house plants that are happy in low light. Many foliage plants, in particular, grow on shady rainforest floors in the wild, and will cope well in a north-facing room, especially if you mist them regularly to imitate their natural environment. Others, especially those that produce beautiful flowers, grow best in lighter conditions, but will tolerate a good deal of shade.

☼ full light   ☀ partial shade   ☀ full shade
◌ water lightly – only when the top few centimetres of soil is dry   ● water frequently – once or twice a week in the growing season

❶ Parlour palm, *Chamaedorea elegans*; ↕1m (3ft) ↔30cm (12in) ☀ ☀ ● ❷ *Peperomia caperata* 'Luna'; ↕30cm (12in) ↔30cm (12in) ☀ ☀ ● ❸ Painted net-leaf, *Fittonia albivenis* Verschaffeltii Group; ↕30cm (12in) ↔30cm (12in) ☀ ● ❹ Zebra plant, *Calathea zebrina*; ↔1m (3ft) ↕1m (3ft) ☀ ● ❺ Peace lily, *Spathiphyllum* 'Mauna Loa'; ↕90cm (36in) ↔60cm (24in) ☀ ● ❻ Miniature tree fern, *Blechnum gibbum*; ↕50cm (20in) ↔1m (3ft) ☀ ☀ ● ❼ Mother-in-law's tongue, *Sansevieria trifasciata*; ↕1.2m (4ft) ↔40cm (16in) ☀ ☀ ◌ ❽ *Philodendron bipinnatifidum*; ↕3m (10ft) ↔3m (10ft) ☀ ☀ ● ❾ Flamingo flower, *Anthurium andraeanum*; ↕50cm (20in) ↔50cm (20in) ☀ ● ❿ Prayer plant, *Maranta leuconeura*; ↕30cm (12in) ↔40cm (16in) ☀ ●

Add flower power to your home

Recreate a holiday atmosphere in your home with a selection of vibrant or scented tropical flowers that hint at beach-front promenades. Flowers provide colourful contrasts to cool, contemporary interiors, and many bloom for months without too much fuss — just keep them well fed and watered.

BRIGHT BRACTS

Like colourful neon lights, vibrant bromeliad flowers and bracts make a bold statement that can't be ignored. To show off these peacocks of the house plant world to full effect, present them against a clean, simple backdrop, such as a white windowsill. The bright bracts of most bromeliads last for many months, and the flowers peep out between or above them.

SURVIVAL STRATEGY

Most bromeliads, including *Guzmania*, *Tillandsia* and *Vriesea*, are from the tropics and love the warmth of a heated home, but suffer if the humidity is low. Plant them in free-draining compost and water them regularly when in growth, reducing the frequency in winter. Take care not to overwater bromeliads, as soggy soil can kill them. To provide humidity, mist them once or twice a week with soft water or rainwater, applied at room temperature.

∧ *Water with care*
When watering Vriesea, *pour into the central cup formed by the rosette of leaves. Also water the compost to keep it moist.*

TOP TIP: FEEDING TILLANDSIA

Tillandsia has few roots and clings to trees in its natural habitat, absorbing water and nutrients through its leaves. Provide similar conditions by misting the leaves once a month with a quarter-strength balanced liquid fertilizer, ideally diluted in rainwater.

∧ *Tropical pots*
Hot-hued glazed pots bring out the colours of these three vivid bromeliads: Guzmania dissitiflora, Tillandsia cyanea, *and a flaming red* Vriesea. *Although they prefer bright light, they dislike direct sun, so avoid hot, south-facing windowsills.*

Long-lasting blooms

Flowers in the home deserve pride of place, so if you have space for just one or two, choose plants that will sparkle for several months.

LONG-TERM COLOUR

For prolonged flower power, *Streptocarpus* (*see pp.368–369*), which come in many colours, can bloom almost all year. Other good choices include the orange-flowered dwarf pomegranate, *Punica granatum* var. *nana*, statuesque *Lantana*, and *Plumbago*, with its blue summer flowers.

PLANT OPTIONS

Hibiscus rosa-sinensis
Kalanchoe
Lantana camara
Persian violet, *Exacum affine*
Plumbago auriculata
Streptocarpus hybrids

∧ **Persian queen**
Masses of tiny fragrant blue flowers adorn the Persian violet, Exacum affine, *for many months from spring and throughout the summer.*

Floral scents

Why buy flower-scented air fresheners when you can have the real thing, and enjoy colourful blooms into the bargain? Take care when choosing a fragrant plant, as the intense perfume of some can be overpowering in a small room.

PERFUMED PRIZES

Choose between the compact gardenia, prized for its white, deliciously scented flowers and shiny dark foliage; an indoor jasmine, *Stephanotis*; and the wax plant, *Hoya carnosa*. The wax plant and jasmine are climbers and need space to grow, or train them around a wire hoop. All are highly fragrant and need bright light.

PLANTING OPTIONS

Brugmansia x *candida*
Gardenia jasminoides
Hoya carnosa and *H.lanceolata*
 subsp. *bella*
Jasmine, *Jasminum polyanthum*
Stephanotis floribunda

∧ **Fragrant wax flower**
Hoya lanceolata subsp. bella *has the same sweet scent as its climbing cousin,* H. carnosa, *but reaches just 45cm (18in).*

Holiday care

Take a few precautions before you go on holiday to avoid the disappointment of returning home to find your house plants flagging, or dead.

SET THEM OUTSIDE

One way to keep plants happy while you are on holiday is to set them outdoors in the shade on a tray of pebbles. Many will tolerate summer night temperatures, and enjoy the fresh air and humidity outside. Check plant labels first for their minimum temperature requirements.

WATERING TRICKS

If keeping plants in the garden is not an option, try the plastic bottle trick. Cut the bottom off a bottle and make a small hole in the lid with a skewer. Invert the bottle and push the lid into the compost. Fill the bottle, and water will slowly seep into the compost while you are away.

∧ **Trick number two**
Another option is to put your pots on a wet towel on the draining board. Place one end of the towel in the sink. Fill the sink with water and it will seep up the towel and keep the compost in the pots damp.

Bathroom oasis

Hot and steamy, the bathroom is an ideal environment for ferns. Their delicate fronds soften the lines of ceramic, metal, and glass, and a quick shower once a week helps to keep them in excellent health. If you have no shelf space to fit a fern or two, suspend a hanging basket from the ceiling (*see pp.370–371*).

TIME TO COMPLETE
 30 minutes

YOU WILL NEED
- Decorative containers
- Plastic pots that fit inside
- Pieces of polystyrene
- House plant compost
- Slow-release fertilizer granules
- Gravel or moss
- *Adiantum capillus-veneris*
- *Asplenium nidus*

1 POT UP THE FERNS
If you bought your ferns in pots that fit perfectly into your decorative containers, simple add slow-release fertilizer granules to the compost. If not, repot them. In a new plastic pot, put pieces of polystyrene in the base, then add a layer of compost. Tip a fern out of its old pot and place it on top. Fill in around it with more compost and fertilizer granules.

2 SITING AND AFTERCARE
Fit the potted ferns into your decorative containers, add a layer of gravel or moss on top of the compost, and place them in a shady spot. Water the *Adiantum* well throughout the year – the leaves will shrivel if the compost dries out. The *Asplenium* needs plenty of water in spring and summer, but keep the compost just moist in the winter months.

< *Hungry ferns*
Feed the bird's nest fern (Asplenium) and delicate maidenhair fern (Adiantum) regularly in summer with a balanced liquid fertilizer.

Fern choices

Most, but not all, ferns like the moist conditions in a bathroom, so check individual plant labels before buying. Match your plants with smooth ceramic, glass, or rust-proof metal containers that contrast well with the textured fronds.

FOLIAGE EFFECTS
For large bathrooms, the spreading, bushy foliage of a dwarf tree fern works well, but if your space is limited, try small, slow-growing brake or button ferns (*Pteris* and *Pellaea*). Asparagus ferns, with their feathery foliage, look delicate but are deceptively easy to keep. They are not, in fact, true ferns at all, and adapt to a wide range of conditions. If you opt for a hanging basket, the tree-dwelling staghorn fern will provide a focal point.

❶ *Asparagus setaceus* 'Nanus'; ↕↔30cm (12in) ❷ Dwarf tree fern, *Blechnum gibbum*; ↕75cm (30in) ↔60cm (24in) ❸ *Pteris ensiformis* 'Evergemiensis'; ↕↔30cm (12in) ❹ *Pellaea rotundifolia*; ↕30cm (12in) ↔60cm (24in) ❺ Staghorn fern, *Platycerium bifurcatum*; ↕90cm (3ft) ↔1.2m (4ft) ❻ *Asparagus densiflorus* 'Myersii'; ↕40cm (16in) ↔30cm (12in)

Create a desert bowl

Cacti have a reputation for sitting around in corners getting dusty and barely growing, but use them in a new way and they come to life. They look great planted in small groups, and given a sand mulch such a group becomes a funky and kitsch desert scene. All it needs is a miniature cowboy.

 WHEN TO START
Spring
AT ITS BEST
Early summer

 TIME TO COMPLETE
1½ hours

 YOU WILL NEED
Shallow planting bowl
Crocks or pebbles
Cacti compost
Washed sand
Newspaper
Spoon
Heavy-duty gloves
Watering can

Miniature cacti
This selection includes
Cleistocactus strausii,
Mammillaria hahniana,
Opuntia tuna, and
Rebutia species

1 BEFORE YOU START
Cacti famously survive on little water, but if you want them to grow and flower they should actually be watered regularly during the growing season. Giving them a thorough watering before planting will help the roots to make good contact with the new compost, and they should grow well.

2 AID DRAINAGE
All cacti hate to sit in water, so make sure it will run freely through the growing medium, and out of the bottom of the pot. The container should have lots of drainage holes, covered by a layer of pebbles or crocks, to prevent the compost from clogging up the holes.

3 SET OUT THE PLANTS

Don your protective gloves and start arranging your plants. If you have chosen the position for each of your cacti before you start, planting will be easier and you are more likely to end up with a good overall effect. It makes sense to put smaller ones at the front and larger ones at the back, but also consider planting those with different habits, textures and flower colour next to each other.

4 PLANTING TIPS

Wrap a folded strip of newspaper around the top of the plant. This will help you to slide it out of its pot and manoeuvre it into the larger planter without getting spines or fine hairs in your fingers. It also protects the plant.

5 FILL IN THE GAPS

Once the plants are in position, use a spoon to carefully fill the gaps between them with a cacti compost. Add small amounts of compost at a time and keep firming it down with the back of the spoon to ensure that there are no air holes left around the plant roots.

6 BRUSH OFF COMPOST

No matter how careful you are, some compost will inevitably get caught in the cactus spines and hairs. Use a soft brush to remove it and to keep the plants looking clean and tidy.

7 WATER IN

Water all the plants in well. In summer, they can be watered whenever the surface of the soil dries out. In winter, they should be left dry; start watering again sparingly when you see signs of growth in spring.

8 APPLY A SAND MULCH

Use the spoon to spread fine sand around the surface of the planter. This helps water to quickly drain away from the surface, so preventing rot, and gives the planter an authentic desert-like appearance. Set your arrangement in a bright, sunny position.

TOP TIP: WATERING OVERFILLED POTS

Cacti are often sold when the plants are almost overflowing the sides of their pots, making it tricky to water them properly before planting. Sit these in a container of water until the root ball is damp.

Desert dwellers

Cacti create intrigue with their weird shapes, fierce spines, and surprisingly vivid flowers. Together with succulents, these easy plants are perfect for a sunny windowsill. Most remain small when grown as houseplants, but others, like the silver jade plant, will make sizeable specimens. Water from spring to summer, allowing the compost to dry between doses, and in winter, reduce this to once a month for succulents and not at all for cacti.

All of these plants need a sunny site and minimal watering (*see opposite*) **1** *Haworthia attenuata* f. *clariperla*; ‡12cm (5in) ↔12cm (5in) **2** *Parodia penicillata*; ‡30cm (12in) ↔12cm (5in) **3** *Parodia magnifica*; ‡15cm (6in) ↔45cm (18in) **4** *Echinocereus pulchellus*; ‡5cm (2in) ↔15cm (6in) **5** Plush plant, *Echeveria pulvinata*; ‡30cm (12in) ↔50cm (20in) **6** Living stone, *Lithops pseudotruncatella* subsp. *dentritica*; ‡4cm (1½in) ↔ 4cm (1½in) **7** Flaming Katy, *Kalanchoe blossfeldiana*; ‡40cm (16in) ↔40cm (16in) **8** Silver jade plant, *Crassula arborescens*; ‡60cm (24in) ↔60cm (24in) **9** *Echinopsis multiplex*; ‡25cm (10in) ↔30cm (12in) **10** *Aloe aristata*; ‡12cm (5in) ↔30cm (12in) **11** *Mammillaria blossfeldiana*; ‡5cm (2in) ↔5cm (2in)

Perfect presents

Poinsettias are classic Christmas plants, bringing a splash of festive red and green to the table or windowsill. An attractive bowl, planted up with one or two, makes a cheery winter gift.

1 FIND THE IDEAL SPOT
To keep them looking good, poinsettias need a sunny, south-facing windowsill, or bright filtered light. Don't press them close up against a cold windowpane though, as this can damage the leaves. Keep them at about 20°C (68°F) during the day, and cooler at night, to prolong the display.

2 WATERING AND FEEDING
Poinsettias should be watered regularly and kept evenly moist. Never let plants sit in water; always empty their saucers or planters shortly after watering.

3 RE-FLOWERING METHOD
With year-round care, you can get a plant to perform again. Water it until mid-spring, then let it dry out and allow the stems to shrivel. Keep it cool. At the end of spring, cut all growth to a few centimetres above the soil and repot it in new compost. Water well and keep it warm, feeding it with houseplant fertilizer when new growth appears. A month later, move the plant outside to a shady spot, pinching out the growing tips in midsummer, before returning it indoors. Give it a sunny spot, watering and feeding regularly. From mid-autumn, keep the plant in total darkness between 5pm and 8am. It will then soon re-flower and produce colourful bracts.

TOP TIP: LEAF DROP

It is common for a few poinsettia leaves to turn yellow and drop off when you first bring them home. Don't be alarmed, the plant is just reacting to its new living conditions.

Poinsettia gallery

Many colourful cultivars are available, and grow to about ‡30cm (12in) ↔40cm (16in).

❶ *Euphorbia pulcherrima* 'Freedom White'
❷ 'Red Fox Infinity Red'
❸ 'Sonora'
❹ 'Spotlight Pink'

Bring plants into flower

There are some house plants that will flower prolifically whatever you do with them. However, there are others that, having been chosen for their glorious flowers, only ever seem to sprout more leaves. Every house plant requires slightly different care to make it bloom again, plus a degree of patience.

Peace lilies

This plant is one of the trickiest to encourage back into bloom. If you try these tips, and still have no luck, keep it and grow it for its attractive, sword-like leaves instead.

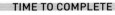
WHEN TO START
Spring
AT ITS BEST
Spring

YOU WILL NEED
Peace lily, *Spathiphyllum*
Container
House plant compost

TIME TO COMPLETE
🕐 1 hour

1 ASSESS THE PROBLEM
Take care not to feed your peace lily too much. Feeding may initiate flowering, but it often has the opposite effect, leading to more leaves at the expense of blooms.

2 REPOT IF CRAMPED
Peace lilies will tolerate small pots unless their roots are severely cramped, causing the plant to become water-stressed. Transferring it to a slightly larger pot can lead to a flush of new flowers.

3 CHOOSE A BRIGHT LOCATION
Poor light is the main reason why peace lilies don't re-flower. Although these plants will tolerate quite deep shade, and grow reasonably well in dull corners, they actually require soft, indirect light in order to flower. Position them on a north-facing windowsill, or somewhere within a few feet of a brighter window, but shielded from direct sunlight. The plant will then flower at various intervals throughout the year.

Other difficult plants

House plants originate from all over the world, and naturally require different conditions in order to flower. The trick is to mimic these at home to coax reluctant types to bloom.

BROMELIAD

The main part of a bromeliad dies after flowering, leaving new shoots to take its place. These can either be grown on as a group, or divided and grown on for a few years until mature. Once the bromeliad is as large as your original plant was when it flowered, place a clear plastic bag over it for a week, with a ripe apple inside. The apple releases ethylene, a gas that initiates flowering.

CLIVIA

For this beautiful spring- and summer-flowering bulb to flower, it needs a period of cold dormancy. While it likes a warm spot for most of the year, from late autumn to late winter, keep it dry and at around 10°C (50°F). Water again from early spring, and give it a liquid feed every other week. As growth

begins, move the plant to a warmer spot to flower, after which you should water it slightly less and begin the cycle again. Clivias like to be pot-bound, so repot infrequently.

CHRISTMAS CACTUS

To flower well, Christmas cacti, *Schlumbergera*, need plenty of light during the summer. If grown indoors, keep them on a sunny windowsill. If placed outside, shade them a little to prevent them from scorching. To persuade them to flower, they then require short days and long nights. So, from autumn to Christmas, keep them in a room that is not lit at night, such as a spare room or a child's bedroom.

MOTH ORCHID

If the growing conditions are right, it is fairly easy to get beautiful moth orchids, *Phalaenopsis*, to re-flower. They don't like too much light, so grow them on a west- or east-facing windowsill during winter, and in a shadier spot in summer. Water weekly in summer with rainwater, taking care to avoid the crown. Reduce watering in winter. If you have a plant in flower, just as the last bloom is fading, trim the spike slightly below where the first flower opened. A bud there will sprout a second flower spike, which itself can be trimmed to give a third. To encourage a moth orchid to flower again from scratch, keep it humid (*see p.374*), give it a diluted feed once a month, and keep it at around 15°C (59°F) at night and 21–25°C (70–77°F) during the day. This fluctuation, combined with feeding and humidity, will initiate new flowers.

Silver splash

Begonias come in many forms, and these elegant foliage types make handsome features in a modern indoor arrangement (*right*). Choose tall simple containers to contrast with the heavily textured leaves, partner them with small-leaved trailing plants, and set them in a line or up a few steps.

WHEN TO START
Any time

AT ITS BEST
All year round

TIME TO COMPLETE
2 hours

YOU WILL NEED
- Silver-leaved *Begonia rex* hybrids
- *Pilea depressa*
- Tall metal container
- Plastic tray, such as vegetable packaging, or thick plastic bag
- Plastic pots
- Gravel
- House plant compost

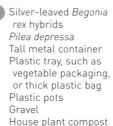

1 LINE THE CONTAINERS
If your container has drainage holes, place a deep plastic tray in the bottom to prevent water leaking out, or line it with a thick plastic bag. Then add some gravel to the bottom. Also buy plastic plant pots that fit neatly into the container.

2 ARRANGE THE PLANTS
Cover the drainage holes of the plastic pots with gravel, top up with compost, and plant the begonias and *Pilea* (one in each pot). Water and allow to drain. Arrange the pots in the container, adding more gravel to raise them up to the correct level, as required.

Caring for begonias

Begonia rex hybrids come in many colours and forms, but all require the same treatment. Feed them fortnightly in summer and once a month in winter, and keep them away from bright sunlight to prevent the foliage from scorching.

FOLIAGE NEEDS
Although they dislike strong sun, begonias produce the best colours in bright, diffused light, and prefer a temperature of 18–21°C (64–70°F). Watering is the key to success, since they are prone to rotting if given too much or too little. Every two weeks, remove the plastic pots from the container, and place them in a bowl of water that reaches just below the rims. Allow moisture to seep up from the bottom, and when the top of the compost is wet, take them out and leave to drain.

Begonias come in an array of spectacular colours and forms. Specialist nurseries offer the widest choice, and most offer a mail-order service:

❶ 'Martin Johnson'
❷ 'Benitochiba'
❸ 'Tiny Bright'

Winter flowers

When it's cold and grey outside, you need some indoor colour to brighten things up. Lots of house plants flower over winter, and you will appreciate them all the more for their excellent timing. From dependable stalwarts, such as primulas and African violets to exotic clivias, there is a winter-flowering house plant to suit every taste. Some, such as jasmine, provide delicious scents that will remind you of the warmer months to come.

SELECTIONS》

☀ full light   ☀ partial shade (bright but filtered light)   ☀ full shade
◐ water lightly – only when the top few centimetres of soil are dry   ◆ water frequently – once or twice a week in the growing season

① *Pentas lanceolata*; ‡50cm (20in) ↔40cm (16in) ☀◆   **②** African violet, *Saintpaulia*; ‡15cm (6in) ↔40cm (16in) ☀◐   **③** *Cyclamen persicum* 'Sierra White'; ‡23cm (9in) ↔20cm (8in) ☀◐   **④** *Clivia miniata*; ‡45cm (18in) ↔30cm (12in) ☀◐   **⑤** Flaming Katy, *Kalanchoe blossfeldiana*; ‡40cm (16in) ↔40cm (16in) ☀◆   **⑥** *Cymbidium* 'Showgirl'; ‡45cm (18in) ↔45cm (18in) ☀◐   **⑦** *Primula obconica*; ‡30cm (12in) ↔25cm (10in) ☀◐   **⑧** Winter-flowering begonia, Begonia elatior Catkin; ‡30cm (12in) ↔45cm (18in) ☀◐   **⑨** Jasmine, *Jasminum polyanthum*; ‡up to 3m (10ft) ↔1m (3ft) ☀◐   **⑩** Flamingo flower, *Anthurium andraeanum*; ‡60cm (24in) ↔30cm (12in) ☀◆

Plant Care

To care for your plants well it's important to provide them
with sufficient water and fertilizer, and to keep your garden
free of weeds. Shrubs and some trees also benefit from an
annual prune to keep them tidy and boost new growth. You
may also like to try propagating plants. Dividing up perennials
couldn't be easier; taking cuttings requires a little more skill
but you will soon master the techniques. Finally, learn to
recognize and treat common pests and diseases.

Dealing with weeds

Thug-like grasses, such as couch, scutch and twitch grass, as well as broad-leaf weeds, including thistle, dandelion, and chickweed, all compete with your plants for nutrients, water, and sunlight. They also spoil the look of displays and take up valuable planting space, so it is vital that you weed them out.

REMOVING ANNUALS AND PERENNIALS

The way in which you control the weeds in your garden depends partly on whether they are annual plants that grow, make seed, and die in one year, or perennial types, which survive winter via tough root systems. Some annuals flower almost continuously for most of the year and produce vast amounts of seed, so try to clear them at the start of the growing season before they bloom. After weeding, apply a mulch and dig over the soil as little as possible so that you don't uncover more weed seeds.

Perennial weeds, like dandelions and couch grass, also flower and seed, but it is their tough roots that make them difficult to eradicate. Any root fragments that you miss when digging them up will regrow into new plants, so try to remove every piece.

METHODS OF CONTROL

Most annual weeds are easy to dig up or pull out by hand. On large areas, use a hoe to sever the stems from the roots just below soil level, taking care not to cut off your plants too. Hoe on a dry day, and leave the weeds to die on the soil surface. Some weeds, such as buttercups, spread by long stems, called runners, which root when they touch the soil. Ease out the root systems of young plants with a hand fork.

Contact weedkillers are useful for controlling annual weeds in paths and gravel, and on bare soil before planting. Always follow the manufacturers' instructions. Use a systemic, glyphosate-based weedkiller for perennial weeds as this kills the roots, preventing plants from regrowing.

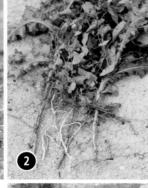

❶ Oxalis is a perennial and produces hundreds of tiny bulbils that split off and regrow when you try to dig them up.
❷ Many perennial weeds have drought-resistant tap roots that survive extreme conditions.
❸ Annuals have fibrous roots that can be pulled up easily.

❶ Set aside one watering can to apply weedkiller, and keep it well away from those you use for watering.
❷ A hand fork is useful for digging up the roots of weeds, as it loosens the soil, making them easier to extract.
❸ Move your hoe back and forth along the soil surface so the blade slices through the lower stems.

Persistent troublemakers

The following rogues gallery will help you to identify and control some of the most troublesome weeds. If you do not want to use weedkillers, eradicating some will be very difficult. Your options are either to starve their roots by continually removing the leafy shoots, or try blocking out light by covering the ground with black plastic or matting for two years.

❶ GROUND ELDER

This perennial forms a low mat of dark green leaves. Dig up young plants before they flower (*above*), or cover them with weed matting or carpet. If they persist, treat repeatedly with glyphosate weedkiller.

❷ OXALIS

The clover-like leaves spread rapidly, and can invade lawns. Annuals have explosive seed pods; perennials have bulbils. Yellow oxalis in lawns resists selective weedkillers, so try autumn scarifying (*see p.423*).

❸ HORSETAIL

The roots of this perennial are hard to pull out since the stems snap easily. A water-resistant coating on the stems also helps them shake off weedkiller, so crush them before treating with glyphosate in late summer.

❹ DOCK

Treat plants when young: dig the tap root out with a fork, or use a weeding tool in lawns. Don't allow mature plants to flower, and use a glyphosate-based weedkiller to kill their extensive root systems.

❺ NETTLES

Perennial stinging nettles form a network of root runners that support a colony of plants. Wear thick gloves to dig out the whole root system, or spray with systemic weedkiller. Or leave large groups as they are valuable wildlife refuges.

❻ JAPANESE KNOTWEED

Any root fragments of this bamboo-like thug will regrow. Repeatedly dig them out over several seasons; dry and burn the removed roots. If this fails, spray with glyphosate-based weedkiller repeatedly from late spring to early autumn.

❼ BINDWEED

This pretty but persistent twining perennial disappears in winter, only to resprout from fleshy white roots in spring. Digging it up can spread the roots; instead, train it up canes set away from ornamentals, and spray with glyphosate.

❽ BRAMBLES

The thorny stems spread rapidly over other plants and the tips will root where they touch any soil. Dig out seedlings and rooted runners. Cut back larger plants and dig out the woody base and roots. Spray unplanted areas with brushwood killer.

Feeding your plants

No matter how good your soil, it will probably need extra nutrients to help plants with specific needs, or to boost them at key times, like flowering. Always follow the instructions on the label, as too much, or the wrong type of fertilizer, can cause problems, such as plants with all leaves and no flowers.

UNDERSTANDING NUTRIENTS

The three basic elements that plants require are nitrogen (N), phosphorus (P) and potassium (K). Nitrogen is needed for leaf and shoot growth, phosphorus for roots, and potassium helps flowers and fruits to develop. Fertilizer manufacturers list the nutrient content as a ratio: a general purpose fertilizer has an N:P:K ratio of 7:7:7, while a tomato feed has a high concentration of potassium to boost fruit production, and a fertilizer for lawns or leafy crops contains mostly nitrogen. Many fertilizers also include various trace elements or micro-nutrients. A plant's nutrient requirements can depend on their phase of growth, with most needing a general boost in the spring, and more potassium as they fruit or flower.

❶ Nitrogen (nitrate) is needed for healthy leaves. ❷ Potassium (potash) boosts the production of flowers and fruit. ❸ For strong root development, choose a fertilizer rich in phosphorus (phosphate).

FERTILIZER CHOICES

Your local garden centre will offer both organic (derived from plants and animals) and inorganic (chemically manufactured) fertilizers. Most are concentrated for convenience and available as liquids, powders that you dilute in water, or granules. Typical examples of organic fertilizers are pelleted chicken manure; blood, fish and bonemeal; liquid seaweed fertilizer; and homemade plant feeds, such as the diluted liquor from a wormery, or fertilizers made from soaking comfrey leaves. Inorganic feeds include sulphate of potash, Growmore and granular rose feeds.

❶ Blood, fish, and bonemeal is a balanced organic fertilizer, applied through the growing season around flowers and vegetables; cease applications in early autumn. ❷ Slow-release granules, activated by warmth and moisture, give a steady supply of nutrients in containers and borders. ❸ Well-rotted manure or garden compost is rich in trace elements and soil-conditioning substances. Dig it in or apply as a surface mulch. ❹ Growmore is a balanced chemical feed used to enrich the soil for sowing or planting, and as a top dressing.

Mulching

Materials spread on top of the ground, usually around plants, are called mulches. They can be practical — feeding the soil, suppressing weeds, retaining moisture, or insulating roots in winter — or mainly decorative, applied for visual effect.

APPLYING ORGANIC MULCHES

Mulches are applied at different times depending on their purpose. For example, bark chips are spread over the soil after planting to suppress weeds. An organic mulch, such as manure, garden compost, chipped bark, or cocoa shells, must be laid over moist soil, either in spring, following autumn and winter rains, or after watering.

Some mulches, especially bark, use up nutrients temporarily as they decompose, so before laying them, apply a nitrogen-rich fertilizer, such as fish meal. Lay organic mulches in a layer 10cm (4in) deep so they continue to provide cover as they slowly decompose and feed the soil. Replenish these mulches every year.

∧ *Moist mulch*
Organic mulches help to retain moisture but if laid too close to plant stems can cause them to rot, so keep them at a safe distance.

∧ *Useful coverings*
Spread landscape fabric over the soil prior to planting to prevent weed growth (left). *Use straw to keep strawberries clean and dry* (right).

PRACTICAL SOLUTIONS

Man-made mulches offer many benefits. Weed membrane or landscape fabric is a semi-permeable material that blocks light but allows moisture through. Use it on low-maintenance beds, or on weed-ridden soil. Lay it before planting (*see also pp.76–77*) and cover with bark, gravel, or a decorative mulch. Black polythene does not allow moisture through, but it warms the soil and kills off weeds when laid over vegetable beds in spring.

Straw insulates the soil, and protects tender plants in winter. It is also used to raise crops, such as strawberries, off the ground, reducing fungal and slug problems. A thick layer of straw will protect the roots of vulnerable plants from frost.

DECORATIVE OPTIONS

Mulches that don't decompose are useful as decorative garden surfaces. They are particularly effective when laid over landscape fabric or membrane, which reduces weed growth and helps to prevent soil mixing in with the mulch and spoiling the effect. For a modern feel, try coloured crushed glass or slate shards. Cover small areas, like the tops of pots and containers, with beads, crushed and whole shells, or polished pebbles. Natural cobbles and pebbles blend well with gravel or shingle over larger areas, and can create a beach effect when laid in swathes.

❶ Pebbles and cobbles come in different colours and sizes. Ask to see a sample out of the bag, wetted to show the true colour.
❷ Crushed glass is usually a recycled product, milled to take off the sharp edges. Use bright colours for design highlights.
❸ Slate chips in various grades and subtle shades of dark grey have sharp edges, so are unsuitable for children's areas.
❹ Crushed shells are recycled from the seafood industry.

Watering your plants

All plants need watering, but some need more than others. Concentrate on plants in containers, where the compost dries out relatively quickly; newly planted specimens that haven't yet developed a strong enough root system to cope on their own; and fruits and vegetables at key stages in their growth cycle.

PRESERVE WATER SUPPLIES

Water is a precious commodity, but if you irrigate only those plants that need it, and water in the cool of the morning or in the evening, you can greatly reduce your impact on supplies.

Other ways to minimize water usage are to add moisture-retentive gel crystals to containers, and mulch borders every year after it has rained. Trees, shrubs, and perennials will also need watering less frequently during the first few months if you plant them when the soil is naturally moist in autumn, winter, and early spring. Lay turf in late winter and early spring, too, and it will usually establish well without the need for extra irrigation.

After planting, encourage deep rooting by watering thoroughly and then leaving for 7–14 days before watering again, rather than giving frequent small doses. The water will then sink deep into the soil and encourage roots to follow. Also, if planting in the rain shadow of walls and hedges use drought-tolerant species.

∧ *No buts about water butts*
Save water by installing water butts around your property, connecting them to the rainwater downpipes. Metal or plastic butts are widely available, or choose something more attractive like this wooden barrel.

Watering methods

Make the most of your water supplies and save yourself time and energy by using a watering method that suits the job at hand. A watering can is ideal for small areas where you want to target water accurately; hoses are best for large beds, but use them with care to avoid wastage.

WATERING BY HAND

If you only have a few plants or pots to water, use a watering can, and pour slowly so it has a chance to soak into the roots; remove fine roses from cans unless watering new plantings. Direct water to the roots of your plants — they do not absorb water through their leaves so spraying overhead is not only wasteful but means that less moisture reaches the soil. Also avoid flowers and fruits, which may rot if too wet. Mound up the soil around the base of large plants to create a reservoir in which water will collect and sink down to the root area.

When hosing beds and borders, focus the spray on the soil, and turn it off as you move between planted areas. Long-handled hoses are useful if you have lots of pots and baskets to reach — again, turn the flow off between each container.

∧ *Spraying from a distance*
Long-handled hoses allow you to reach hanging baskets with ease, and also to direct water to less accessible plants, such as vegetables in a large bed, without treading on the soil.

AUTOMATIC SYSTEMS

Relatively easy to install, automatic watering systems can save hours of work in the garden; attach a timer, and they will water your plot in your absence. Most come in kit form and allow you to design a system that suits your garden. Kits typically include a network of main pipes into which you insert fine feeder pipes that take water directly to individual plants or pots. These terminate in small drip nozzles, held just above soil level, that gradually release water, which drains down around the roots. Check your watering system every few weeks to ensure plants aren't being under- or over-watered, and adjust individual flow regulators as necessary. Turn off nozzles when no longer required.

< Timed to perfection
Set water timers to come on every day or week, in the morning or evening to minimize evaporation, and alter the program if the weather changes.

LEAKY AND SEEP HOSES

Less sophisticated than automatic irrigation systems, these perforated hosepipes are perfect for watering lots of plants at the same time. Unlike a regular hosepipe, water gradually seeps out at soil level and penetrates deeply. Lay one along a row of thirsty vegetables, or weave it between newly planted shrubs and perennials. Attach the hose to a water butt, which may need to be raised up to provide a gravitational flow of water, or fit on to an outdoor tap. Lift your hose and reposition it as needed.

Slow-release watering >
The most efficient watering method if used correctly, seep hoses trickle water into the soil exactly where it is needed.

WATERING CONTAINERS

Although large containers need watering less frequently than small ones, they may still require water every day in summer. Porous terracotta pots dry out quickly, so consider lining them with plastic before planting (*see p.409*). Don't rely on rain to water your pots as the compost often remains dry after a shower. When planting, leave a gap of at least 2cm (1in) between the compost and the pot's rim to allow water to collect there. A bark or gravel mulch helps retain moisture.

< Preventing soil erosion
Direct water onto a piece of broken pot to help prevent compost being washed off the roots.

TOP TIP: WATERING TREES

Help trees to establish by inserting perforated drainage tubing into the hole, close to the roots, at planting time. Water poured into the exposed end is directed to the root area with no wastage. Mulch, or use a tree mat, to deter weeds and to seal in moisture.

Frost protection

Some plants and containers need a little help to get them through cold winters but they can be left outside if you provide some protection when temperatures dip below freezing.

The big cover-up

Tender plants must be brought inside in winter because they die when exposed to freezing temperatures, but those that can survive a few degrees of frost (given two stars in this book) should survive outside in all but the coldest regions.

PLANTS TO PROTECT

Many slightly tender plants survive low temperatures but not cold, wet soils, so ensure yours drains freely before planting (*see pp.14–15*). Other plants are not killed by frost, but their flowers may be damaged. Examples include peach trees, magnolias, and camellias, which suffer when frosted blooms thaw too quickly in warm morning sun. Young leaves and buds of hardy plants can also be sensitive to frost, so don't feed in late summer because it promotes this vulnerable new growth. Also, allow herbaceous plants to die down naturally so that the leaves fall over the plant, creating a protective blanket, and apply a thick mulch over those that may suffer in low temperatures, like *Alstroemeria* or diascias.

∧ Ice-laden maple
Acer palmatum *cultivars are hardy, so just enjoy the sparkle of their vibrant deciduous autumn leaves laced with frost.*

∧ Straw blanket
Use chicken wire to secure a straw blanket over frost-sensitive plants that prefer dry soil conditions.

< Star fright
The flowers of star magnolias are damaged by frost; protect them with garden fleece.

TOP TIP: OVERWINTER BANANAS AND TREE FERNS

Popular for tropical gardens, *Musa basjoo* is one of the hardiest bananas and tolerates winters outside if protected from cold, wet conditions. First, cut down the stems and remove the leaves. Attach chicken wire to bamboo canes set around the plant to form a cage, and pack it with straw. Treat tree ferns in the same way: make a cage around the plant, fold the fronds over the top of the stem, and pack straw around it.

∧ Make a waterproof hat
Both bananas and tree ferns suffer in wet winters, so top the wire cage with a waterproof covering, such as clear plastic sheeting. In very cold regions you can also add a fleece wrapper. Remove the protection in late spring or when you see new growth.

Cloches for crops

Some vegetables that overwinter in the soil benefit from a protective cloche or a layer of straw. Likewise, crops that are sown early in spring may grow more quickly if kept snug when frosts strike. A wide variety of cloches is available to buy, or make one yourself from recycled materials.

CHOOSING A COVER

Winter root crops, such as parsnips, carrots, and leeks are difficult to lift when the soil is frozen, so cover them with a layer of insulating straw in autumn. Cold frames are ideal for spring-sown frost-hardy seedlings in trays or pots, which will be transplanted outside later in the year, while a cloche is best for crops that are sown *in situ* in early spring, such as lettuce, rocket, and Oriental greens, or for overwintered vegetables like broad beans.

Cloches can be bought ready-made and as kits, or if you want frost protection for just a few weeks each year, a home-made type constructed from a few sheets of clear plastic may suffice. Alternatively, make a more permanent tunnel from wire hoops covered with clear polythene; leave one end open for ventilation.

∧ Shop-bought option
Cloches are an investment and should last for many years; choose from pricey decorative glass types to cheaper plastic models.

< Home-made solution
This cloche is easy to make with two sheets of clear plastic pinned together with pegs.

Wrap up your pots

Container plants can suffer in winter on two fronts: roots are more vulnerable in pots because they afford less insulation than the soil in the ground, and the pots themselves may crack or break during icy periods.

CONTAINER CARE

Some containers are more vulnerable to frost damage than others. Stone, metal, and plastic pots will sail through winters unscathed, while terracotta often cracks in frosty conditions. Terracotta suffers because it is porous and when moisture from the soil and rain leaches into it and then expands as it turns to ice, the pot cracks. So, unless you pay a premium for containers that have been fired to high

∧ Pot protection
Line terracotta pots with bubble plastic to prevent them absorbing moisture and cracking when the water turns to ice in cold weather.

< Hessian wrapper
Wrap tender plants and vulnerable pots with hessian or bubble plastic to keep them warm.

temperatures to reduce their porosity, you will need to take steps to ensure yours stay intact. Either remove plants and compost and store pots inside, or, if they are housing a prized plant, wrap them up with hessian or bubble plastic. Cover the compost, too, so that it does not become saturated. Another tip is to line the pot with bubble plastic before you plant it up, thereby forming a barrier between the soil and the terracotta.

Slightly tender potted plants are best wrapped in horticultural fleece in the winter. Also tie together the leaves of strappy plants, such as cordylines, to protect their crowns from snow and ice.

Basic pruning techniques

Some shrubs and trees require little pruning apart from removing dead or damaged stems, but for many others an annual trim is essential. Regular pruning can improve a plant's appearance, stimulate the production of fruit and flowers, keep specimens youthful and vigorous, and encourage bolder foliage.

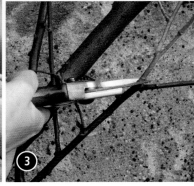

WHAT TO PRUNE

Routine pruning maintains the health and appearance of woody plants. In late winter or early spring, before the leaves of deciduous shrubs and trees appear, look at their overall shape in detail and identify branches that need removing or shortening. Also note any congested growth in the centre, which can encourage disease. Then, cut away dead or damaged stems to healthy tissue; crossing branches that are rubbing and liable to create a wound; and stems that are no longer producing fruit or flowers.

❶ Remove stems and branches growing at odd angles that look unsightly and may rub against one another, creating entry points for infection. ❷ Cut back to young wood, which is often a different colour and texture to the older, thicker stems. ❸ Remove dead or infected wood to prevent further die-back or disease entering healthy tissue.

HOW TO PRUNE

When pruning, use sharp secateurs for thin stems, or a pruning saw for wood that is thicker than a pencil. Loppers are useful for chopping up prunings into manageable pieces. Always make your cut just above a bud to avoid the stump dying back into healthy wood, and make clean cuts that will heal more quickly and are less prone to infection. To avoid wood ripping or splitting when cut, take the weight off long branches in stages (see opposite).

∧ *Slanting cut for alternate buds .*
Cut to an outward facing bud, slanting the cut so that water will run away from the bud.

∧ *Straight cut for opposite buds*
Where buds are arranged in pairs, cut straight across the top. Two shoots will emerge.

Cutting branches

Where possible, remove tree branches when they are young, as the cuts heal more quickly. Most should be pruned in late winter, but wait till mid- to late summer to prune hornbeam (*Carpinus*), pears (*Pyrus*), plums and cherries (*Prunus* species).

1 MAKE AN UNDERCUT FIRST
Take some weight off the branch first to prevent it tearing close to the trunk. Cut partly through the underside of the branch; then saw from the top a little further up. Allow the branch to snap off.

2 CUT CLOSE TO TRUNK
Remove the final stump by cutting close to the trunk, but not flush with it. Make an angled cut away from the tree, just beyond the crease in the bark where the branch meets the trunk.

3 ALLOW THE WOUND TO HEAL
The result is a clean cut that leaves the tree's healing tissue intact, speeding up its recovery. The wound may bleed after pruning, but will soon form a layer of protective bark.

TOP TIP: KEEP SAFE

Wear thick gardening gloves when pruning or trimming, and use well-maintained tools appropriate to the task. Wear goggles and ear protectors when using a hedge trimmer. Don't cut above head height; use ladders or platforms and make sure that they are stable and secure. Undergo approved safety training and wear specialist clothing before using a chainsaw.

Spur pruning

This technique encourages climbers, wall shrubs, and trained fruit trees to flower and fruit more freely. Shortening the shoots that grow from the main stems promotes the remaining buds to produce far more productive stems than would normally appear.

1 FIND A HEALTHY SHOOT
Identify strong growing shoots and trim back to two or three buds from the main stems to form short branches or "spurs". Make a slanting cut to channel rainwater away from the chosen bud. This helps to prevent disease and die back.

2 CREATE SHORT SPURS
The "spurs" of this climbing rose will each produce two or three flowering stems in the forthcoming season. You can also spur prune wall-trained *Chaenomeles, Pyracantha,* and *Ceanothus* to keep plants neat and blooming well.

Pruning shrubs

The best time to prune deciduous climbers and shrubs depends on whether they bloom on growth produced in the same or previous years. Generally, those that flower after midsummer are pruned hard in spring. Winter-, spring- and early summer-bloomers are normally pruned soon after flowering.

EARLY-FLOWERING SHRUBS

This group contains spring show-stoppers, such as forsythia and flowering currants (*Ribes*), as well as early-summer bloomers, including *Philadelphus, Weigela, Deutzia* and *Spiraea* 'Arguta'. These all flower on stems that were produced the previous year; prune them just after flowering so that new growth can ripen throughout the summer. Remove dead and diseased growth, and cut back old flowering stems, leaving new shoots to take over. Thin overcrowded growth, cutting a third to a fifth of the oldest stems to ground level. Apply an all-purpose granular fertilizer, water well, and lay a deep organic mulch.

1 ENCOURAGE FLOWERING
Prune early-flowering shrubs, such as honeysuckle, *Lonicera* x *purpusii*, in early summer after flowering. Cut a third of the oldest stems to 30cm (12in) from the ground with a pruning saw, reducing the length gradually to prevent tearing.

2 MAINTAIN VIGOUR
Trim back tall stems to stimulate new buds to shoot lower down the stems and make a bushier plant. This also gives new growth room to develop and mature, and still leaves sufficient old wood to bloom the following year.

LATE-FLOWERING SHRUBS

This group contains shrubs and climbers that flower in late summer and autumn, such as butterfly bush (*Buddleja*), shrubby mallow (*Lavatera*), *Hydrangea paniculata, Perovskia*, and hardy fuchsia, as well as late-flowering clematis, like *C. viticella* (*see p.414*). Prune all the stems back hard in late winter or early spring to promote lots of new flowering shoots.

1 SHORTEN STEMS
To prevent tall, fast-growing shrubs, such as butterfly bush, *Buddleja*, from being damaged by autumn storms, prune the tallest stems after flowering. Then carry out the main pruning in spring.

2 CUT BACK HARD
In spring, remove long whippy stems and thin twiggy growth with secateurs to reveal the main framework of branches. Using a pruning saw, cut back to create a low structure of healthy stems.

3 ENCOURAGE LARGER BLOOMS
Pruning encourages more flowers and healthier growth. It breathes new life into old shrubs, and can even increase the longevity of short-lived plants, like shrubby mallow, *Lavatera*.

PRUNING EVERGREENS

Many evergreens are not as hardy as deciduous shrubs and grow more slowly. They are best pruned sparingly to reduce their size and keep them tidy after the frosts, between late spring and late summer. To avoid removing any blooms, prune summer-flowering evergreens, such as *Escallonia*, when the flowers have finished. Never prune evergreens in autumn because any new growth will not have enough time to harden off before the frosts return, and could be damaged. If any stems are harmed by frost, leave them until the following spring before removing them.

TRIM PLANTS LIGHTLY

Shrubs, such as *Ceanothus*, should be pruned lightly after flowering, as they may not make new wood if cut back too hard. Maintain a compact, flower-filled shrub by pruning long, straggly branches by 25–30cm (10–12in), but leave some of the shorter stems unpruned to help the plant maintain its strength. Cut above a leaf bud to prevent die-back, and to stimulate new growth below the cut (*see p.410*).

Stay in shape >
Spring-flowering ceanothus grow very quickly, and without annual pruning they soon fill out their allocated sites and become untidy.

< ∧ Cut down to size
To improve the appearance and performance of this overgrown mahonia, prune hard after flowering (midwinter to early spring). Renovate other evergreen and deciduous shrubs in the same way.

RENOVATING SHRUBS

Old and overgrown deciduous or evergreen shrubs can be cut back quite severely to rejuvenate them, and help them to become productive once more. Those flowering on wood made the previous year may take a couple of years to bloom again.

CUTTING BACK AN OVERGROWN MAHONIA

Shorten the main stems to 60cm (2ft) above ground level. First, remove dead, damaged, and diseased stems. Then, imagine the re-grown plant and maintain a balanced shape while you cut out the oldest growth, to leave around 5 or 6 strong young stems. Prune these to 30–40cm (12–16in) from the ground, making sloping cuts to deflect the rain.

PRUNE FOR FOLIAGE DISPLAYS

Many deciduous shrubs are valued for their brightly coloured foliage, which grows on young stems and can be encouraged by hard pruning. Some shrubs should be cut back severely every year, such as the coloured-leaved forms of elder (*Sambucus*), spiraea, Indian bean tree (*Catalpa bignonioides*), and smoke bush (*Cotinus*). Others, like the purple filbert (*Corylus maxima* 'Purpurea'), should be pruned every two years. To aid their recovery after pruning, water them well and apply an all-purpose fertilizer. Then add a thick mulch.

CUT BACK A SMOKE BUSH

Prune the shrub down to a stout framework of branches in spring, before the leaf buds burst. Use a pruning saw to reduce the height initially, then cut all the healthy stems to 60cm (2ft) from the ground. Pruning also keeps the shrub more compact.

∧ > Larger and brighter
The regrowth on this previously hard-pruned smoke bush, Cotinus, (above) has larger, more colourful leaves, giving a glowing autumn display.

How to prune clematis

Clematis are some of our best-loved flowering climbers but although they are generally easy to grow given the right conditions, there is often confusion about how best to prune them. Some flower well if pruned lightly, while others thrive when cut back hard. The trick is to identify what type you have.

IDENTIFYING CLEMATIS

Clematis species and cultivars are divided into three main pruning groups; the plant label should tell you what type you have. A broad rule of thumb, as with many deciduous flowering shrubs and climbers, is that early-flowering (spring and early summer) types require just a light tidy-up, while late-flowering (mid- to late summer and autumn) clematis should be pruned hard in late winter.

PRUNING GROUP 1

This group contains the vigorous, late-spring-flowering, *Clematis montana* and earlier blooming evergreen, *C. armandii;* the late-winter-flowering *C. cirrhosa,* and dainty *C. alpina* and *C. macropetala* which both flower in mid-spring. These need little pruning once established, except to remove dead and damaged stems.

∧ *Trim back lightly*
After flowering, remove any wayward shoots and damaged growth. This also helps to reveal the attractive fluffy seedheads.

PRUNING GROUP 2

This group includes the flamboyant large-flowered cultivars, like 'Nelly Moser'. Wood made the previous year bears flowers in early summer, but these plants can also bloom again in late summer on stems made the same year. In early spring, follow the stems from the top down to new growth, and cut just above it.

Prune to a healthy shoot >
Remove the dead and damaged tops of the stems, which will look brown and dry, and cut back to green buds from which flowering side shoots will grow.

PRUNING GROUP 3

Clematis that flower from midsummer through to the autumn make up this group, and include the prolific small-flowered *C. viticella* hybrids, and forms of *C. texensis*. The yellow autumn-flowering *C. tangutica* and *C. orientalis* also belong here.

1 PRUNE BACK TOP GROWTH
When left unpruned, these clematis form flowers at the top of the plant, leaving long, straggly bare stems beneath. To prevent this, cut back the tangle of shoots, removing them from their supports. Do this in late winter before the buds have started to break.

2 PRUNE TO HEALTHY BUDS
Then cut all the stems back hard. It may look drastic, but pruning the stems to within about 30cm (12in) of the ground encourages plants to develop a strong network of new shoots. Cut to just above a pair of healthy buds. Prune less radically if you want to maintain height.

Pruning roses

Modern floribunda and hybrid tea roses benefit from hard pruning to encourage new flowering shoots, while shrub roses require relatively gentle treatment. Pruning also helps to control the disease blackspot.

FLORIBUNDA ROSES

Also known as cluster-flowered roses, floribundas produce flushes of blooms through summer and early autumn. Compact dwarf floribundas are also called patio roses, and can be grown in pots. In early spring, remove dead, diseased, and crossing stems. Prune the other stems to outward-facing buds 20–30cm (8–12in) from the ground using sloping cuts.

EXAMPLES OF FLORIBUNDA AND PATIO ROSES

'Arthur Bell'
'English Miss'
'Fellowship'
'Fragrant Delight'
'Pretty Lady'
'Princess of Wales'
'Remembrance'
'Sunset Boulevard'
'Sweet Dream'
'Tall Story'
'Trumpeter'

< Make a low framework
When pruning, aim to leave a framework of between eight and ten strong, healthy stems.

HYBRID TEAS

These are large-flowered roses, with some varieties that repeat bloom, although they produce just one flower per stem. Prune in early spring, removing dead, diseased, and crossing stems. Cut the oldest stems to the ground, and shorten the remainder to 15cm (6in) from the base. In late autumn reduce their height by one third to prevent root damage caused by wind rock.

EXAMPLES OF TEA ROSES

'Alexander'
'Blessings'
'Deep Secret'
'Elina'
'Ingrid Bergman'
'Just Joey'
'Lovely Lady'
'Paul Sherville'
'Savoy Hotel'
'Tequila Sunrise'
'Troika'
'Warm Wishes'

< Slanting cuts
Leave three to five strong young stems after pruning with cuts angled to allow water to drain off the buds.

SHRUB AND SPECIES ROSES

Usually flowering once on wood made in previous years, these should be pruned lightly in early spring. Thin out congested stems to improve air flow, and remove dead, weak, damaged or diseased wood. Also prune some of the oldest stems to ground level. Cut main stems back by a quarter and slightly reduce side shoots by a few centimetres. These roses often grow quite tall and benefit from being cut back by a third in late autumn to prevent root damage caused by wind rock.

Prune lightly to prevent disease >
Shorten the main stems by about a quarter to produce an open-structured framework, allowing in light and air to help prevent fungal diseases.

EXAMPLES OF SHRUB AND SPECIES ROSES

'Blanche Double de Coubert'
'Boule de Neige'
'De Resht'
'Fantin-Latour'
'Graham Thomas'
'Louise Odier'
'Madame Isaac Pereire'
'Madame Pierre Oger'
'Maiden's Blush'
Rosa gallica 'Versicolor'
'Souvenir de la Malmaison'
'William Lobb'

Propagating plants

There are many simple techniques to propagate all types of garden plants, from perennials, shrubs, and climbers to fruit trees. You don't need specialist equipment, as divisions, layers, and some cuttings can be left to root in the ground with little additional help, although a cold frame is useful for some plants.

Dividing perennials

This easy method can be used to propagate most herbaceous perennials, and to rejuvenate large, tired clumps that are no longer flowering well. You can also divide newly-bought perennials, providing they are large enough, to make the most of your purchases.

PLANTS TO DIVIDE

Achillea	Heuchera	Phlox
Aster	Hosta	Polemonium
Bergenia	Iris	Pulmonaria
Campanula	Ligularia	Rudbeckia
Geranium	Monarda	Sedum
Helenium	Nepeta	Veronica

Bargain borders >
Dividing perennials, such as Achillea *and* Helenium, *in early spring is an easy and economical way to fill large borders. After replanting, they will soon bulk up to form new flowering clumps.*

1 DIG UP PLANT
In early spring, select a healthy clump of plants and water them well. Cut back any top growth to the ground. Using a fork, lift the clump, taking care to keep the whole root ball intact.

2 DIVIDE WITH FORKS
Cut solid crowns into portions with a spade or old bread knife. If you can't prise other pieces apart by hand use two forks back-to-back to split the clump into smaller sections, ready for replanting.

3 REPLANT
Discard dead central portions of overgrown clumps. Replant healthy hand-sized pieces with strong buds in soil improved with well-rotted organic matter, such as manure. Water in well.

Layering shrubs and climbers

The stems of climbers and shrubs sometimes root when they touch the soil, and you can harness this tendency to make new plants. This is useful for shrubs, such as rhododendrons (*above*), that can be difficult to propagate in other ways.

1 MAKE A SLANTING CUT
In spring, from the base of the plant select a flexible stem that bends to the ground. Remove side stems and make a shallow slanting cut on the underside, 30cm (12in) from the tip. Dip the cut in hormone rooting powder.

2 PEG DOWN STEM INTO SOIL
Use wire staples, or a large stone, to firmly anchor the wounded section of stem just below the soil surface. To aid rooting in poorer soils, pin the stem into a shallow depression filled with moist potting compost.

PLANTS TO LAYER

Aucuba	Magnolia
Chaenomeles	Passiflora
(above)	Skimmia
Cotinus	Syringa
Erica	Viburnum
Fothergilla	Weigela (right)
Lonicera	Wisteria

OTHER LAYERING TECHNIQUES
Basic layering works for a wide range of shrubs, and by varying the technique, you can also use it to propagate woody climbers and fruit bushes.

IVY AND HONEYSUCKLE
Climbers, such as ivy (*Hedera, below*), and honeysuckle, *Lonicera*, often root where their stems are in contact with the soil. Either pin stems down yourself in autumn or spring, or check your plants for any stems that have rooted naturally. Use a hand fork to lift any stems with roots, and cut them between each rooted section to make new plants, which you can then grow on.

∧ *Climbers for free*
Many climbers will root along their stems where they come into contact with the soil. Peg them down at intervals to produce new plants.

BLACKBERRIES
In summer, propagate blackberries and their hybrids by burying the tip of a healthy, young stem (*below*) in a hole 10cm (4in) deep. In a few weeks a new shoot will appear; transplant it the following spring.

How to take cuttings

Given the right conditions, plants can be persuaded to root from stem cuttings in spring or summer, or in winter from pieces of root. Seal collected cuttings and root material in a plastic bag to keep them fresh.

Root cuttings

With the exception of variegated plants, which produce only green shoots from root cuttings, many perennials can be propagated using this method. Never take more than a few roots from each plant, and quickly replace the plants in the soil. Thin roots, such as those of phlox (*Phlox paniculata*), should be laid horizontally on the compost to root.

SUITABLE PLANTS

Anemone x *hybrida*
Bear's breeches, *Acanthus*
Campanula
Crambe
Dicentra
Globe thistle, *Echinops*
Plume poppy, *Macleaya*
Oriental poppy, *Papaver orientale*
Sea holly, *Eryngium*
Tree poppy, *Romneya*
Verbascum

1 TRIM OFF HEALTHY ROOTS
In midwinter, lift the plant, or scrape away soil from larger plants to expose the roots. Cutting close to the stems (crown), remove three or four fat, healthy roots, avoiding brittle, damaged, or woody pieces. Seal in a plastic bag.

2 CUT TOP AND BOTTOM
Cut each root into 5–8cm (2–3in) segments with a sharp knife. Trim the top end (nearest the crown) straight across and the bottom at an angle. This ensures you plant them the right way up. You do not need to do this with thin roots.

3 PLANT UP
Insert the root cuttings vertically in pots of compost (with the blunt end at the top), spacing them 5cm (2in) apart. Lay thinner roots on the surface, covering them with 1cm (½in) of coarse sand or grit. Water the roots with diluted fungicide and move pots to a sheltered spot outside.

4 AFTERCARE
Cover pots and trays with fleece, or place them in a cold frame, and keep the compost damp. The cuttings should be well-rooted in about six months. They may produce shoots beforehand but wait until roots appear at the holes at the bottom of the pots before transplanting.

Hardwood cuttings

These are the easiest cuttings to grow, but you need patience, as rooting can take more than a year. Find a sheltered spot where the cuttings won't be disturbed, such as the back of a border. Use this method for deciduous shrubs, trees, roses and fruit.

1 TAKE A HEALTHY STEM
In autumn, select straight stems, about the thickness of a pencil and with plenty of buds, taken from the current year's growth. Strip off any leaves and side shoots. You may be able to take several cuttings from a single stem.

2 CUT INTO SECTIONS
Make individual cuttings about 25cm (10in) long. Cut straight along the bottom just below a bud, and make a slanted cut above a bud at the top. The cuts differentiate the top from the bottom, and allow you to plant the right way up.

3 PLANT IN GROUND
Make a narrow V-shaped trench by inserting a spade about 20cm (8in) in the soil and pushing it forwards. On heavy soil, add horticultural sand to the base to aid drainage. Insert cuttings 15cm (6in) apart, leaving a few buds above the surface. These will form the branches of the new shrub. Firm lightly, label, and water.

4 POT-GROWN CUTTINGS
For less hardy plants, such as *Cistus*, *Perovskia*, and *Santolina*, plant cuttings in pots of free-draining compost. Trim cuttings to 8–10cm (3–4in) long and plant with the top bud exposed. Protect from frost by placing pots in a cold frame or unheated greenhouse until spring. Plant in autumn once rooted.

∧ *Worth the wait*
It can take two or three years for a shrub grown from a cutting to reach flowering size, so take a few each year for a constant supply of new plants. If you don't have room for them yourself, your gardening friends will appreciate a gift.

SUITABLE PLANTS

Box, *Buxus*
Butterfly bush, *Buddleja*
Deutzia
Dogwood, *Cornus*
Elder, *Sambucus*
Forsythia
Flowering currant, *Ribes*
Mock orange, *Philadelphus*
Rose (including bush types)
Spiraea
Viburnum
Weigela
Willow, *Salix*

Softwood cuttings

Non-flowering shoots of many tender perennials and patio plants, as well as some herbaceous perennials, including delphinium and lupin, will root in six to eight weeks in warm, humid conditions in summer. Cuttings are prone to disease, so sterilize knives, pots, and trays used in their preparation, and root them in fresh, sterilized compost. Use tap water for cuttings.

SUITABLE PLANTS

Argyranthemum	*Impatiens*
Begonia	*Lantana*
Chrysanthemum	*Lupin*
Delphinium	*Nepeta*
Dianthus	*Passiflora*
Erysimum	*Pelargonium*
Felicia	*Penstemon*
Fuchsia	*Salvia*
Hebe	*Verbena*

Find the right material >
Flowering shoots, such as those on this lupin, are unlikely to root, even if the blooms are removed, so look for young leafy stems for the best results.

1 SELECT HEALTHY STEMS
In summer, collect healthy, leafy shoots, about 7–12cm (3–5in) long, from plants that you have watered well the evening before. Take your cuttings in the morning, before the plants are stressed by high temperatures, and seal them in plastic bags to keep them fresh.

2 TAKE OFF LOWER LEAVES
Pre-fill pots and trays with moist cutting compost to avoid any delay once cuttings have been prepared. Using a sharp knife, cut just below a leaf joint and trim off lower leaves neatly to leave just two or three healthy ones at the top. Dip the cut ends in hormone rooting powder.

3 POT UP
Push the cuttings into the compost, leaving the upper half exposed. Root singly in small pots or fit several into large pots or trays, ensuring the leaves are not touching. Firm lightly, water, and cover with a clear plastic bag, or root in a propagator, and keep at 15–21°C (59–70°).

Semi-ripe cuttings

These are gathered later in summer when the bases of the stems are firmer. You can pull off side shoots with a little tear or "heel" of stem, and they will root in about ten weeks, or the following spring. This method is used mainly for evergreen shrubs, like box (*Buxus*), and woody herbs, such as sage (*Salvia*).

1 CHOOSE A HEALTHY STEM
Select shoot tips or side shoots that are firm at the base, soft and leafy at the top. Cut just below a leaf joint or gently pull side shoots downwards to leave a heel of stem tissue still attached.

2 PREPARE THE STEM
Use a sharp, sterilized knife to trim off the soft shoot tip just above a leaf joint. Discard this section. Removing the shoot tip helps to reduce moisture loss from the cutting.

SUITABLE PLANTS

Abutilon	*Erica*
Artemisia	*Lavandula*
Buxus	*Mahonia* (pictured
Calluna	above)
Ceanothus	*Rosmarinus*
Choisya	*Salvia*
Cytisus	*Sarcococca*

3 REMOVE LOWER LEAVES
Remove the leaves and side shoots from the lower half of the cutting, and trim back any heels at the base that are particularly long. If your cutting has no heel, simulate one by cutting a 2.5cm (1in) slice from one side of the stem.

4 POT UP
Dip the cut ends in hormone rooting powder. Either root in pots of moist cutting compost, inserting them up to the base of the lower leaves, or set hardy types, such as box (*above*) 8cm (3in) apart in sandy soil in a cold frame.

5 KEEP WARM
Place your pots of cuttings in a covered propagator set to 18–21°C (64–70°F), or seal them in clear plastic bags, propped up with canes to keep the plastic off the leaves. Keep compost moist. Harden off (*see p.109*), and plant out once rooted.

Lawn care

A verdant lawn makes a wonderful foil for flower borders and creates an emerald focal point in winter when colour is in short supply. There are different types of turf for different situations (*see p.206*) but all lawns benefit from regular mowing, and care and attention in the spring and autumn.

MOWING AND WATERING

Mow grass whenever it is growing, provided the ground isn't too wet or icy to walk on. In spring, mow once a week with the blades at their highest setting, and gradually lower them as growth accelerates. Use a box to collect the clippings, which can be composted, or use a "mulching mower" which doesn't remove the grass but chops it into fine pieces, returning nutrients to the lawn. Rake off thick patches of clippings, which will damage the turf. In summer, a high-quality lawn may need cutting three times a week, but in autumn, as growth slows, once or twice a week should suffice. In dry periods, water newly laid turf, freshly sown areas, and high-quality lawns. Leave established lawns unwatered, but stop mowing, as longer grass helps protect the roots. The grass may turn brown, but will recover once rain returns.

< *When to water*
Water a new lawn every week in dry spells, until it is established. You can tell when fine lawns need watering as they lose their spring when walked on. Reduce water evaporation by using sprinklers early in the morning or at night. Move seep hoses by 20cm (8in) every half an hour.

FEEDING

The amount of fertilizer you need to maintain lush green grass depends on how rich the underlying soil is, and if you occasionally leave the clippings on the lawn, which help top up the soil nutrients. Apply granular or liquid lawn fertilizer at least once a year. Spring and early summer feeds are high in nitrogen to boost leaf growth; products for use in early autumn are low in nitrogen but high in potassium to aid grass roots in winter. Do not overfeed as this can result in weak growth and fungal problems.

∧ *Applying fertilizer*
Divide the lawn into a grid of metre squares using canes. Apply fertilizer at a rate according to the pack. Hire a calibrated spreader for large lawns, and water if it doesn't rain within three days after feeding.

TOP TIP: HOME-MADE TOP DRESSING

Applying a sandy top dressing (*see opposite*), helps to rejuvenate lawns, especially those grown on heavy soils, by increasing drainage and encouraging strong root growth. Mix your own dressing by spreading out a sheet of plastic close to the lawn. Then, using a bucket as a single measure, combine three parts good-quality top soil or sandy loam with six parts horticultural sand and one part peat substitute, such as coir or ground composted bark. Let the mixture dry slightly so you can spread it more easily, and then work it thoroughly into the surface of the lawn.

Autumn treatment

After a summer of heavy use many lawns start showing signs of wear and tear by the end of the season. Early autumn is a great time to repair the damage and to ensure that your turf is in good condition for the year ahead.

1 RAKE OUT MOSS
Kill off any moss with a lawn moss herbicide before vigorously scratching out dead material (thatch) from the lawn with a spring-tined rake; hire a motorized scarifier for large lawns. Raking improves the look and health of the turf.

2 AERATE THE SOIL
Open up air channels in a compacted lawn by pushing a border fork into the soil, or use a hollow tiner, which pulls out plugs of soil. Work across the lawn at 10cm (4in) intervals. Repeat this process every two years.

3 APPLY TOP DRESSING
After raking and aerating the lawn, work a top dressing into the holes. You can buy this premixed from garden centres and DIY stores, but it's easy and cost effective on large lawns to make your own (*see Top Tip, opposite*).

4 BRUSH IN DRESSING
Work in the top dressing thoroughly using a stiff brush or besom, lightly filling the new aeration channels, and covering the ground to encourage strong rooting. Apply it evenly and make sure the grass isn't smothered.

5 FEED AND SOW
Wearing gloves, apply a granular autumn lawn fertilizer evenly over marked out squares (*see Applying fertilizer, opposite*). Water in if no rain falls within three days of applying it. In early autumn, the soil is sufficiently warm and moist to sow grass seed too. Sprinkle seed to match your lawn type at half the recommended rate for new lawns to help thicken up any bald spots.

TOP TIP: WEEDING OPTIONS

Acidic lawns are prone to moss and weed growth. Check soil pH in winter, and raise it by applying ground chalk or limestone at a rate of 50g per sq metre (2oz per 10 sq ft). Apply a lawn weedkiller in spring or summer, and repeat in early autumn to remove any remaining weeds. Organic gardeners can grub out creeping buttercups, daisies (*below*), and tap-rooted weeds, like dandelions, using an old knife.

Pest control

By encouraging natural predators, following good garden practice, and making regular checks on your plants, you can keep many pests at bay. Aim to create conditions that support a healthy balance of predators and their prey, and you will limit the damage and need fewer chemical controls.

KEEPING PESTS AT BAY

Pest patrol should begin when you buy new plants or accept leafy gifts. Unwelcome visitors also fly or crawl in from neighbouring gardens, so keep your eyes peeled and take prompt action.

REDUCING THE RISK

To prevent a plague of pests, avoid growing large areas of one type of plant. It is more difficult for pests to home in on their target when confronted by a variety of different plants, such as perennials, annuals, and shrubs, as well as herbs, vegetables, and fruit. The abundant nectar also draws in beneficial insects (*see opposite*). Don't overfeed plants, either, as aphids love the resulting soft growth.

∧ *Make a home for pest predators*
This water garden, surrounded by borders planted with a wide range of flowering perennials, makes the perfect home for beneficial bugs, slug-hunting amphibians, and insect-eating birds.

BE VIGILANT

Use a hand lens to scan flower buds, shoot tips and the undersides of leaves for mites, aphids, and whitefly. Also look for grubs or nibbled roots when you take plants out of their pots, and search for caterpillars on rolled or skeletonized leaves. A night-time foray with a torch will reveal nocturnal pests, such as slugs and snails; seek them out during the day by checking under pots. Weed regularly, and look out for pest hideaways.

❶ Tidy potential slug and snail roosting sites. ❷ Check buds and shoot tips for aphids. ❸ Pick off larger pests, such as lily beetle, by hand.

Garden friends

There's often a frustrating lag between the appearance of pests, like aphids, and their natural predators, such as ladybirds, lacewings and hoverfly larvae. So, don't be too quick to reach for insecticides, as killing off natural predators' food sources may drive them away. Chemical pesticides also kill friendly bugs, as well as unwanted insects.

∧ *Flowering feast*
Simple, open nectar-rich flowers, such as blanket flower (Gaillardia), are a magnet to bees and hoverflies, which appreciate an easy meal.

IDENTIFYING PREDATORS

It is important to recognise the chief insect predators; they are often the larvae of more familiar adults, like ladybirds and hoverflies, but some are quite different in appearance (*see ladybird, below*). By knowing what these insects look like, you will be less likely to confuse them with pests, and may be able to move them to badly infested plants. Some predators hide under leaf litter and bark mulch, and are invisible during the day, actively feeding at night. One example is ground beetles, which attack slugs. Visit internet websites to identify mystery bugs or seek advice at your garden centre.

ENCOURAGING FRIENDLY BEASTS

Lure beneficial insects into your garden by providing hibernation sites, such as a log pile, and simple flowers, which attract nectar-feeding types (*see pp.352–353*). Grow leafy ground cover to shelter slug-munching frogs and toads, and add a small pond with grassy margins. Delay cutting herbaceous plants till spring for winter cover, and provide food, water, and nesting sites for birds.

❶ Ladybirds and their larvae (*inset*) both gorge on aphids. Encourage them to visit in spring by avoiding insecticides, and provide cover, such as evergreen shrubs on a south wall, a hedge base, bark crevices, or leaf litter, for overwintering adults. ❷ Frogs and toads eat slugs and flies, and even without a pond, will colonize a garden if there is shady ground cover, and a log or rock pile. ❸ Garden spiders, especially web-building species, trap and eat large numbers of flying insect pests including aphids and crane flies. ❹ Hoverflies vary enormously. Larger species are sometimes confused with wasps, despite their hovering flight. Adults pollinate flowers and crops, and most larvae have a keen appetite for aphids and other pests. Adults prefer yellow, orange, and white blooms. ❺ Lacewing adults are most often seen seeking shelter indoors in autumn. Provide cover as for ladybirds. Green lacewing larvae, called "aphid lions", also have a voracious appetite for other pests. ❻ Thrushes are one of the few birds that eat snails. Most birds, including seed-eaters, feed nestlings on insects and caterpillars. Encourage them with a year-round water supply, supplementary food, and roosting and nesting sites.

Common pests and their control

Slugs and snails are a bugbear for most gardeners, but simple preventive treatment, such as erecting barriers, encouraging predators, and the use of biological controls, can significantly reduce attacks in gardens. Tackle other pests with similar organic controls and guards to reduce the need for chemicals.

SLUGS AND SNAILS

Although these are annoying plant pests, much of their activity, such as devouring rotting vegetation, is actually beneficial. Unfortunately, they do not discriminate and are equally happy to chomp through desirable plants and crops.

These nocturnal nibblers have rasping mouthparts, and chew the margins of leaves and petals, as well as leaving holes in them. They also strip off chunks of stem, causing young plants to collapse, and graze the skin and peel of fruit and vegetables. Seedlings and any juicy young shoots of established plants, flower and leaf buds, and newly unfurled foliage are particularly vulnerable. Snails can climb up walls and tall plants to reach their food, while some slugs live underground.

< Snail targets
Snails are fearless climbers, making your hanging baskets, wall troughs and window boxes just as vulnerable as your beds and borders.

< Key signs
Look out for tattered leaves and ragged flowers that indicate the presence of slugs and snails.

ORGANIC CONTROL

Check under and around the rims of pots, beneath ledges, in piles of rocks or timber, and on evergreen shrubs where slugs and snails roost, and pick them off. Beer traps will lure them in at night. Slugs and snails are also deterred by copper strips, which give them an electric shock when they pass over them, and cloches made from plastic bottles. If all else fails, sprinkle pellets sparingly around key plants.

❶ Beer in a cut-off plastic bottle lures and traps slugs. ❷ Use the top half of the bottle to protect seedlings. ❸ Fit copper tape around pot rims. ❹ Surround vulnerable hostas with copper slug collars.

APHIDS

These pests are commonly known as greenfly, though other colours exist and some have a woolly wax coating. Aphid species number over 4,000 worldwide, and many favour specific plants. They reproduce rapidly in spring and summer.

SIGNS OF ATTACK

Shrivelled and distorted shoots, leaves, and flowers are the main signs of aphid attacks. You may also see a residue of a sticky honeydew excretion, which can lead to black sooty mould (see p.433). Also look for aphids' white discarded skins, which they shed as they grow.

Aphids transmit viruses, and yellow mottling and colour streaks in leaves and flowers indicate possible infection. These tiny insects give birth to live young that immediately start feeding, so soft plant tips rapidly become infested. Pinch off heavily affected shoots or blast them with water from a hosepipe.

❶ Adult female aphids can produce five live babies per day for up to 30 days. ❷ Aphids can be green, black or other colours, but all do the same damage if left unchecked. ❸ Clear infestations with fatty acids or plant oil sprays. Keep a ready-to-use spray handy for spot treatments.

BIRDS AND SMALL MAMMALS

Mice and other rodents dig up spring-sown seeds in the kitchen garden, and in autumn munch on ripening fruits and gnaw newly planted bulbs. Some birds are also a nuisance, pecking flowers, pulling up seedlings, eating brassicas, and stealing fruit.

AVOIDING DEVASTATION

Rabbits, squirrels, and pigeons can lay waste to newly planted beds, borders and pots. To avoid scenes like that shown (right), erect barriers or netting, or cover seedlings and pots of bulbs with chicken wire. To prevent cats from scratching in the finely tilled soil of seed beds, lay thorny twigs across the surface, or insert short bamboo canes between crops or flowers. Sow large seeds, such as peas and beans, in pots away from hungry mice, and protect trees and shrubs with rabbit guards.

Physical barriers >
If birds and other animals persist in wrecking crops, sow within a protective enclosure.

TOP TIP: BIOLOGICAL CONTROL

Slugs, vine weevils, chafer grubs, and crane fly larvae can all be controlled with microscopic nematode worms that kill the pests without harming the environment. Mix the nematodes with water and apply at specific times of year, following the supplier's instructions. Treatments may need to be repeated. You can buy nematodes to control a range of pests on the internet or via mail-order companies.

Identifying common pests

You can identify pest damage in one of two ways: either you see the beast, or the damage it causes. Use chemical sprays only as a last resort: wear gloves when mixing and spraying them, and follow manufacturers' instructions. Where possible, try pest traps and barriers, biological controls, and organic sprays first.

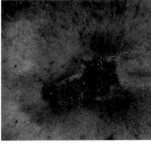

❶ GALL MITES
These microscopic mites suck sap and cause abnormal growths. These include raised pimples or clumps of matted hairs on leaves, or enlarged buds. Most are harmless and can be tolerated.

❷ BOX SUCKER
The wingless nymphs of box psyllids are covered in a waxy coat, and found inside the ball-shaped shoot tips in spring. Control the pest by cutting off affected growth; then bin or burn it.

❸ CODLING MOTH
To avoid maggots in apples, spray emerging caterpillars twice using bifenthrin, starting in midsummer. Also hang pheromone traps in late spring to catch male moths and prevent them from mating.

❹ WINTER MOTH
In spring, the leaves of fruit trees are webbed together and hide green caterpillars inside. Holes are visible when leaves expand. Apply sticky grease bands to the trees and stakes in autumn to trap adult moths.

❺ SCALE INSECTS
Tiny blister or shell-like bumps on leaf backs result in poor growth. Other symptoms are sticky excretions and sooty mould on evergreens. Wash off mould, and spray with plant oils, fatty acids or thiacloprid.

❻ GLASSHOUSE WHITEFLY
Under glass, hang yellow sticky pads to trap these tiny white flying adults which suck sap from plants; use a biological control (*Encarsia* wasp) on larvae, or spray with thiacloprid or organic chemical controls.

❼ VIBURNUM BEETLE
Both the adults and larvae eat holes in the leaves, mainly on *Viburnum tinus* and *V. opulus*; this can slow growth and looks unsightly. Spray badly affected plants in spring using bifenthrin or thiacloprid.

❽ THRIPS
These tiny black sap-suckers, known as "thunder flies", cause white patches on the petals and leaves of indoor plants, and also peas, leeks, onions, and gladioli. Spray with bifenthrin or use biological controls.

❾ VINE WEEVIL

Small cream grubs with a brown head (*top*) feed on plant roots, especially those growing in containers or with fleshy roots. This can cause plants to suddenly collapse. The adult beetle (*below*) is nocturnal, flightless, and makes notches in leaves. Use a biological control (nematodes).

❿ CATERPILLARS

The larvae of butterflies and moths attack many plants. Cabbage white caterpillars (*top*) decimate brassicas and nasturtiums, while those of the tomato moth (*below*) damage fruits. Cover plants to prevent adults laying eggs, rub off egg clusters, and pick off any caterpillars you find.

⓫ SAWFLIES

The caterpillar-like larvae (*top*) devour the foliage on plants such as roses, gooseberries, and Solomon's seal (*Polygonatum*). Look out for the first signs of attack, such as leaf rolling (rose leaf-rolling sawfly, *below*). Pick caterpillars off by hand or spray with bifenthrin or pyrethrum.

⓬ LEAF MINERS

The larvae of various flies, moths, sawflies, and beetles feed within the leaves, creating discoloured blotches (*top*), or linear mines (*below*). Most are relatively harmless and can be left untreated. However, if necessary, you can spray leaves with thiacloprid.

⓭ RED SPIDER MITES

The tiny mites live under leaves and suck sap, causing yellow mottling. Fine webs are sometimes visible. Raise humidity and use a biological control under glass. Otherwise try organic sprays or bifenthrin.

⓮ WOOLLY BEECH APHID

Seen in early summer, these white fluffy aphids coat shoots and the undersides of leaves. They suck sap, and excrete honeydew that supports black sooty mould. Spray severe infestations with thiacloprid.

⓯ HORSE CHESTNUT LEAF MINER

This new, but widespread, pest attacks mature trees where control is difficult. Leaves show brown marks between the veins, which result in slow growth and early leaf drop.

⓰ EARWIG

Mostly beneficial, earwigs are nocturnal and feed on dahlia, chrysanthemum, and clematis flowers. Lure them into upturned flower pots filled with straw and set on canes; release them elsewhere.

Plant diseases

The best way to keep plants free from disease, is to grow them in the right conditions, so that they are strong enough to fight off any infections. Clean and sterilize tools and equipment, and prevent diseases spreading by taking prompt action. Also check symptoms carefully, as they may just be signs of stress.

PREVENTING DISEASES

Before buying a plant, check that it is healthy, and where species are susceptible to certain problems, buy cultivars that are disease resistant, where available.

Try to plant in ideal conditions in well-nourished soil of the correct type, pH, and drainage for your chosen plants, and with sufficient sun or shade (*see pp.14-15*). Also keep them well watered, especially after planting while they establish. At the first sign of trouble, cut off affected parts, and either burn them or take them to your local recycling centre.

Regularly remove yellowing leaves and fading flowers, as well as diseased leaves that have fallen to the ground, which may cause reinfection if the spores blow onto healthy plants. If space allows in the vegetable garden, practice crop rotation to prevent disease building up in localized areas.

CLEANING SOLUTIONS

Clean cutting tools, including pruning saws, shears, and secateurs, regularly with disinfectant to lessen the risk of disease spreading from one plant to another. Clean and sterilize pots, trays and other equipment used for sowing to prevent damping-off disease, which causes seedlings to suddenly collapse and die. Use new compost and tap water when sowing seeds.

^ *Check plants regularly*
Keep plants healthy by removing any yellowing or marked leaves, fading flowers and dead stems. Pay particular attention to bedding plants (above) *and greenhouse crops.*

^ > *Clean tools and sterilize equipment*
Scrub sap from cutting blades with warm soapy water, and use household disinfectant to sterilize them (above). *This reduces the risk of passing infection between plants. Rinse off old compost and use a baby bottle sterilizing tablet to cleanse containers used for sowing* (right).

STRESS AND VIRUSES

It can be diffficult to work out what is wrong with a plant, but some worrying symptoms are a sign that the plant is stressed, perhaps due to a lack of nutrients, or because it has suffered physical or chemical damage.

ASSESS YOUR PLANTS

Some plants discolour if not properly hardened off (*see p.109*), or if grown at too cool or high a temperature. Leaves may turn white or develop red or purple tints. Starved plants also show leaf discolouration and stunted growth.

Viruses are commonly spread by sap-sucking insect pests, such as aphids. Typical symptoms are pale-streaked or mottled leaves, and leaf curling or distortion. Flower petals may also be streaked, and fruit and flower production reduced or growth stunted. Remove affected plants and throw in the bin or burn them.

∧ *Virus attack*
Streaked foliage that does not improve after feeding may indicate a virus. Kill any sap-sucking pests that spread viruses, and bin or burn infected plants.

∧ *Frost damage*
Brown or blackened shoot tips in spring are signs that a shrub has been scorched by frost. Leave stems to re-sprout and then cut off the dead material.

Signs of stress >
Some plants, including box (right), show unusual leaf colouring when suffering after a hot, dry summer, or following root damage due to waterlogging.

TREATING DISEASES

Taking the right care of your plant patient is an important step towards its recovery. Spraying or removing affected parts all play a part in the process, but ailing plants should also be fed and watered to help them regain their strength. Watch out for pests, which may attack your plant as it recovers, causing it to decline once more.

CHEMICAL CONTROL

Use fungicides sparingly, and follow the manufacturers' instructions and recommendations for protective clothing. On small and wall-trained fruit trees, where practical to spray, a programme of preventive treatment can be helpful to counter a range of diseases (*see pp.432–433*). Also, reduce the need for spraying by growing disease-resistant cultivars and providing good growing conditions. If early sowings suffer from damping off, consider drenching your compost with a preventive copper-based fungicide.

∧ *Spraying fungicide*
If organic methods have failed, spray affected plants with a fungicide recommended for the plant. Wear gloves and follow the instructions on the label.

∧ *Cutting out disease*
Prune out diseased wood as soon as you see it, to prevent infections spreading to healthy tissue.

REMOVING THE PROBLEM

Keep a look out for dead wood and torn branches and prune back to healthy tissue. Prune to a bud to reduce the risk of die back and infection (*see p.410 for pruning methods*). As well as sterilizing cutting equipment, wash your hands in soapy water after handling diseased material. Regularly check stored fruits, vegetables, and flower bulbs and tubers, and remove any that show signs of decay or damage.

Common diseases and disorders

Some plants are more susceptible to certain diseases than others, so always buy resistant varieties whenever possible. You can also boost a plant's natural resistance by growing it in ideal conditions, and remove infected material and overwintering weeds that may carry diseases into the following year.

① CLEMATIS WILT
The fungus causes wilting and black foliage on large-flowered cultivars. Plant clematis 5–7cm (2–3in) deeper than they were in their pots, and cut stems to the base if the disease strikes.

② APPLE SCAB
Symptoms include brown leaf spots, leaf drop, and scabby and cracked fruit. Cut off scabby shoots, clear fallen leaves, and use a fungicide. Also grow resistant cultivars.

③ APPLE AND PEAR CANKER
Lesions appear on bark, and white fungus grows in summer on the wounds. Avoid growing plants on waterlogged soil. Cut out affected wood and spray in autumn with a fungicide.

④ BLOSSOM END ROT
Dark patches on tomatoes are a symptom of calcium deficiency, caused by a lack of, or irregular, watering. Water more often and apply a tomato fertilizer every week after flowering.

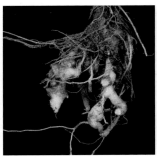   

⑤ CLUB ROOT
This slime mould affects brassicas and causes swollen roots, pale, wilted foliage, and poor crops. Infected soil or plants carry the spores. Plant a different crop on infected soil, or grow brassicas in pots.

⑥ CHOCOLATE SPOT
A common fungal disease that affects broad beans. Brown spots appear on leaves, stems and pods, and yields are poor. Remove and destroy infected material. Improve soil drainage and air flow between plants.

⑦ ROSE BLACKSPOT
Signs are yellowing leaves with black spots and sunken stem lesions. Pick off and burn infected and fallen leaves. Hard prune in late winter, then use a fungicide spray. Also select disease-resistant roses.

⑧ SILVERLEAF
Causes silver sheen on plum, cherry, rhododendron, and rose leaves; affected stems may die. Prune in summer to minimize infection. Prune out and destroy affected wood. Feed to boost plants' vigour.

9 HONEY FUNGUS
Toadstools (*top*) appear in autumn at the base of trees or shrubs, with a white fungus that smells of mushrooms under the bark. Black "bootlaces" (*below*) appear in the soil. There is no cure, so remove the plant and all the roots to prevent the spread of this fatal disease.

10 BOTRYTIS (GREY MOULD)
This fungal disease takes hold in humid conditions, especially on spring and autumn bedding, and under glass. Flowers (*top*) and leaves (*below*) turn yellow or brown, and may have a grey furry coating. Soft fruits and tomatoes also rot. Remove dead material, and injured stems and leaves promptly.

11 POWDERY MILDEW
A white fungus appears on leaves and stems of crops and ornamental plants, especially those growing in pots and planters, or by hedges and walls. Susceptibility increases with lack of water and poor growing conditions. Water well, avoiding the foliage, feed, and mulch to boost resistance.

12 POTATO SCAB/BLIGHT
Scab (*top*) forms if tubers are grown in dry soil; add organic matter and water well to increase moisture. Blight (*below*) is more serious and worse in wet conditions. The foliage browns and wilts, and tubers rot. Destroy all affected plants and don't grow potatoes in the soil for three years.

13 RUST
A fungal disease that causes brown, orange, or yellow pustules on the backs of leaves. The spores increase in humid conditions. Pick off and destroy affected growth. Look out for resistant varieties.

14 SOOTY MOULD
This black fungus is often seen on the upper leaf surfaces of evergreen shrubs. It grows on the sticky mess produced by sap-sucking insect pests. Kill the pests, and wash off the mould with mild soapy water.

15 CORAL SPOT
The orange-pink fungus grows on dead wood but can also infect living tissue if plants are weak or poorly pruned. Cut out and destroy affected wood. Feed and water plants well to boost their immunity.

16 RHODODENDRON BUD BLAST
Buds on infected plants remain unopened and look silvery. In late spring they develop black bristles. Remove affected buds and take to a recycling centre. There is no chemical treatment.

Picture Credits

The publisher would like to thank the following for their kind permission to reproduce their photographs:

(Key: a-above; b-below/bottom; c-centre; f-far; l-left; r-right; t-top)

Garden Library: Jerry Harpur, Design: Ian & Morag Hughes. **342 GAP Photos:** Friedrich Strauss (l). **343 GAP Photos:** Marg Cousens (cr). **344 Marianne Majerus Garden Images:** Marianne Majerus/Susanne Blair (t). **348 Getty Images:** Christina Bollen. **350-351 Marianne Majerus Garden Images:** Yvonne Inne & Olivia Harrison/From Life to Life: A garden for George, Chelsea Flower Show 2008. **352 Getty Images:** Pernilla Bergdahl (l). **356-357 Dorling Kindersley:** Design: Ness Botanic Gardens, A Garden For Bees, RHS Tatton Park 2008. **363 Getty Images:** Richard Bloom (cl). **364-365 GAP Photos:** Flora Press. **367 Getty Images:** Clive Nichols (ca); Polina Plotnikova (cb) (crb). **372 Getty Images:** Evan Sklar (tr). **373 Getty Images:** Mark Bolton (cr); Kelly Kalhoefer (br); Martin Page (l). **378 Getty Images:** Mark Bolton (r). **Photolibrary:** James Guilliam (l). **379 Getty Images:** GAP Photos (br); Rice/Buckland (cr). **381 GAP Photos:** (crb); Visions (cra) (cb). **383 Alamy Images:** Glenn Harper (cr). **384 GAP Photos:** Friedrich Strauss. **385 Getty Images:** Lee Avison (t). **387 Getty Images:** De Agostini (*B. gibbum*); DEA/C. DANI (*P. bifurcatum*). **391 Getty Images:** De Agostini (cra) (br). **392-393 Marianne Majerus Garden Images:** Marianne Majerus. **393 GAP Photos:** Jonathan Need (br); S & O (crb); J S Sira (cb). **Photolibrary:** John W Warden (bc). **394 Caroline Reed** (l). **396 Getty Images:** DEA/C.DANI (br). **399 Alamy Images:** John Glover (cra). **GAP Photos:** John Glover (cr); Friedrich Strauss (br). **400-401 Getty Images:** Richard Bloom. **405 Getty Images:** Hugh Palmer (pebbles). **408 Getty Images:** Clive Nichols (t). **409 Getty Images:** Nicola Browne (cra). **422 Getty Images:** Nigel Cattlin (cla). **424 Dorling Kindersley:** Design: Martin Walker, The HESCO Garden, RHS Chelsea 2009 (cra). **Getty Images:** Mark Turner (cb). **425 Getty Images:** Ben Hall (clb); Dirk Heuer – www.dheuer.net (cr); Elliott Neep (crb); ZenShui/Odilon Dimier (cb). **426 Getty Images:** Steve Hopkin (ca). **427 Getty Images:** FhF Greenmedia (br) (tr); Charles Krebs (tc). **429 GAP Photos:** Andrea Jones (fcla). **Getty Images:** Nigel Cattlin (cla) (tr); National Geographic (br). **432 Alamy Images:** Dr. Ian B Oldham (fcla). **Getty Images:** Nigel Cattlin (clb) (fclb). **433 Getty Images:** Nigel Cattlin (fcra) (ftr); Christopher Fairweather (bl/sooty mould); Mark Turner (cra). **Royal Horticultural Society, Wisley:** (ftl)

All other images © Dorling Kindersley
For further information see: www.dkimages.com

Dorling Kindersley would like to thank:

Andrew Halstead and Beatrice Henricot from RHS Wisley Gardens for their help with the pest and disease sections.

Index: Jane Coulter

Proofreading: Monica Byles

Styling assistance: Alison Shackleton

Suppliers

Reliable tools, plants, and products make gardening easier, cost effective, and more rewarding. Use this list as a starting point and gradually develop your own contacts, based on your own experience.

BULB SUPPLIERS

Bloms Bulbs
01234 709099
blomsbulbs.com
General garden bulbs

de Jager
01622 840229
dejager.co.uk
Familiar and unusual bulbs

Euro Bulbs
01945 430009
eurobulbs.co.uk
Specialist and imported bulbs

Heritage Bulbs
0845 300 4257
heritagebulbs.com
Bulbs for naturalizing and display

Peter Nyssen
0161 747 4000
peternyssen.com
Bulbs in larger quantities

Van Meuwen
0844 557 1850
vanmeuwen.com
Bulbs, plants, and vegetables

FENCING & WALLS

English Hurdle
01823 698418
hurdle.co.uk
Traditional handmade willow hurdles

Forest
0844 248 9801
forestgarden.co.uk
Arches, fencing, and garden buildings

Hilhout Limited
01502 718091
hilhout.com
Decking, fencing, and garden furniture

Jacksons
0800 408 2234
jacksons-fencing.co.uk
Fine fencing, gates and decking

Ready Hedge
01386 750585
readyhedgeltd.com
Hedging and screening

GARDEN SUPPLIES & SUNDRIES

Enviromat
01842 828266
enviromat.co.uk
Sedum green roof matting

Ever Edge
01453 731717
everedge.co.uk
Modular raised bed systems and edging

Garden Products Online
0845 129 7171
gardenproductsonline.co.uk
Furniture, equipment, and features

Harrod Horticultural
0845 218 5301
harrodhorticultural.com
General fruit and vegetable sundries

Quality Garden Tools
0800 783 2202
qualitygardentools.com
Tools, watering, and accessories

Strulch
01943 863610
strulch.co.uk
Mineralised straw for organic gardening

Two Wests & Elliot
01246 451077
twowests.co.uk
Garden and greenhouse equipment

LANDSCAPE MATERIALS

Marshalls
0845 820 5000
marshalls.co.uk
Paving, blocks, and aggregates

Specialist Aggregates
01785 661018
specialistaggregates.co.uk
Gravels, aggregates, cobbles, pebbles

Stonemarket
0247 651 8700
stonemarket.co.uk
Concrete and natural stone paving

The Stone Yard
0845 867 9237
thestoneyard.co.uk
Granite setts, kerbs, posts, and paving

ORGANIC PEST CONTROL

Defenders
01233 813121
defenders.co.uk
Biological control by mail order

Ladybird Plant Care
0845 094 5499
ladybirdplantcare.co.uk
Biological and organic pest control

POTS & CONTAINERS

Italian Terrace
01284 789666
italianterrace.co.uk
Italian-style stone and iron work

Original Stone Troughs
0113 284 1184
stonetroughs.co.uk
Reclaimed antique stoneware

Oxford Planters
01608 683100
oxfordplanters.co.uk
Handmade wooden planters

Pots and Pithoi
01342 714793
potsandpithoi.com
Modern and antique terracotta

Urbis
01759 373839
urbisdesign.co.uk
Contemporary containers and furniture

SEED & PLUG SUPPLIERS

Chiltern Seeds
01229 581137
chilternseeds.co.uk
Familiar and unusual seeds

D.T. Brown
0845 371 0532
dtbrownseeds.co.uk
Vegetables, fruit, and ornamentals

Mr Fothergills
0845 371 0518
mr-fothergills.co.uk
Ornamentals, fruit, and vegetables

Suttons
0844 922 0606
suttons.co.uk
Ornamentals, fruit, and vegetables

Thompson & Morgan
0844 2485383
thompson-morgan.com
Ornamentals, fruit, and vegetables

TREE & PLANT SUPPLIERS

Architectural Plants
01403 891772
architecturalplants.com
Large and architectural plants

Barcham
01353 720748
barchamonline.co.uk
Semi-mature trees and hedging

Big Plant Nursery
01903 891466
bigplantnursery.co.uk
Large and unusual plants

Buckingham Nurseries
01280 822133
buckingham-nurseries.co.uk
Bare-root trees and hedging

Chrysanthemums Direct
0800 056 7443
chrysanthemumsdirect.co.uk
Specialist chrysanthemum supplier

Claire Austin Hardy Plants
01939 251173
claireaustin-hardyplants.co.uk
Specialist perennial supplier

Coblands
01732 350517
best4plants.co.uk
Designer plant nursery

Country Garden Roses
01939 210380
countrygardenroses.co.uk
Specialist rose supplier

Crocus
0844 577 2233
crocus.co.uk
Plants, tools, pots, and furniture

D'Arcy & Everest
01480 497672
darcyeverest.co.uk
Alpine and perennial specialists

David Austin Roses
01902 376300
davidaustinroses.com
Specialist rose and rose care supplier

Dobbies Garden Centres
0131 663 6778
dobbies.com
General plants and garden supplies

Hardy's Cottage Garden Plants
01256 896533
hardys-plants.co.uk
Ferns, grasses, and perennials

Hillier Garden Centres
01794 368733
hillier.co.uk
General plants and garden supplies

Hopleys Plants
01279 842509
hopleys.co.uk
Climbers, perennials, and shrubs

House of Plants
01435 874874
houseofplants.co.uk
House plants and indoor containers

Jekka's Herb Farm
01454 418878
jekkasherbfarm.com
Specialist herb supplier

Keepers Nursery
01622 726465
keepers-nursery.co.uk
Specialist fruit tree supplier

Kings Barn Farm
01403 865405
kingsbarntrees.co.uk
Willow setts and accessories

Knoll Gardens
01202 873931
knollgardens.co.uk
Grasses and perennials

McBean's Orchids
01273 400228
mcbeansorchids.co.uk
Tender, indoor orchids

Notcutts
01934 383344
notcutts.co.uk
General plants and garden supplies

Peter Beales Roses
0845 481 0277
classicroses.co.uk
Specialist rose and rose care supplier

Practicality Brown
01753 652022
pracbrown.co.uk
Trees, screening, and topiary

Raymond Evison Clematis
01481 245942
raymondevisonclematis.com
Specialist clematis supplier

RHS Online Plant Shop
0844 557 2622
rhsplants.co.uk
General plants and garden supplies

Sheila Chapman Clematis
01708 688090
sheilachapman.co.uk
Climbing and herbaceous clematis

Wyevale Garden Centres
0844 800 8428
wyevale.co.uk
General plants and garden supplies

WATER GARDENING

Clear Water: Pond & Lake Management
01442 875616
clearwaterplm.co.uk
Aquatic maintenance and construction

Fairwater
01903 892228
fairwater.co.uk
Water garden specialists

Lilies Water Gardens
01306 631064
lilieswatergardens.co.uk
Garden, bog, and pond plants

Penlan Perennials
01239 711102
penlanperennials.co.uk
Aquatic plants and perennials

Stapeley Water Gardens Limited
01270 623868
stapeleywg.com
Pond, fish, and aquarium specialist

World of Water
01580 243333
worldofwater.com
Pond, fish, and aquarium specialist

WILDLIFE GARDENING

Bird Ventures
01263 710203
birdventures.co.uk
Nest boxes and bird feeders

Garden Organic
0247 630 3517
gardenorganic.org.uk
Organic seeds, plants, and accessories

RSPB
08451 200501
rspb.org.uk
Bird food, feeders, and nest boxes

Designers' details

The following designers and landscape architects have kindly helped us with planting and design plans.

Laurie Chetwood and Patrick Collins
020 7490 2400
chetwoods.com

Fran Coulter
01582 794019
frances.coulter@btinternet.com

Cubed3
Alan Burns 07921 860092
Philip Dugdale 0770 216 2317

Adam Frost
01780 762748
adamfrost.co.uk

Annie Guilfoyle
01730 812943
annieguilfoyle.com

Jeff Hewitt
0208 547 2452
hewittlandscapes.co.uk

Phillippa Probert
07734 157976
outerspaces.org.uk

Hugh Thomas Gardens & Landscapes
01625 531513
hughthomas.co.uk